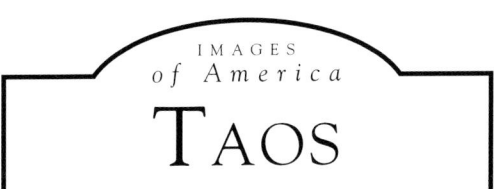

ON THE COVER: Taken on September 30, 1885, this image shows Pueblo residents and visitors enjoying a San Geronimo Day celebration at the Taos Pueblo. This annual religious event includes a traditional buffalo dance, ceremonial foot races, and pole climbing. The sacred Taos Mountain is seen in the background. (Courtesy of Taos Historic Museums.)

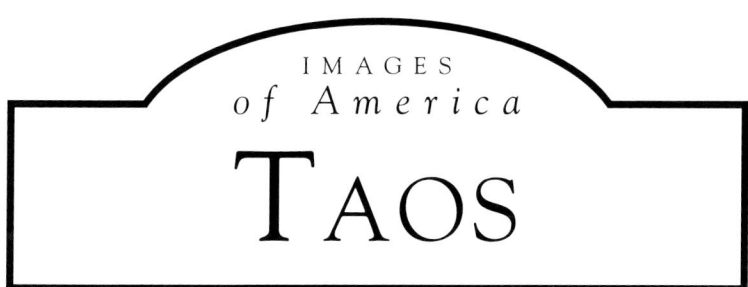

IMAGES of America
TAOS

Lyn Bleiler
Society of the Muse of the Southwest

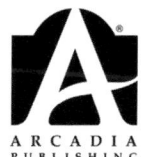

Copyright © 2011 by Lyn Bleiler, Society of the Muse of the Southwest
ISBN 978-0-7385-7959-7

Published by Arcadia Publishing
Charleston, South Carolina

Printed in the United States of America

Library of Congress Control Number: 2010934335

For all general information, please contact Arcadia Publishing:
Telephone 843-853-2070
Fax 843-853-0044
E-mail sales@arcadiapublishing.com
For customer service and orders:
Toll-Free 1-888-313-2665

Visit us on the Internet at www.arcadiapublishing.com

For the people of Taos

Contents

Acknowledgments		6
Introduction		7
1.	Early Taos Pueblo	9
2.	Historic Taos Plaza	41
3.	Fiestas and Parades	53
4.	Taos Society of Artists	75
5.	Mabel Dodge Luhan and Friends	103
6.	Taoseños y Taoseñas	113

ACKNOWLEDGMENTS

Thank you to the Beinecke Rare Book and Manuscript Library at Yale University, Millicent Rogers Museum, Taos Historic Museums, Southwest Research Center, Janet Caldwell-Cannedy, Virginia Couse, the Reyna family, Charles Randall, Cecilia Torres, Nita Murphy, and Larry Torres. Special thanks go to Anita McDaniel, Patricia Mervine, Michael Mooney, Charlie Strong, Olga Torres-Reid, Terry Martin-Hart, and Dori Vinella, and to my editor at Arcadia Publishing, Hannah Carney.

Introduction

Taos, from an Indian word for red willow, has a remarkable history that predates Columbus's arrival in America and the Pilgrims' landing at Plymouth. Puebloan Indians were the first to inhabit the Taos Valley around 1000, and the Taos Pueblo holds the distinction of being the longest continuously inhabited community in the United States. Over the years, the people of Taos Pueblo have had to fight to protect their 99,000-acre land base consisting of the sacred Blue Lake and surrounding mountainous area that the U.S. government seized in 1906 to designate as a national forest. As a result of hard work and diligence on the part of Taos Pueblo tribal leaders and concerned citizens, 48,000 acres, including the sacred Blue Lake, were returned to the Pueblo Indians in 1970. In the early days of photography, Pueblo officials allowed photographs to be taken of ceremonial dances and rituals. Some of these are included in the Taos Historic Museums' extensive archives but are not reproduced here out of respect for Taos Pueblo tribal leaders. Many Taos Pueblo extraordinary celebrations, such as the annual pow-wow, San Geronimo Day, Christmas Eve Procession of the Virgin, and various dances are still open to the public.

The Spanish heritage of many of the oldest families in Taos adds a rich cultural component to the area. Dating back to 1540, when Spanish conquistadors arrived in Taos believing it to be one of the mythical cities of gold, and the Spanish people who followed in 1615, bringing a legacy of the wheel, iron, mules, horses, sheep, cattle, and wheat, began to dramatically influence the Taos landscape. Most of these families left during the Pueblo Revolt of 1680 but returned in 1796 when the king of Spain distributed the Don Fernando Land Grant.

The influx of American artists, many of whom studied in Europe, profoundly influenced the Taos community at the end of the 1800s, as did the arrival of Mabel Dodge and her marriage to Taos Pueblo Indian Tony Luhan. While still just a remote mountain village, Taos was infused with an astonishing number of artistic, literary, and intellectual thinkers of the day.

Finally, like most interesting places, Taos attracted and nurtured an inordinate number of eccentric individuals, some of whom are featured in chapter six. Fortunately, this phenomenon is still true today.

One

EARLY TAOS PUEBLO

The northernmost of all New Mexico pueblos, Taos Pueblo was built between 1000 and 1450, making it the oldest continuously inhabited community in the United States. Taos Pueblo land encompasses 99,000 acres, and includes the sacred Blue Lake from which Taos Pueblo Indians believe they originated. The Pueblo is divided into two large buildings: *Hlauuma* (north house) and *Haukwima* (south house), four and five-story dwellings made of adobe (a combination of earth, straw and water), with large timbers (*vigas*) supporting the multilevel roof structures. For protection against raids by Apache, Navajo, and other nomadic tribes, early Pueblo housing did not have windows or doors, and living quarters were entered through rooftops using wooden ladders.

Spanish conquistadors explored the Taos Valley in 1540, and by the early 1600s Franciscan priests were sent to New Mexico to spread the Catholic faith. Religious interference caused mounting tension between New Mexico Indians and the Spanish. Finally, in 1680 a medicine man named Popé from San Juan Pueblo led the now legendary Pueblo Revolt against Spanish rule and Franciscan missionaries. Of the 400 Spaniards killed by various Pueblo Indians, more than 70, including two Franciscan priests, were killed at Taos Pueblo. As a result of the uprising, missions and other vestiges of Christianity in New Mexico were eliminated. In 1692, however, Don Diego de Vargas led a campaign to regain the Spanish rule of New Mexico and, following years of active resistance, Taos Pueblo surrendered in 1696.

In 1906, the Taos Pueblo's sacred Blue Lake and 48,000 acres of surrounding land were confiscated by the United States government and designated as a national forest. The sacred lake and surrounding mountains have significant ritual and ceremonial importance to the Taos Indians and in 1970, tribal leaders were able to regain possession.

The Taos Pueblo was named a national historic landmark in 1965 and became an official UNESCO World Heritage Site in 1992 as "one the most significant historic cultural landmarks in the world" along with such treasures as the Taj Mahal, the Great Pyramids, and the Grand Canyon.

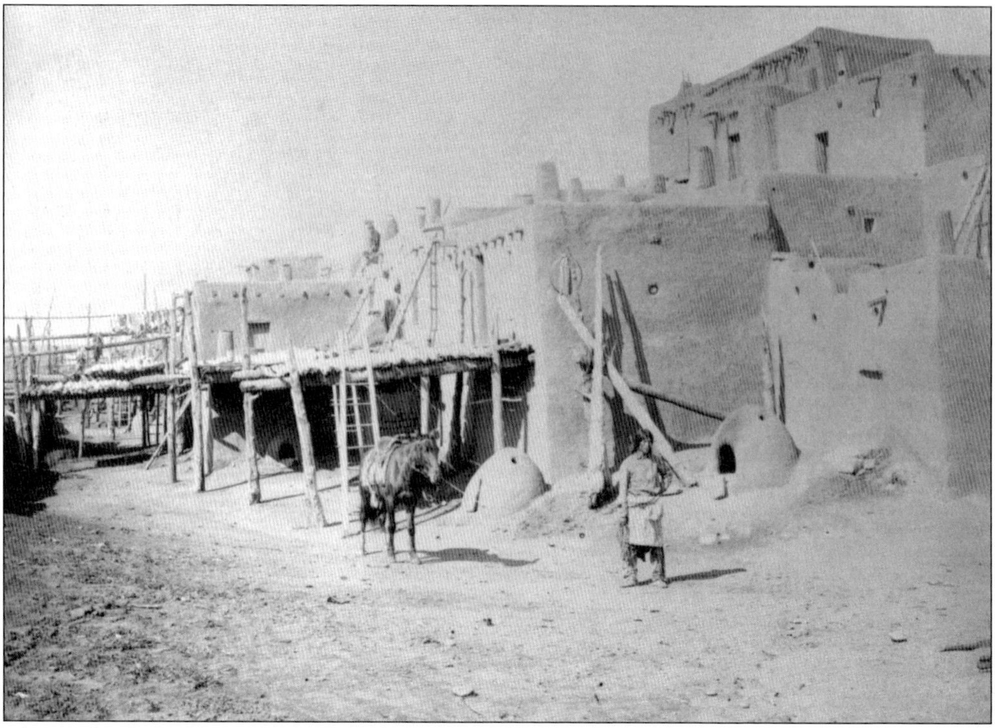

This early photograph of a young Taos Pueblo man leading a horse provides a close-up view of Pueblo dwellings. Domed-shaped baking ovens and wooden drying racks are visible, and wooden *vigas* (timbers) supporting the roof structures can be seen along the rooflines. (Courtesy of Taos Historic Museums.)

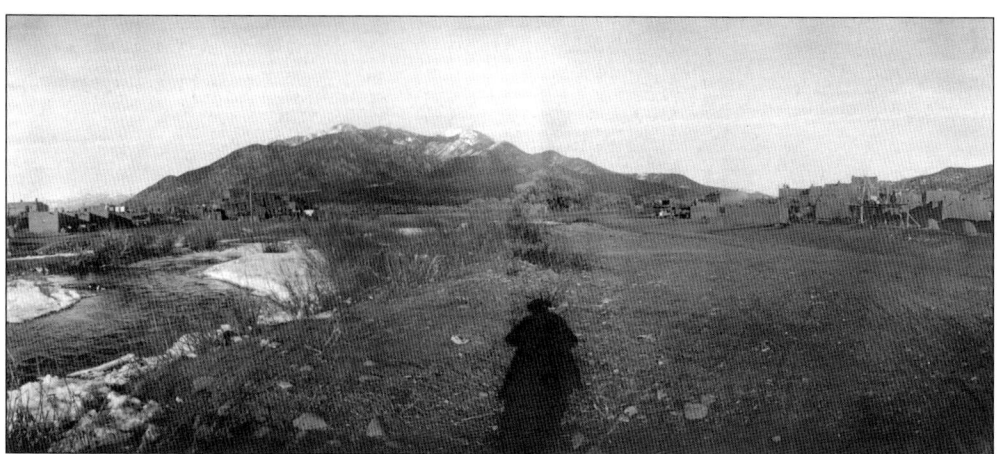

Taken in the 1890s, this sweeping panoramic view shows the *Hlauuma* (north) building to the left, and the *Haukwima* (south) building to the right with an icy Rio Pueblo running between them. The snowcapped Taos Mountain forms a stunning backdrop, while the photographer's shadow forms an interesting image in the front. (Courtesy of Taos Historic Museums.)

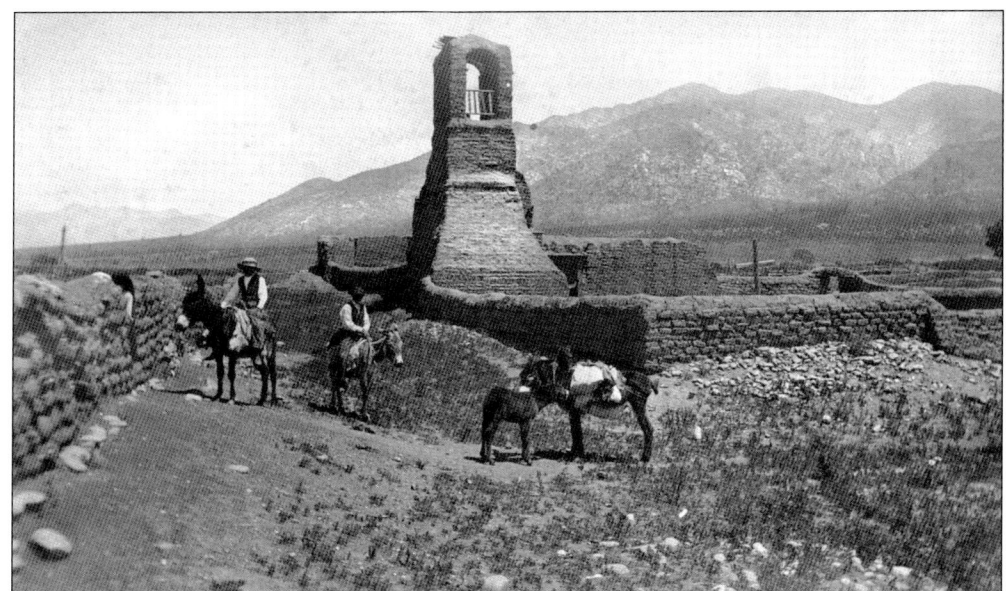

This photograph from the 1880s shows two men on burros next to the ruins of the San Geronimo de Taos church that was destroyed by the U.S. Army in 1847 during the war with Mexico. The original church on the same site was built on the west side of the village in 1619 and was destroyed in the Pueblo Revolt against the Spanish in 1680. These ruins are still standing today. (Courtesy of Taos Historic Museum.)

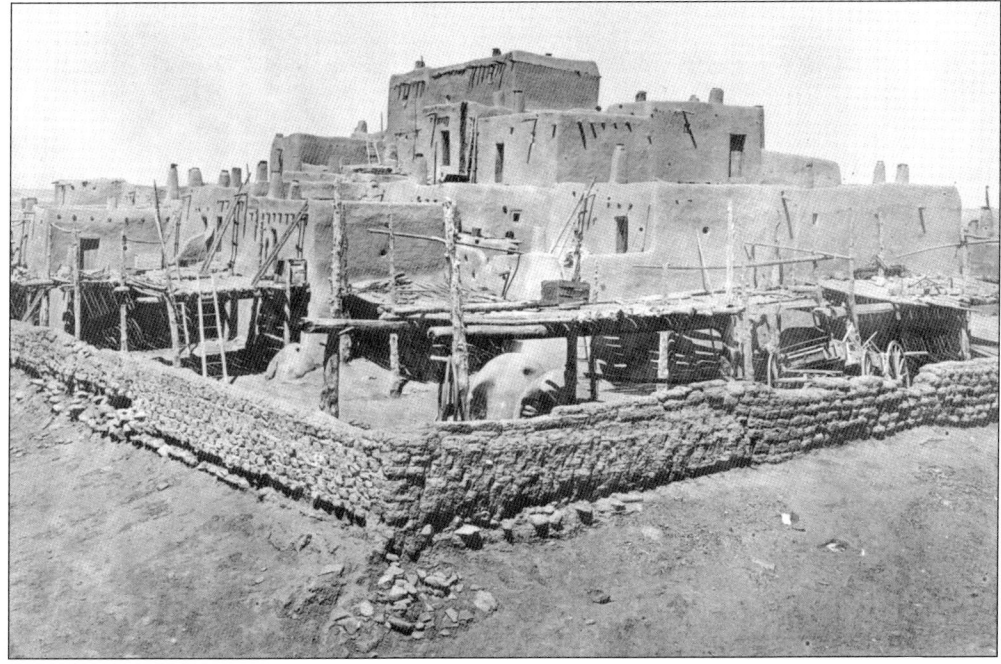

This is a rare view of an original Taos Pueblo building, constructed several hundred feet to the northeast of the existing pueblos and believed to have been abandoned around 1400 due to fire resulting from an attack. The adobe wall shown here once ran through the Pueblo, although only small portions remain today. (Courtesy of Taos Historic Museum.)

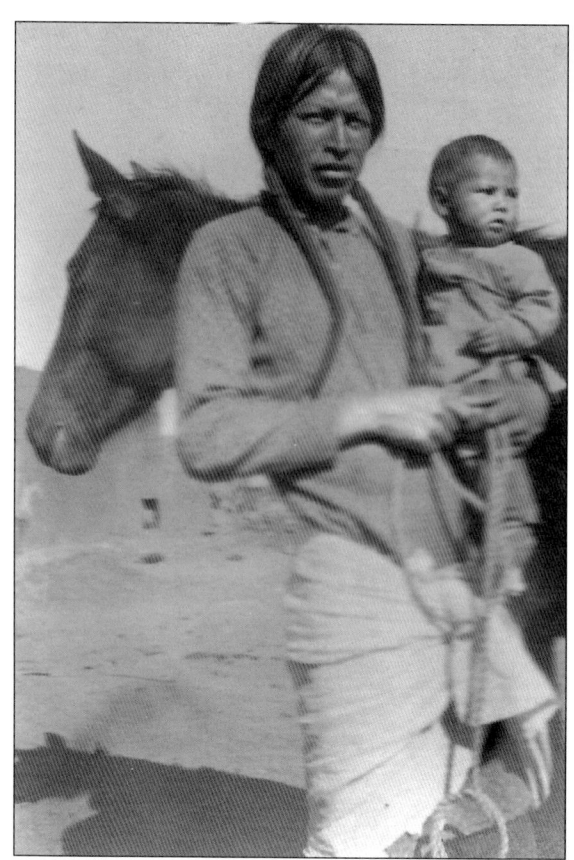

In the photograph at left, a young Taos Pueblo Indian holds a toddler while his horse stands patiently. In the image below, the Pueblo man has lifted the child onto the horse. Behind him is a view of all five stories of the north building, or *Hlauuma*, and drying racks and backing ovens to the left. (Both courtesy of Taos Historic Museums.)

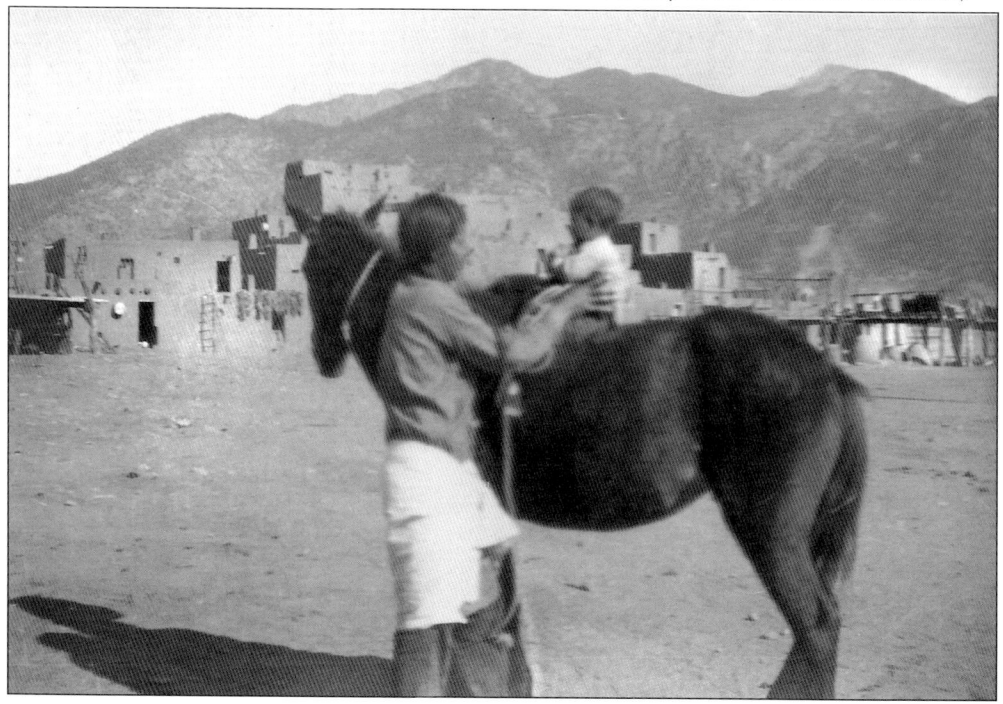

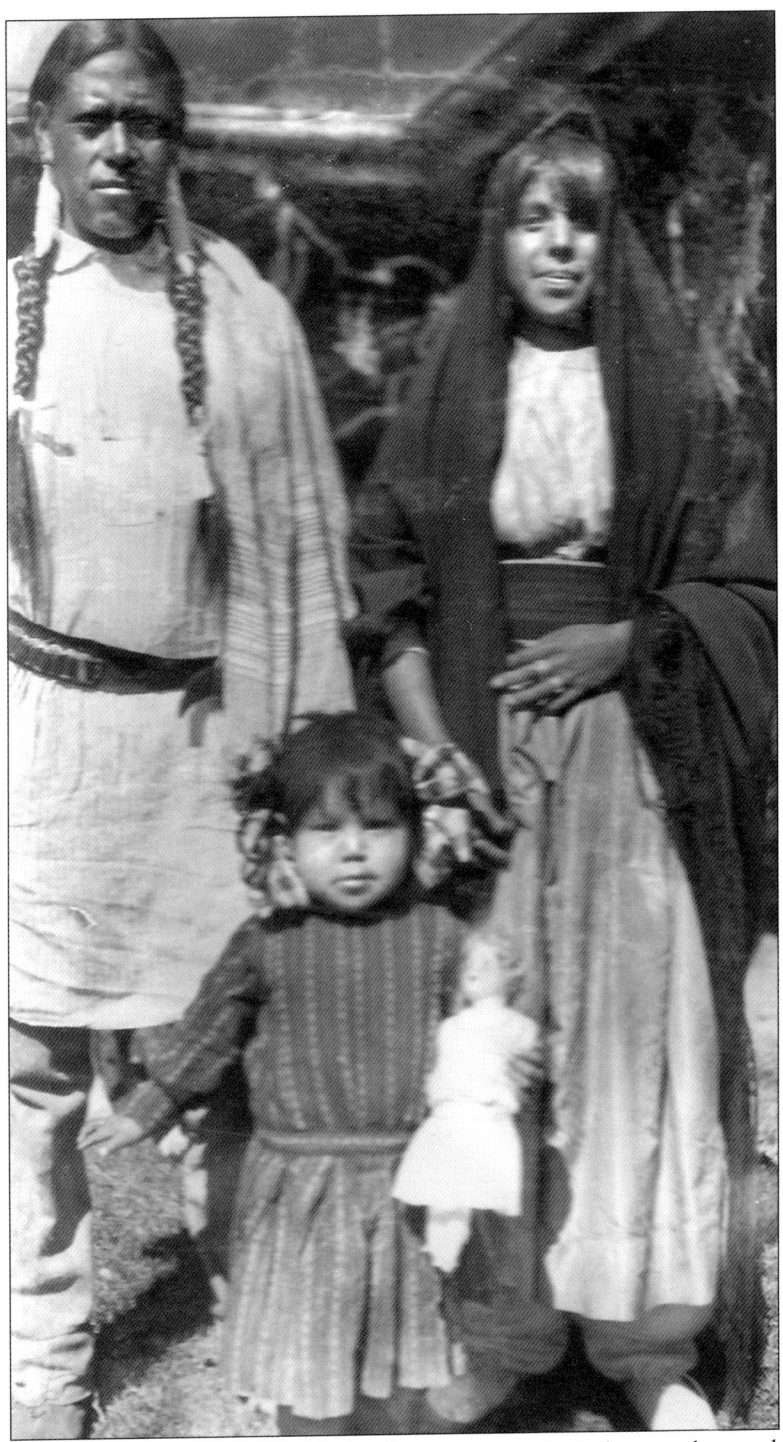
Pictured here is a handsome Taos Pueblo family consisting of a father, mother, and young girl holding an Anglo doll. The woman is wearing ceremonial white deer hide leggings, indicating that this photograph was taken during a special celebration at the Pueblo. (Courtesy of Taos Historic Museums.)

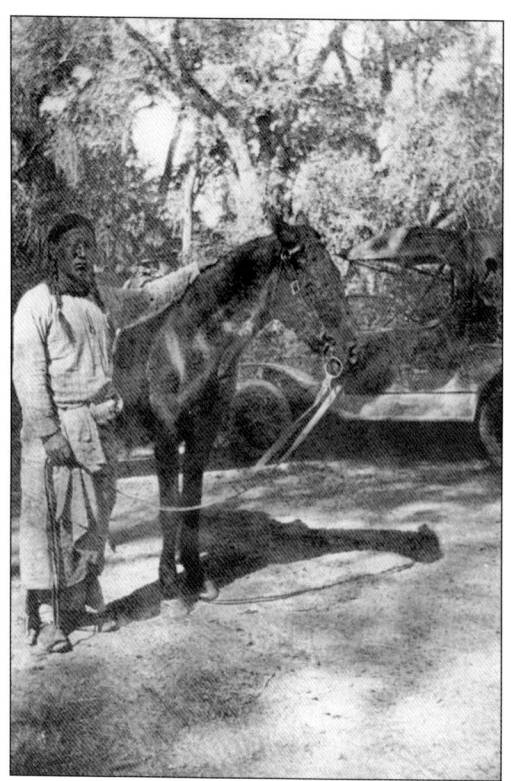

Wearing his hair in long, traditional braids, this solemn Taos Pueblo man poses with his horse next to an early model automobile. The horse casts an interesting shadow in the strong New Mexico sunshine. (Courtesy of Taos Historic Museums.)

This Taos Pueblo man on horseback sits in front of a traditional drying rack festooned with aspen limbs that form a shady bower for the Pueblo residents below. The newly felled branches as well as the non-Pueblo visitor to the upper right suggest that this was a special day of celebration, possibly San Geronimo Day. (Courtesy of Taos Historic Museums.)

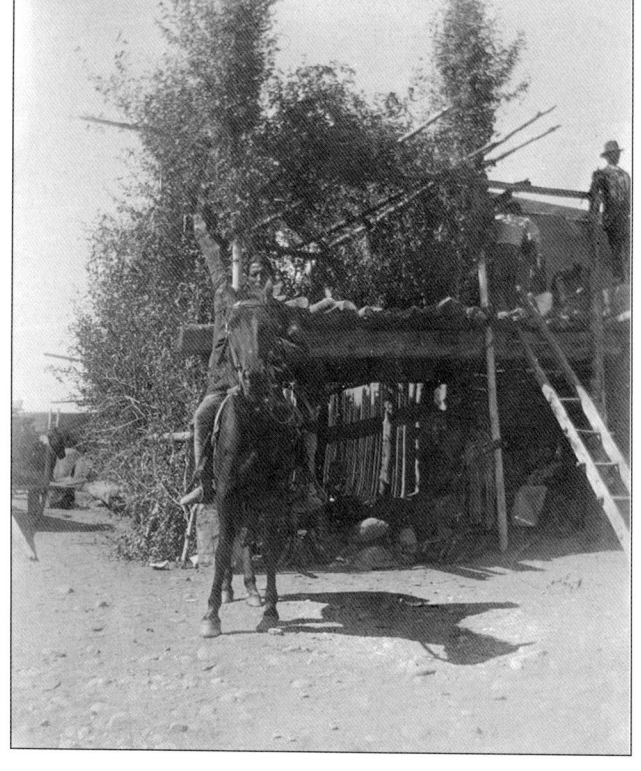

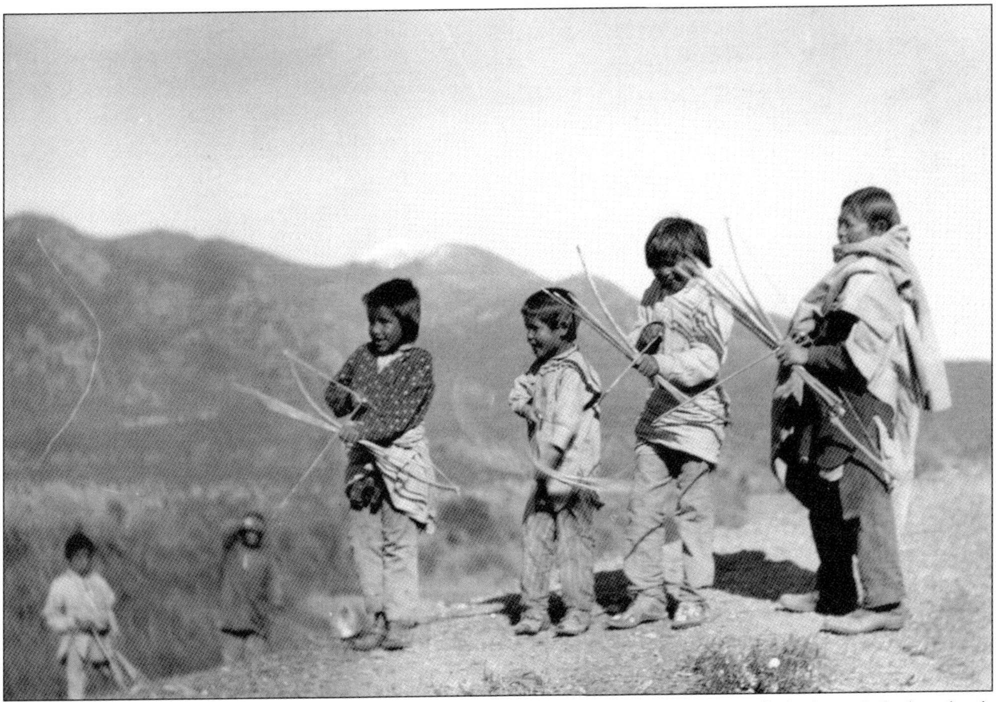

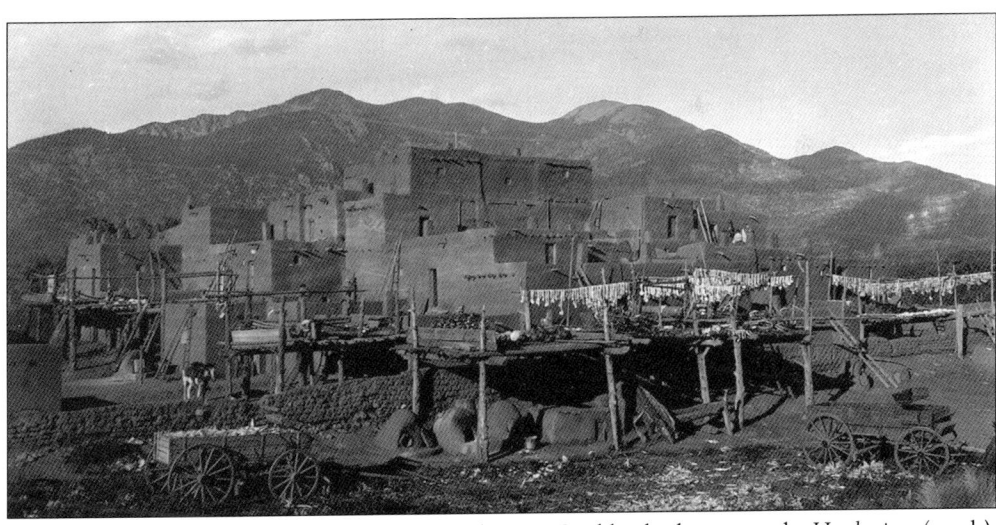

These young Pueblo boys appear to be enjoying a bow-and-arrow lesson, while friends below look on. A snowcapped Taos peak appears in the background. (Courtesy of Taos Historic Museums.)

This is an early photograph of the south side of the Taos Pueblo also known as the *Haukwima* (south). Pumpkin strips hang on ramada racks in the foreground, with domed ovens for baking underneath. The sacred Taos Mountains are seen in the background. (Courtesy of Taos Historic Museums.)

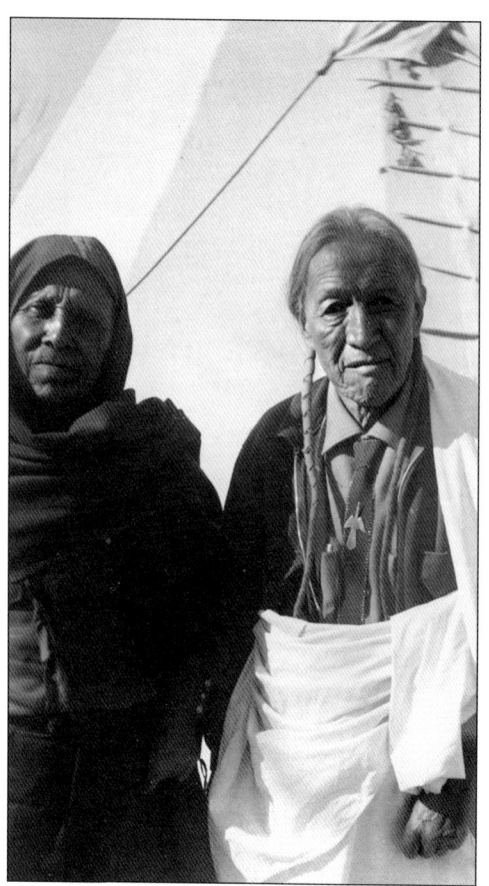

The caption on the original photograph shown here reads, "Jim Mirabel and ? Romero." The distinguished Pueblo man on the right wears a Westernized shirt and tie, yet both are wrapped in traditional blankets. (Courtesy of Taos Historic Museums.)

The agrarian Taos Pueblo Indians were at constant risk of attack by nomadic tribes such as the Navajo, Apache, Ute, and Comanche. This young Pueblo man is wearing a feather headdress, likely made of eagle feathers, which the peaceful Pueblo Indians customarily wore during their Comanche dances. (Courtesy of Taos Historic Museums.)

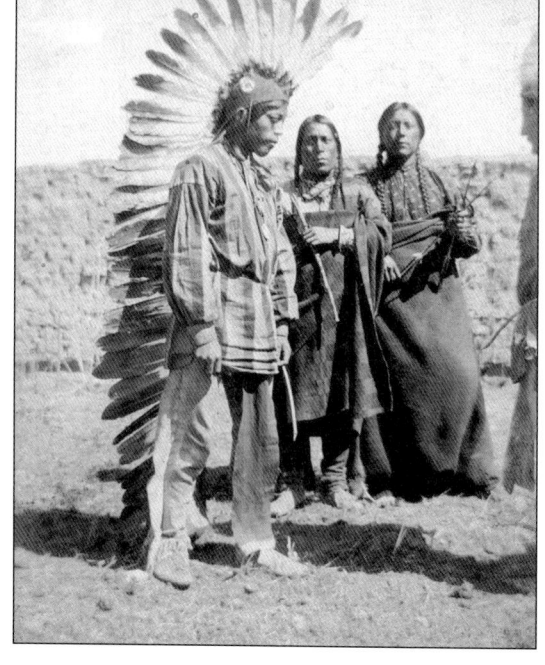

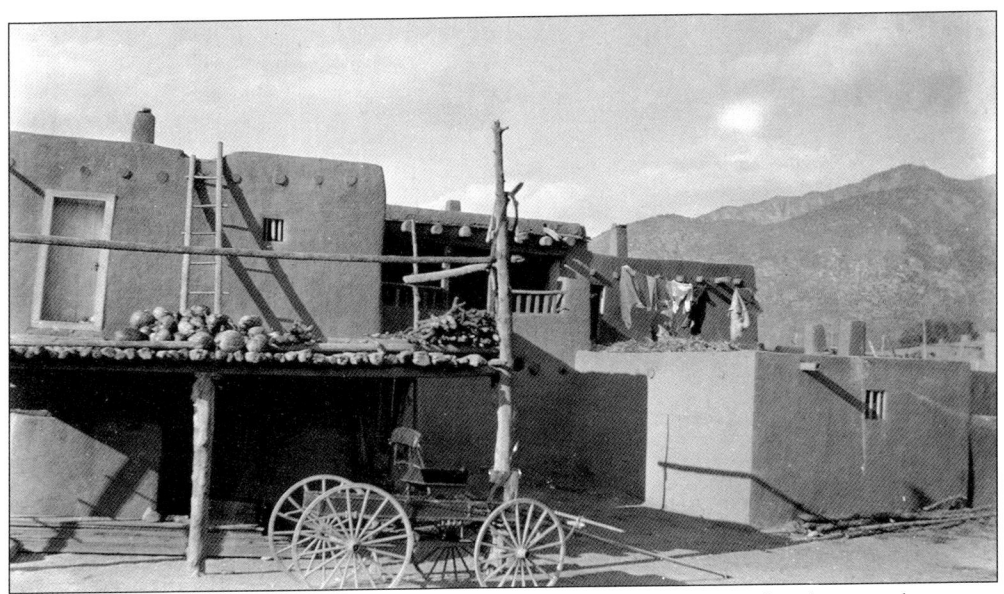

This photograph shows a typical Pueblo home, complete with a pumpkin harvest drying on the racks and a wooden buckboard wagon outside. Early Taos Pueblo dwellings did not have windows, thereby allowing fortress-like protection against enemy attacks. (Courtesy of Taos Historic Museums.)

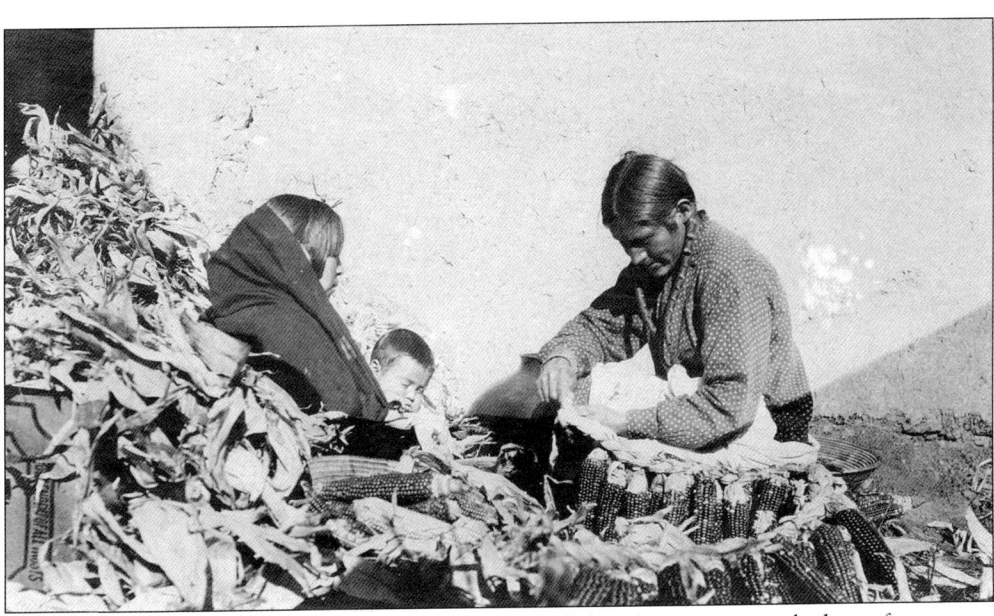

With their infant napping nearby, a Taos Pueblo couple braid corn so it can be hung for storage. Corn was an important staple of the Taos Pueblo Indians, with religious significance and ritual corn dances. (Courtesy of Taos Historic Museums.)

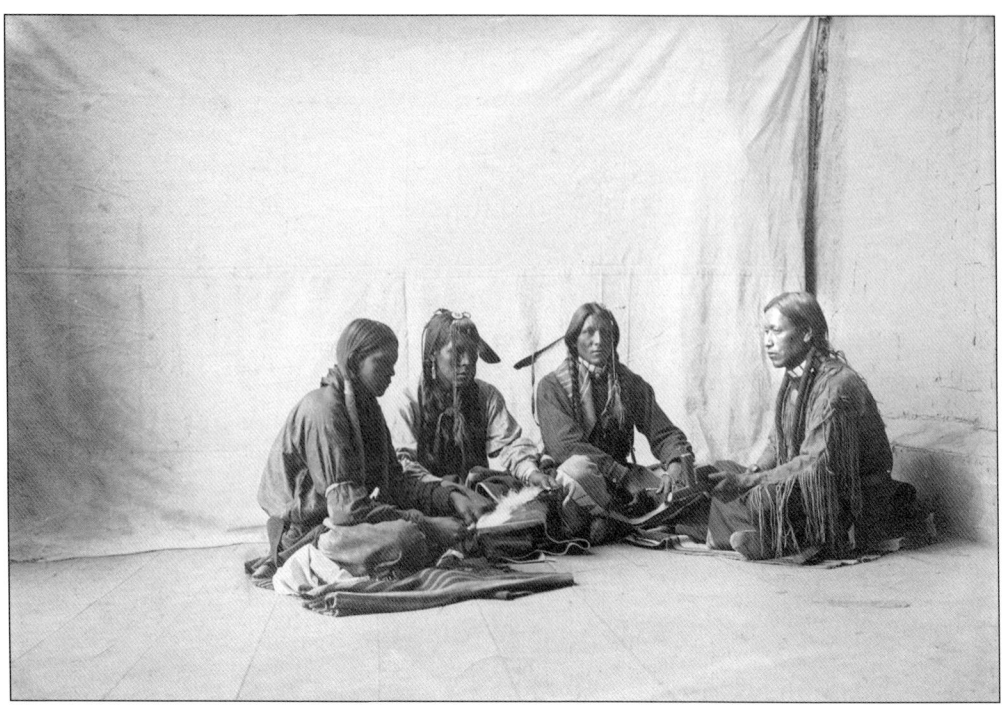

These young Native American men appear to be engaged in a tribal ritual. Since they are seated in a teepee, it is possible they are from a visiting tribe during San Geronimo Day or the annual Taos Pueblo Pow Wow, which served as an Indian trade fair. (Both courtesy of Taos Historic Museums.)

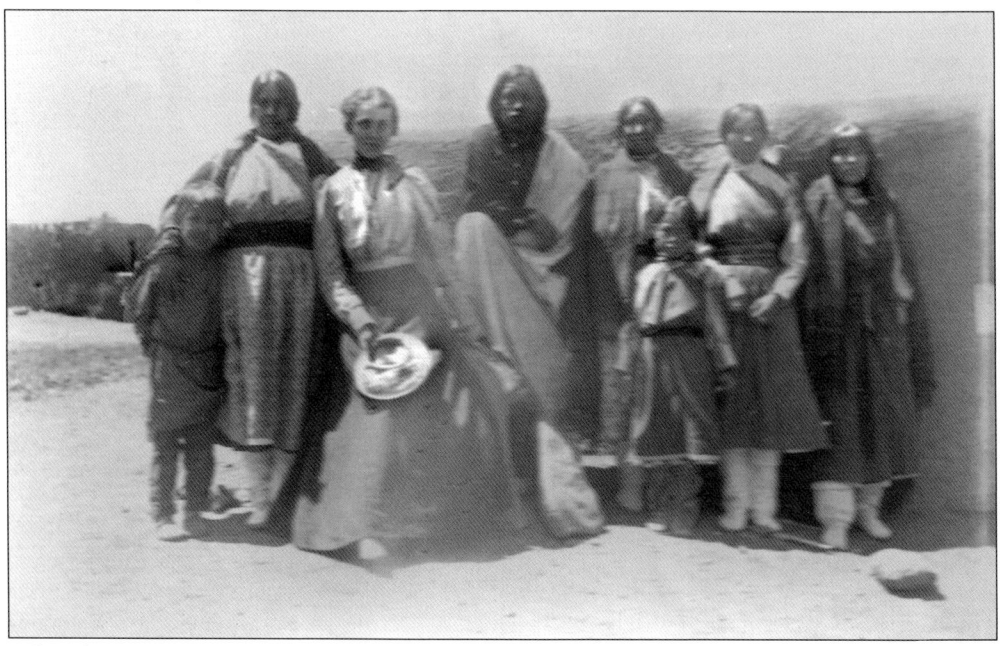

A handwritten note on the back of the original of this photograph reads, "On left of picture are Manuel's aunt and cousin. On the right side of the picture is Manuel, his mother, two sisters, and sweetheart." (Courtesy of Taos Historic Museums.)

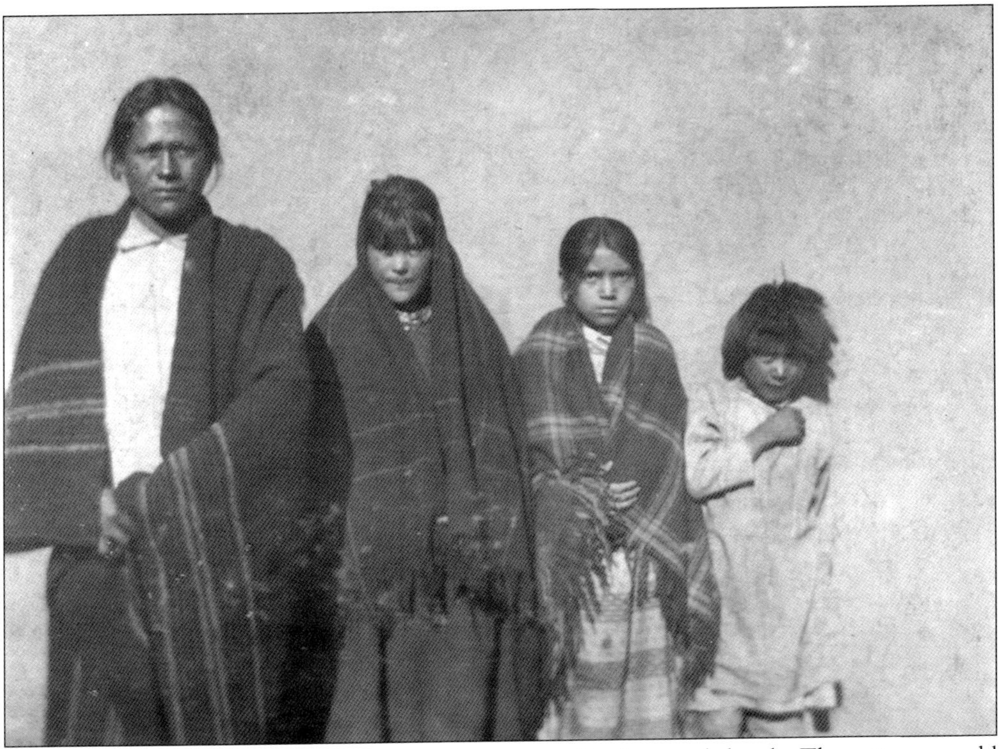

These Pueblo family members are wrapped in woven blankets and shawls. These items would most likely have been acquired through trade with other Pueblos or local Taos Hispanic weavers. (Courtesy of Taos Historic Museums.)

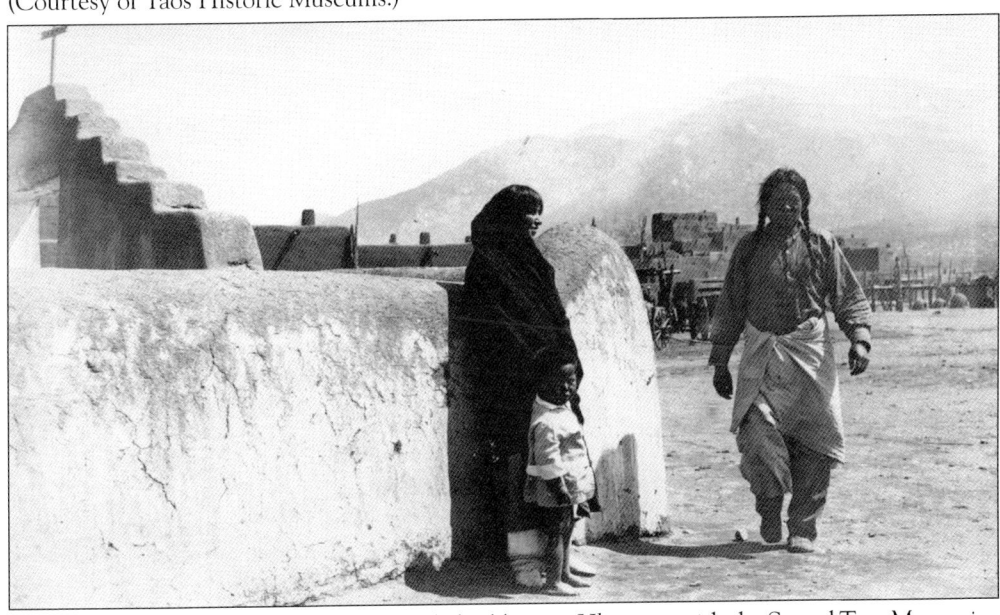

This is an early view facing the north Pueblo building, or *Hlauuma*, with the Sacred Taos Mountains forming a majestic backdrop. The woman and child are standing against the southeast corner of the Catholic St. Jerome Chapel, built in 1850 to replace the original church destroyed by the U.S. Army in 1847 in the 1847 revolt. (Courtesy of Taos Historic Museums.)

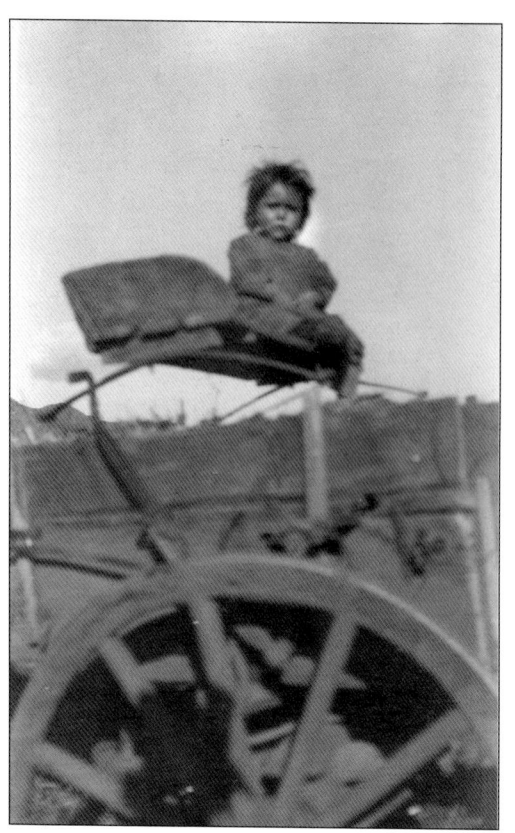

A Pueblo child sits on top of a wooden buckboard wagon. Horse- or mule-drawn, the wagon would likely have been filled with corn, which was an important staple for the Pueblo Indians and had ritual and ceremonial significance. (Courtesy of Taos Historic Museums.)

This photograph, titled "An Early Dance Lesson, Plate #13," was taken by anthropologist Elsie Clews Parsons. Known as the "quiet feminist," Parsons was born into a prominent New York family but vehemently rejected the role of debutante. She attended Barnard College and later earned a master of arts in 1897 followed by a Ph.D. in sociology in 1899 from Columbia University. Her 25 years of research on the Pueblo Indians of the Southwest culminated in the publication of two volumes titled *Pueblo Indian Religion* originally released in 1939 as well as numerous other scholarly publications. (Courtesy of Taos Historic Museums.)

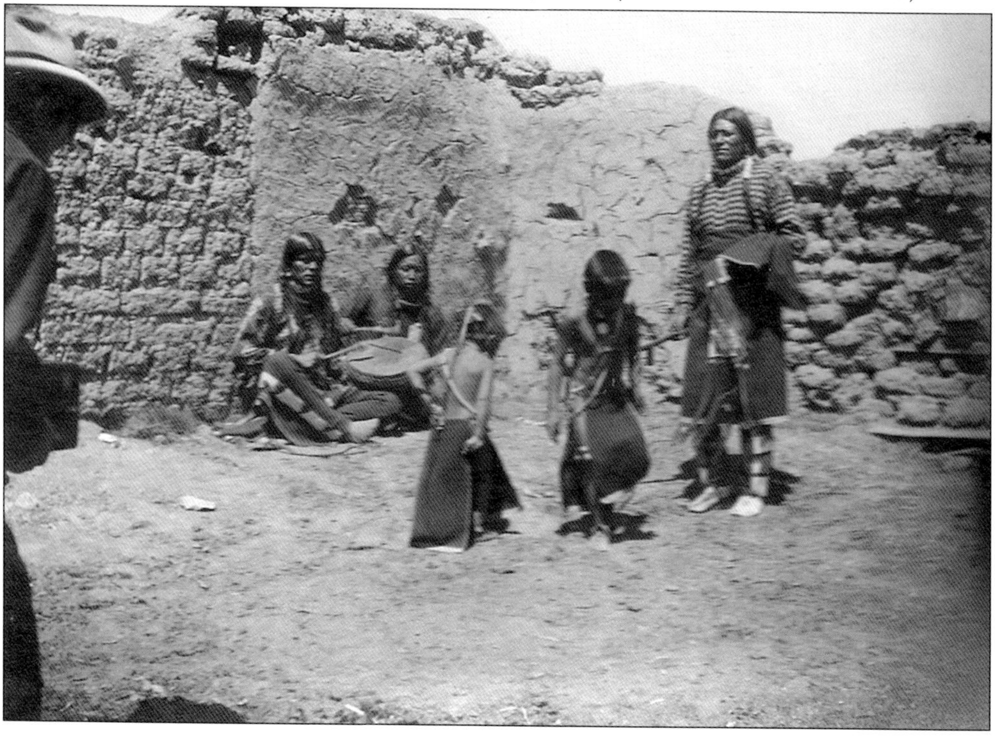

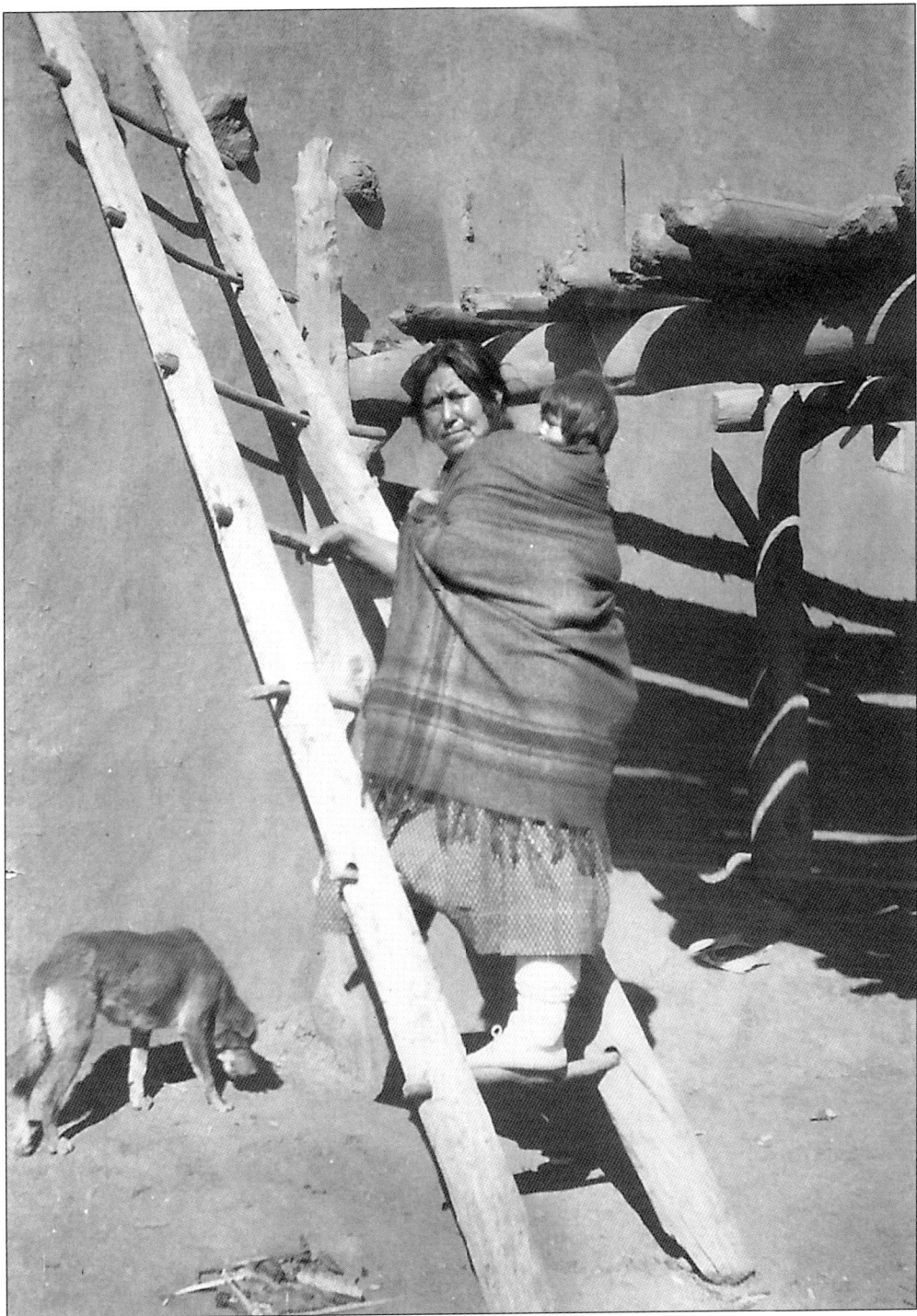

To fortify their dwellings, Taos Pueblo Indians accessed their homes through openings in the roof. Here we see a Native American woman climbing a ladder to the roof with her baby securely wrapped against her back. She is wearing white deerskin boots, usually reserved for special ceremonial occasions. (Courtesy of Taos Historic Museums.)

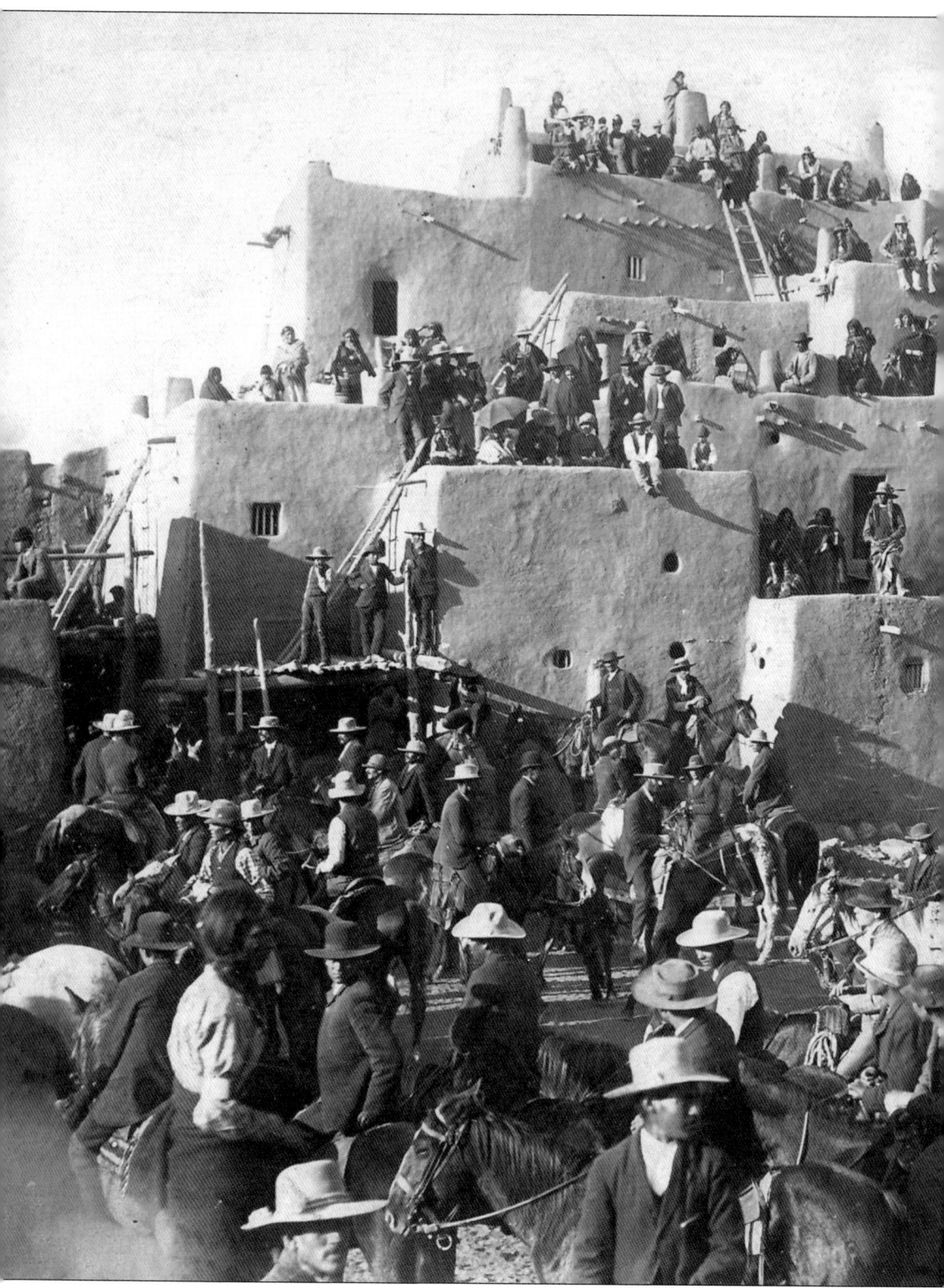

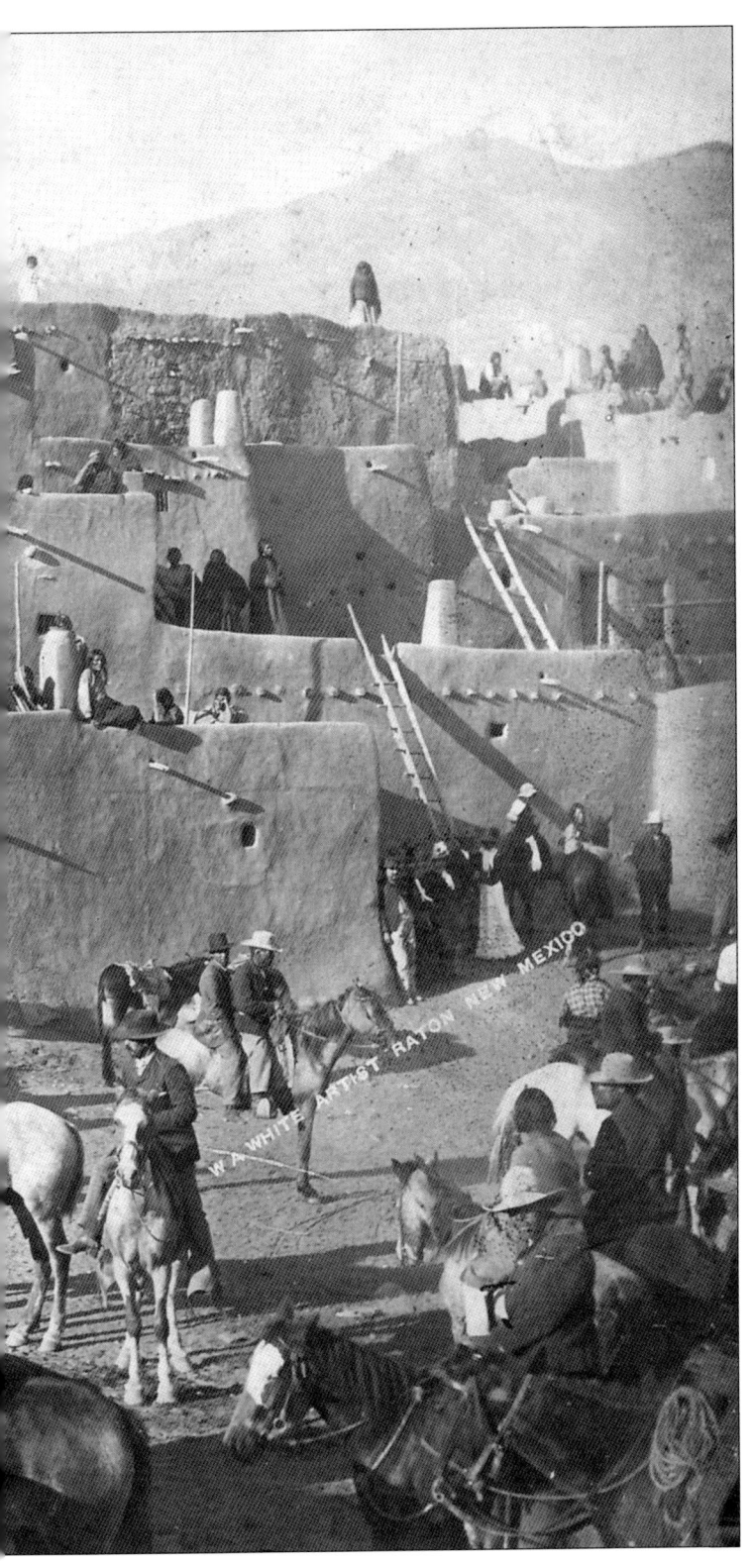

This spectacular photograph by W. A. White of Raton, New Mexico, shows some visitors congregating on horseback while others line the rooftops of the north Taos Pueblo building known as *Hlauuma* to await the beginning of San Geronimo activities. This annual event held on September 30 is named after St. Jerome, the patron saint of Taos Pueblo. Originally, this was an autumn day designated for trading with neighboring tribes. After Spanish colonization, however, San Geronimo incorporated religious ceremony as well. (Courtesy of Charles R. Strong.)

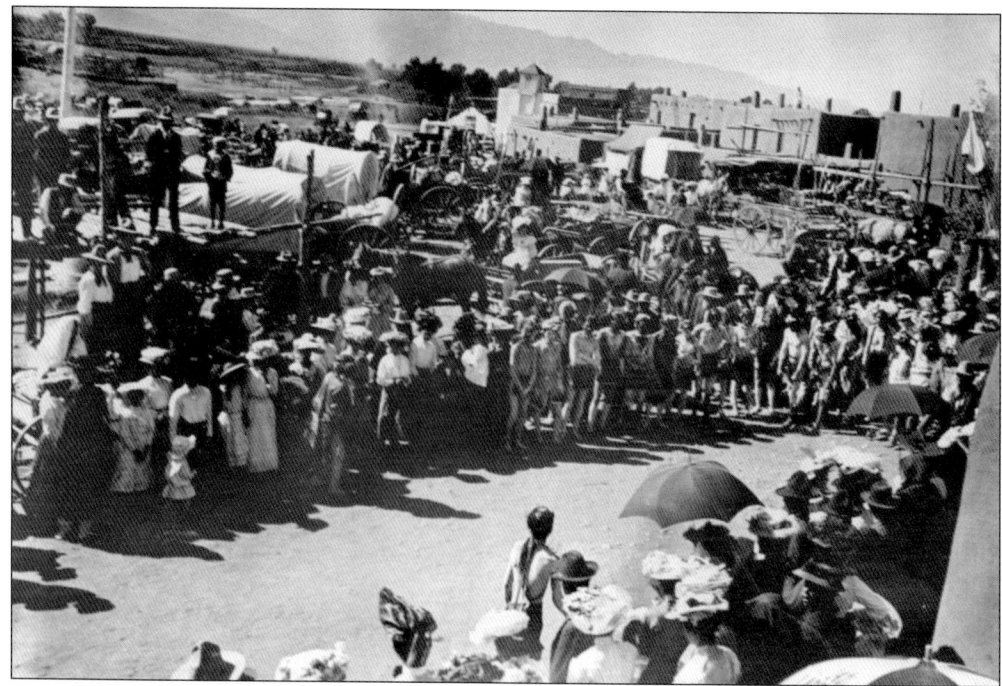

Spectators gather in anticipation of traditional morning footraces at a San Geronimo Day celebration. A tall wooden timber has been erected (see upper right corner) for pole climbing activities that will take place later in the day. The St. Geronimo (also known as St. Jerome) Church is seen in the background, along with covered wagons belonging to visitors. (Courtesy of Taos Historic Museums.)

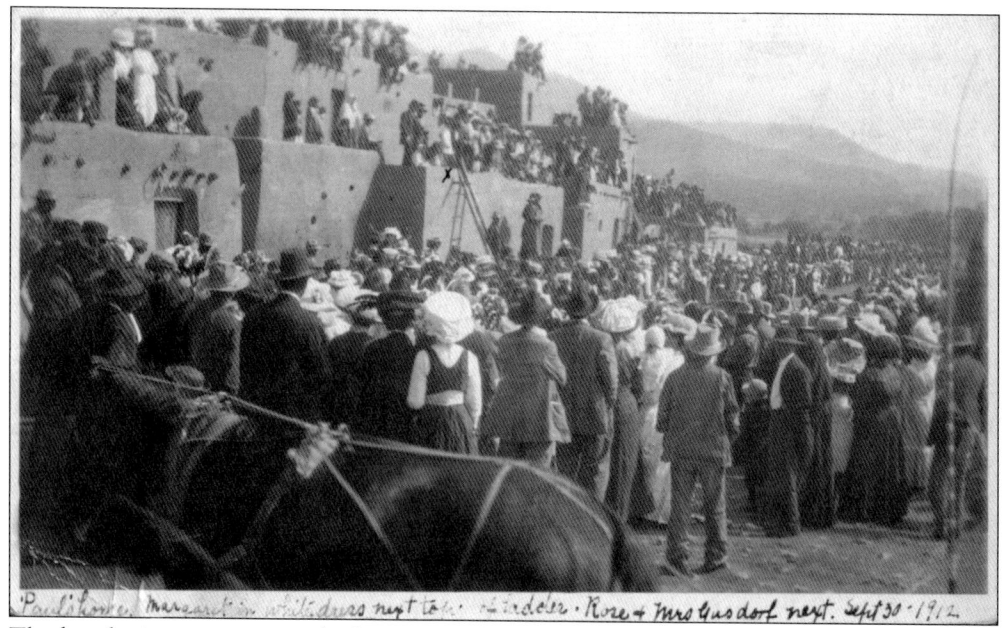

The handwritten caption at the bottom reads, "Paul's home. Margaret in white dress to right of the ladder. Rose and Mrs. Gusdorf next." The Gusdorfs were a prominent Taos family who established the first general merchandise store in the Taos area (see additional photographs in chapters two and six). (Courtesy of Taos Historic Museums.)

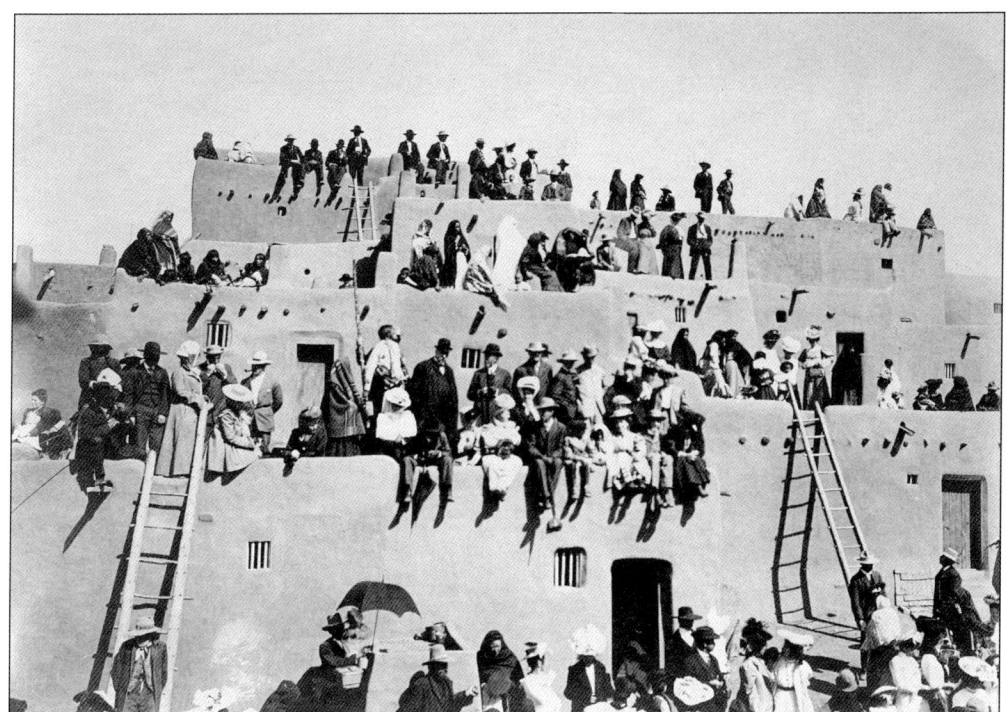

This view of San Geronimo Day at the Taos Pueblo shows Pueblo residents and visitors alike lining the rooftops of the north building known as *Hlauuma* to view the day's festivities. Wooden ladders against the adobe structure provide the only means of access to upper-story dwellings. (Courtesy of Taos Historic Museums.)

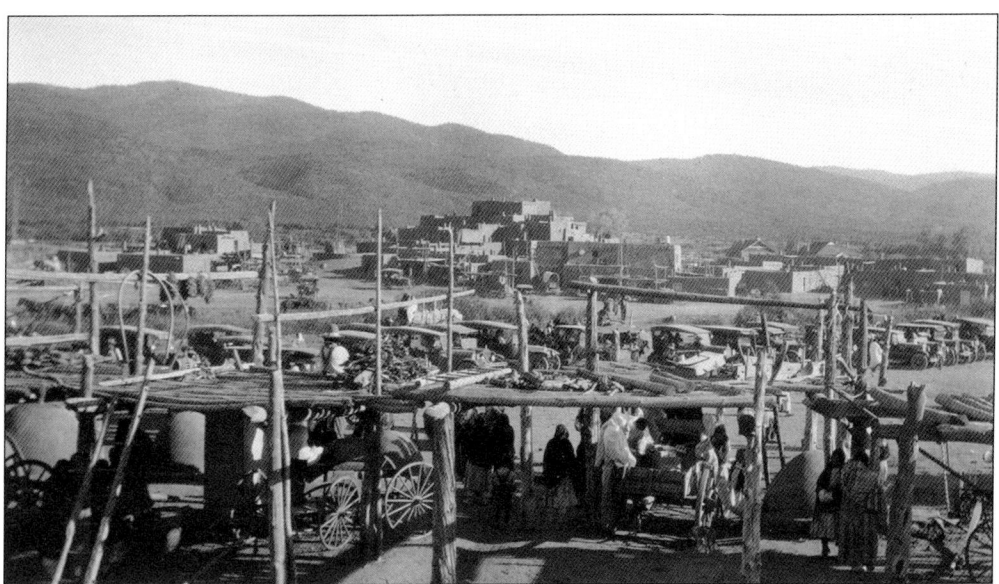

This is a wonderful view of the south, or *Haukwima*, side of the Taos Pueblo taken from a rooftop vantage point from the north building, or *Hlauuma*. Pueblo women are congregating beneath drying racks in the foreground. A row of 1920s automobiles suggests that this is a San Geronimo Day celebration, an event that is open to the public. (Courtesy of Taos Historic Museums.)

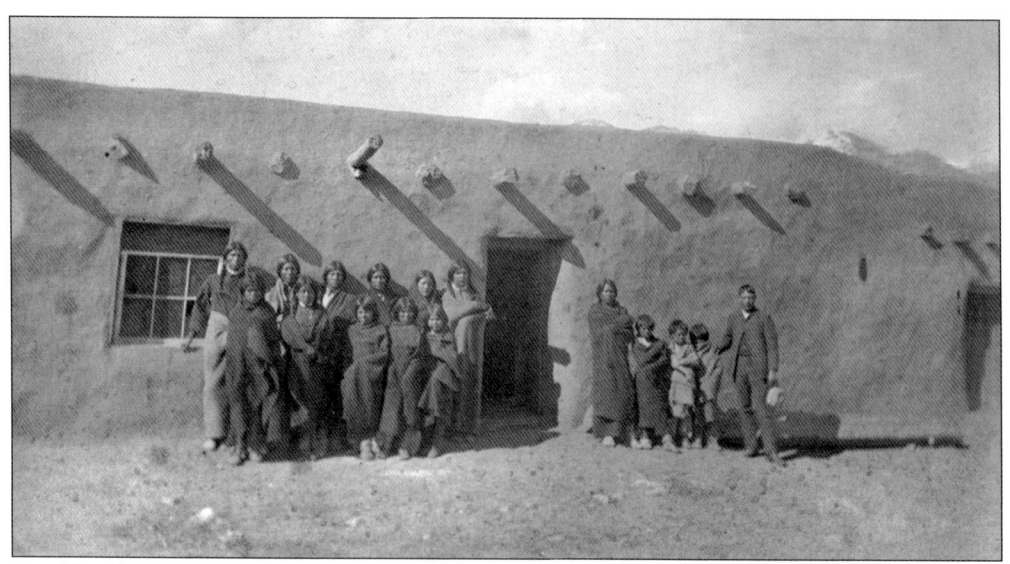

Possibly taken outside of the Taos Day School, this photograph shows several Taos Pueblo children and an Anglo man. (Courtesy of Taos Historic Museums.)

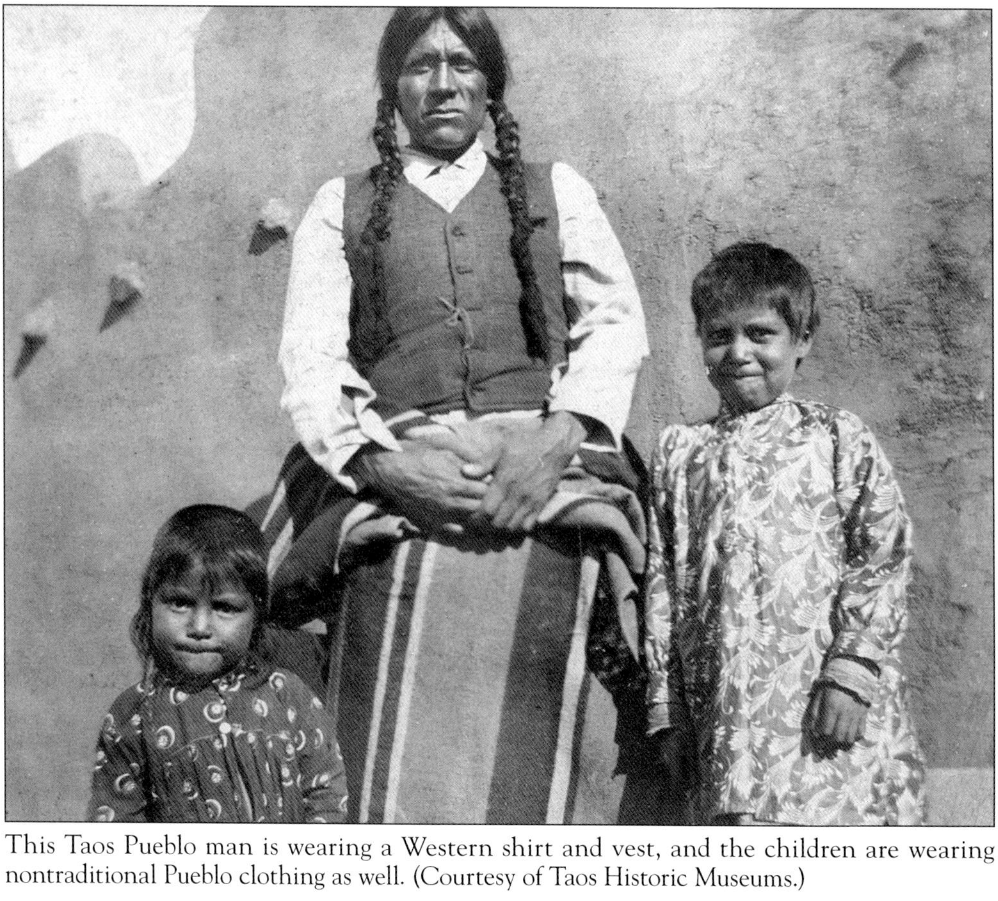

This Taos Pueblo man is wearing a Western shirt and vest, and the children are wearing nontraditional Pueblo clothing as well. (Courtesy of Taos Historic Museums.)

This Taos Pueblo man is wearing a feather headdress with Plains Indian influences. Leather leg straps around his calves are adorned with bells for use in tribal dances. (Courtesy of Taos Historic Museums.)

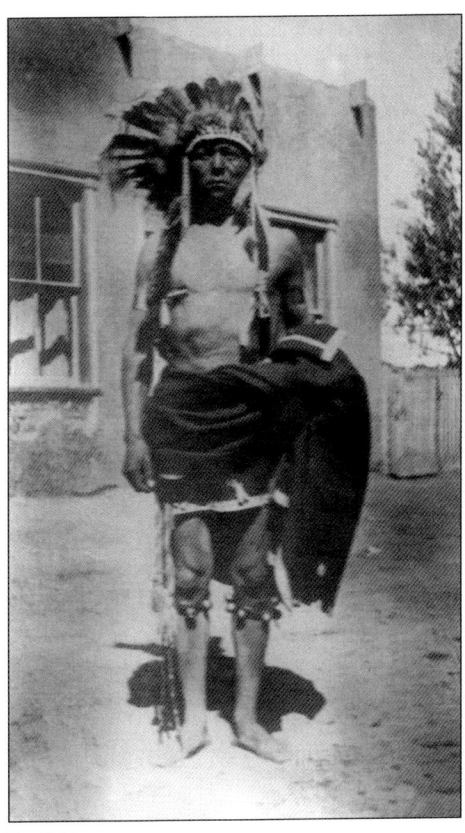

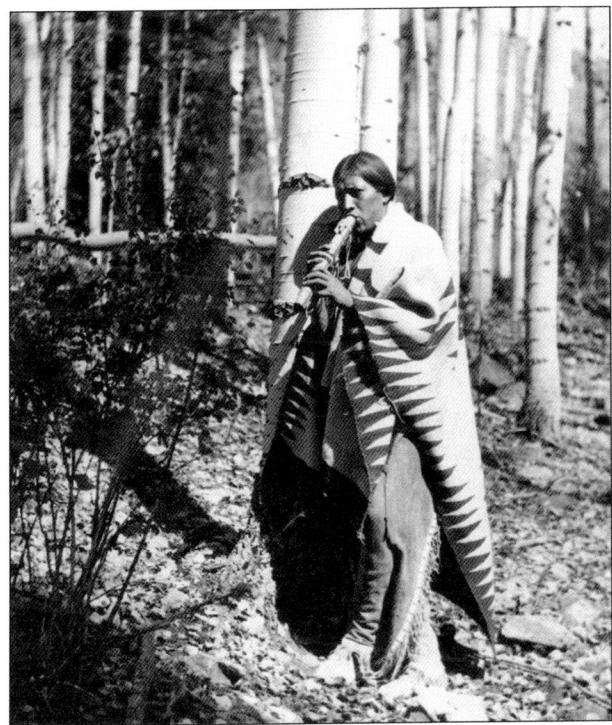

Standing in an aspen grove playing a flute, this Pueblo man is likely to have been posing for one of the early Taos artists. Flute playing was used as a courting ritual among Taos Pueblo Indians. (Courtesy of Taos Historic Museums.)

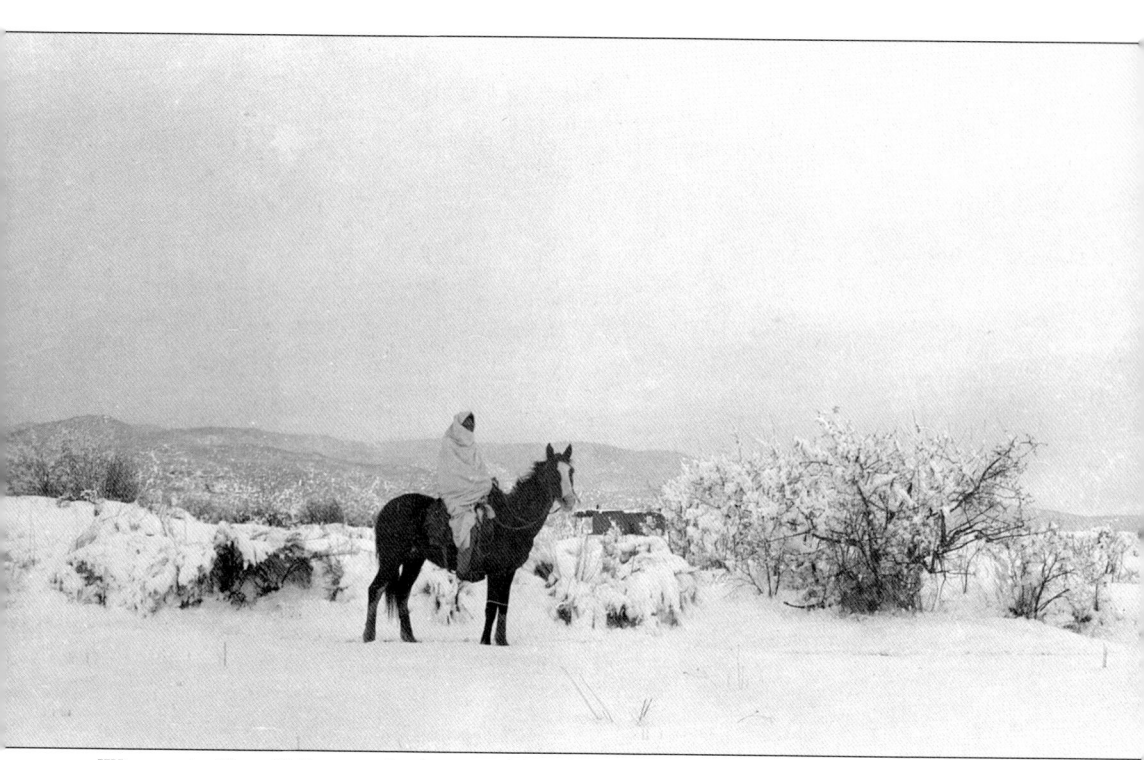

Winters in Taos Valley can be long and harsh. This snowy scene shows a Pueblo man riding a blaze-faced horse. The man is wrapped in a white blanket, a custom of Pawnee Indians. (Courtesy of Taos Historic Museums.)

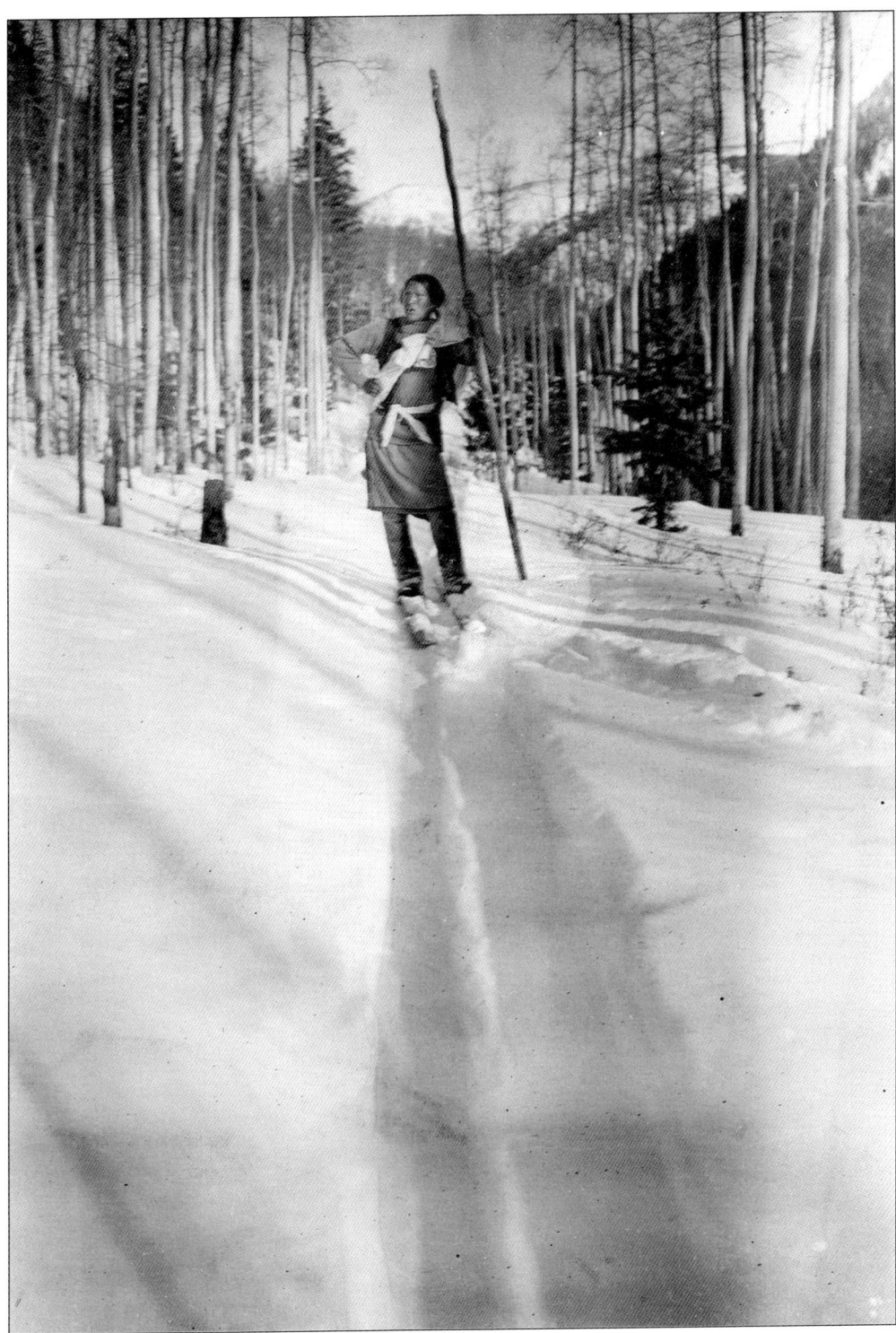
In another winter view, a Pueblo Indian is wearing skis and carrying a tall guiding stick. He is standing in a grove of aspen trees. (Courtesy of Taos Historic Museums.)

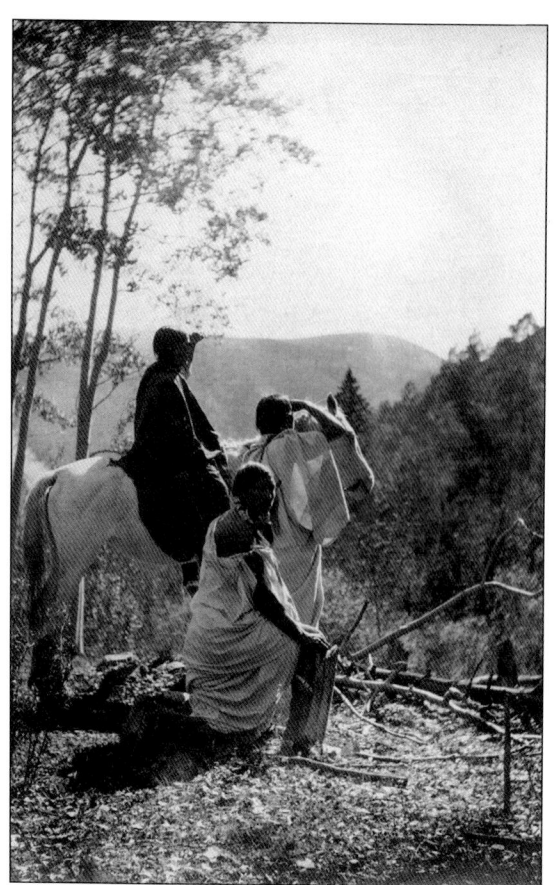

Artists staged many of the early photographs taken of Taos Pueblo. This shot appears to be one of those, with Indian scouts looking over the mountain range. (Courtesy of Taos Historic Museums.)

This Taos Pueblo man is posing for an artist. He is wearing a Plains Indian headdress, which the early Taos artists often substituted for traditional Taos Pueblo traditional clothing. Fields of sagebrush provide an interesting backdrop with chamisa anchoring the right-hand foreground. (Courtesy of Taos Historic Museums.)

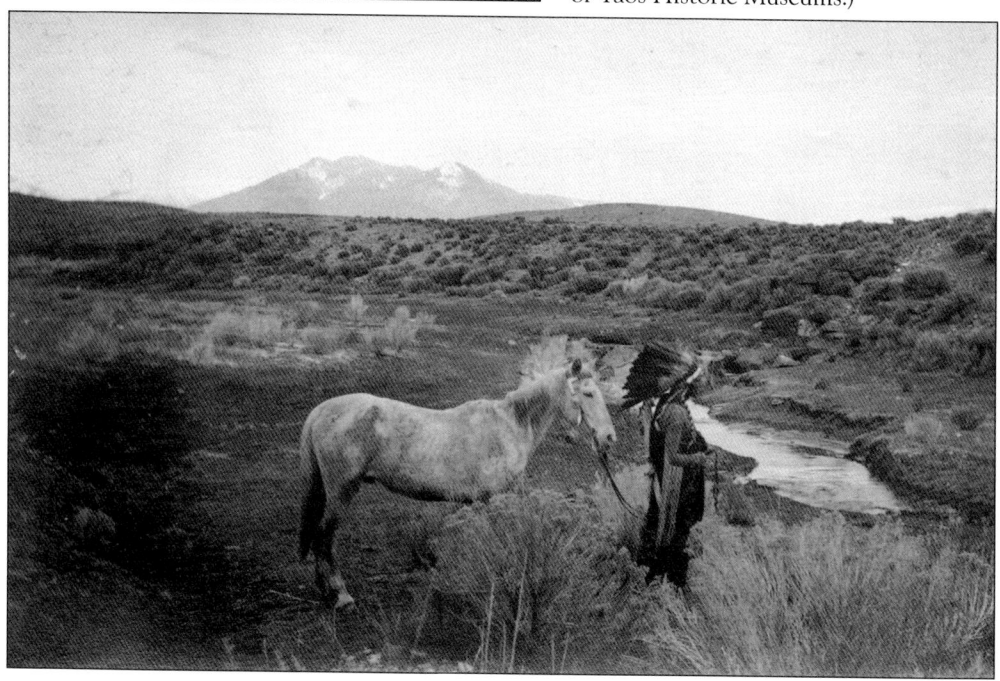

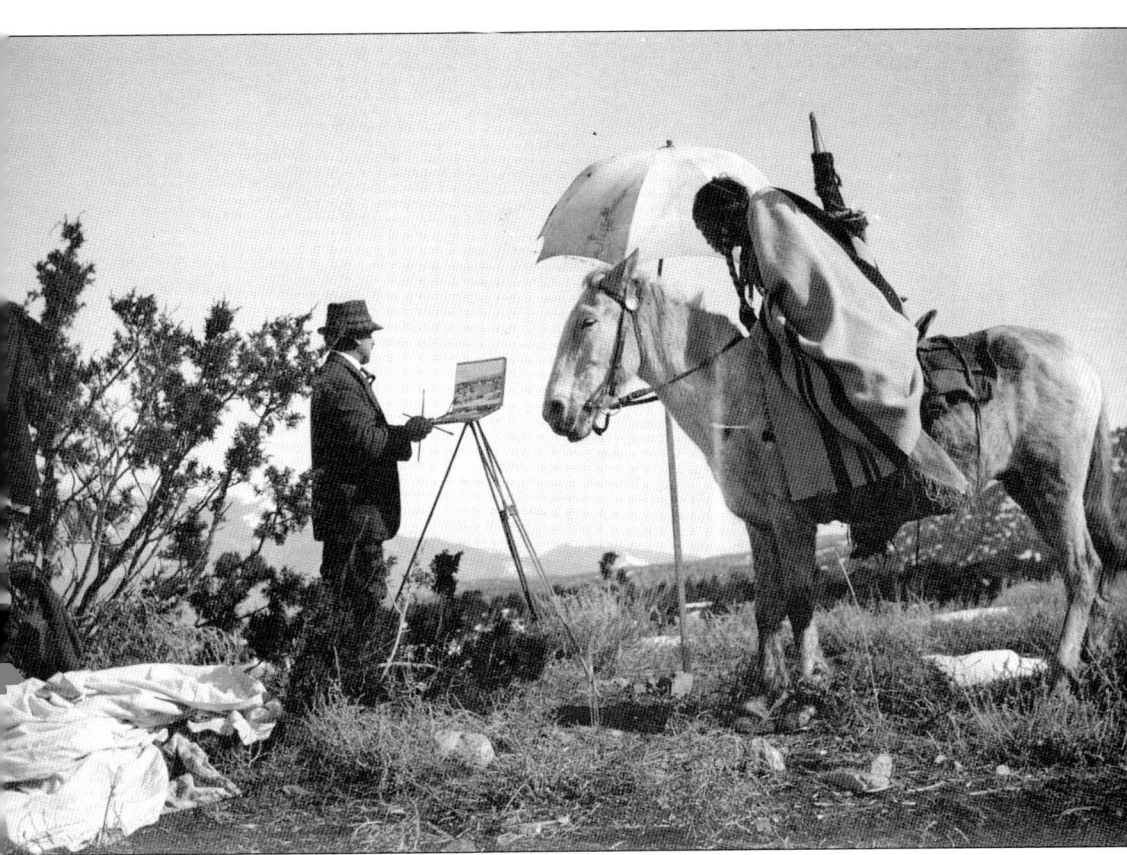

Bert Phillips was one of the founding members of the Taos Society of Artists. (See chapter four.) This photograph shows him using an outdoor easel to paint a Pueblo man on horseback. (Courtesy of Taos Historic Museums.)

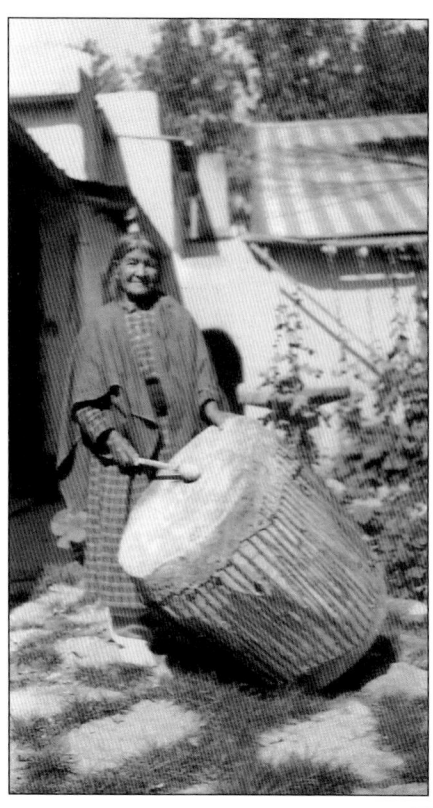

This posed photograph of an elderly Pueblo woman was taken in 1939 in the yard of Taos Society of Artists member Bert G. Phillips. (See chapter four.) The woman appears to be playing a large traditional drum, although in reality in Taos Pueblo it is not customary for women to participate in drumming or traditional dances. (Courtesy of Taos Historic Museums.)

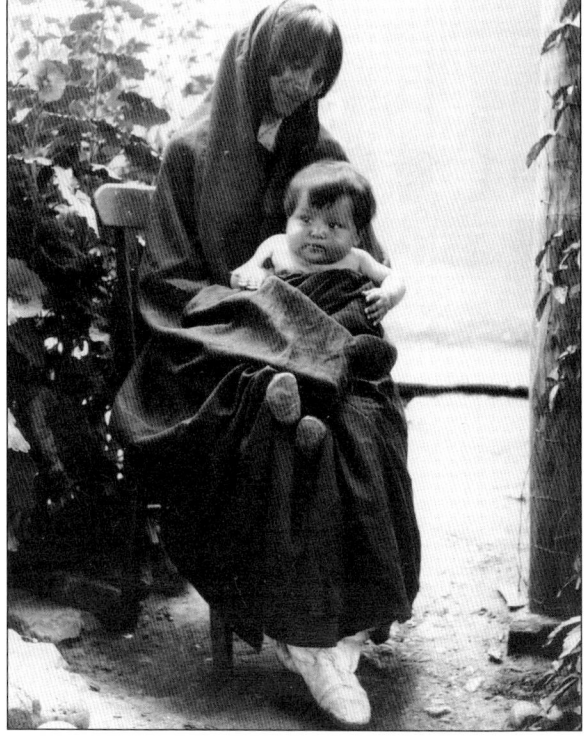

In another staged photograph for the purpose of creating a painting, a Pueblo woman and child are seated in front of a flowering hollyhock bush. Hollyhocks are a common plant found throughout Taos. (Courtesy of Taos Historic Museums.)

The Taos Society of Artists were not always as interested in using authentic Taos Pueblo clothing and props as they were in creating interesting compositions. They often borrowed items from other tribes for use in their paintings. (Courtesy of Taos Historic Museums.)

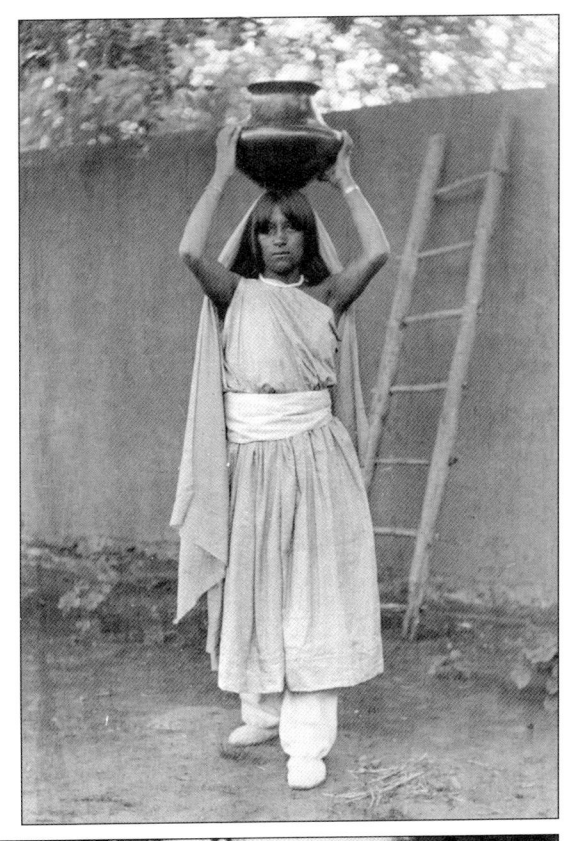

This photograph of a young Taos Pueblo girl with a turkey was taken in town, most likely by an artist creating a painting. She is wearing a buckskin dress and beaded belt not normally associated with Taos Pueblo. Hollyhocks blooming against adobe walls appear in many scenes of Taos. (Courtesy of Taos Historic Museums.)

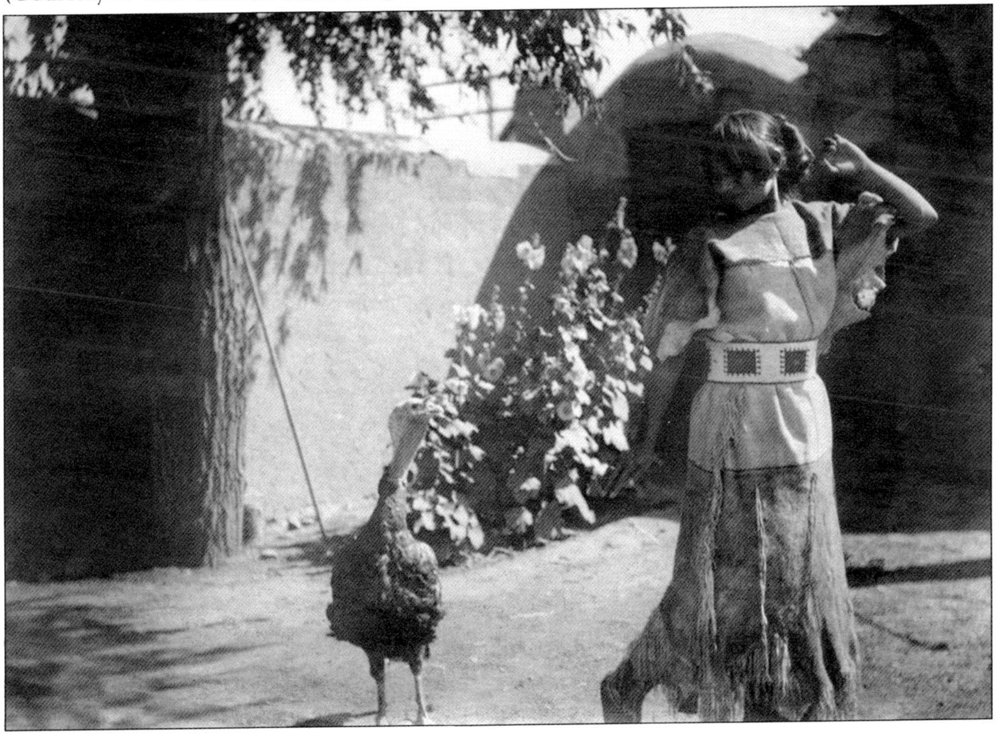

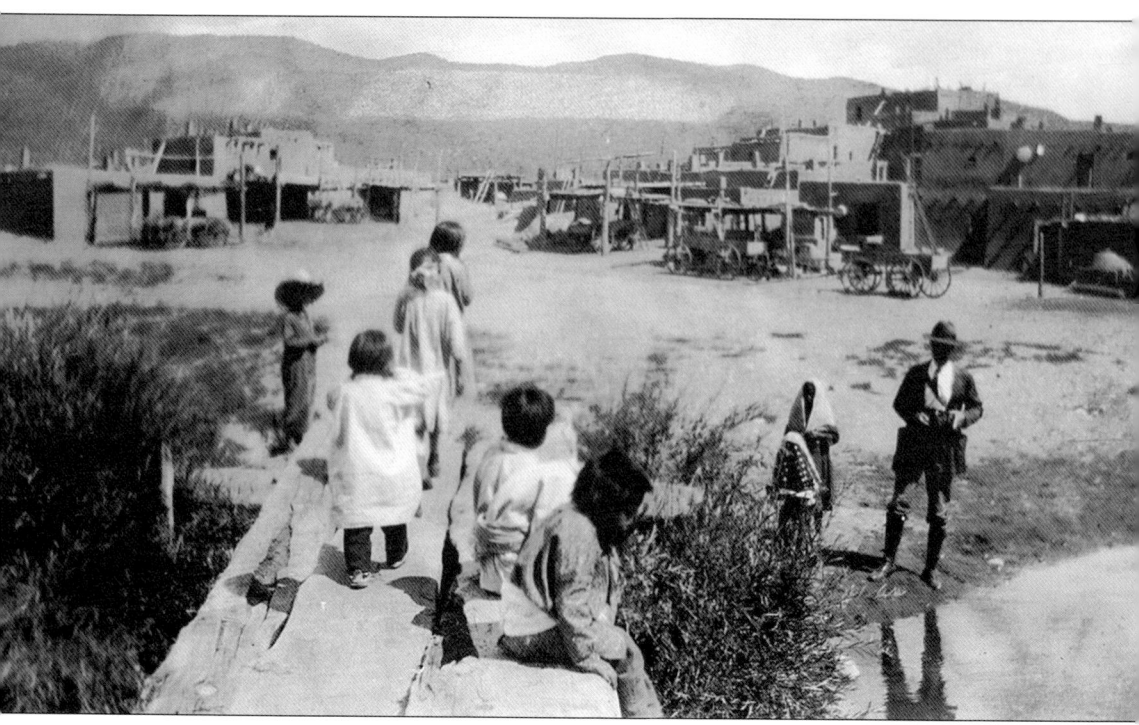

This photograph shows a group of Taos Pueblo children on the wooden bridge crossing the Rio Pueblo that unites the *Hlauuma* (north) to the *Haukwima* (south) side of the Pueblo. (Courtesy of Taos Historic Museums.)

These two photographs were taken on the same bridge over the Rio Pueblo as the one on the facing page. The image at right shows young Pueblo boys fishing from the bridge, with the Taos Mountains visible behind them. The child in the photograph below processes corn while a dog dozes in the sun behind him. (Both courtesy of Taos Historic Museums.)

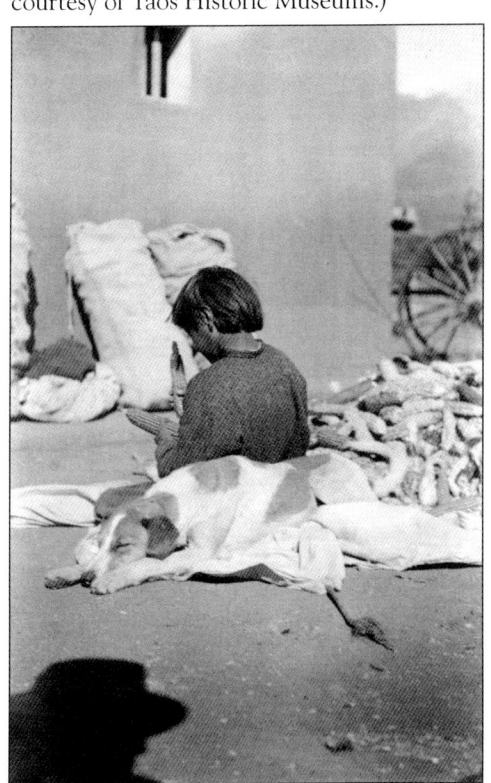

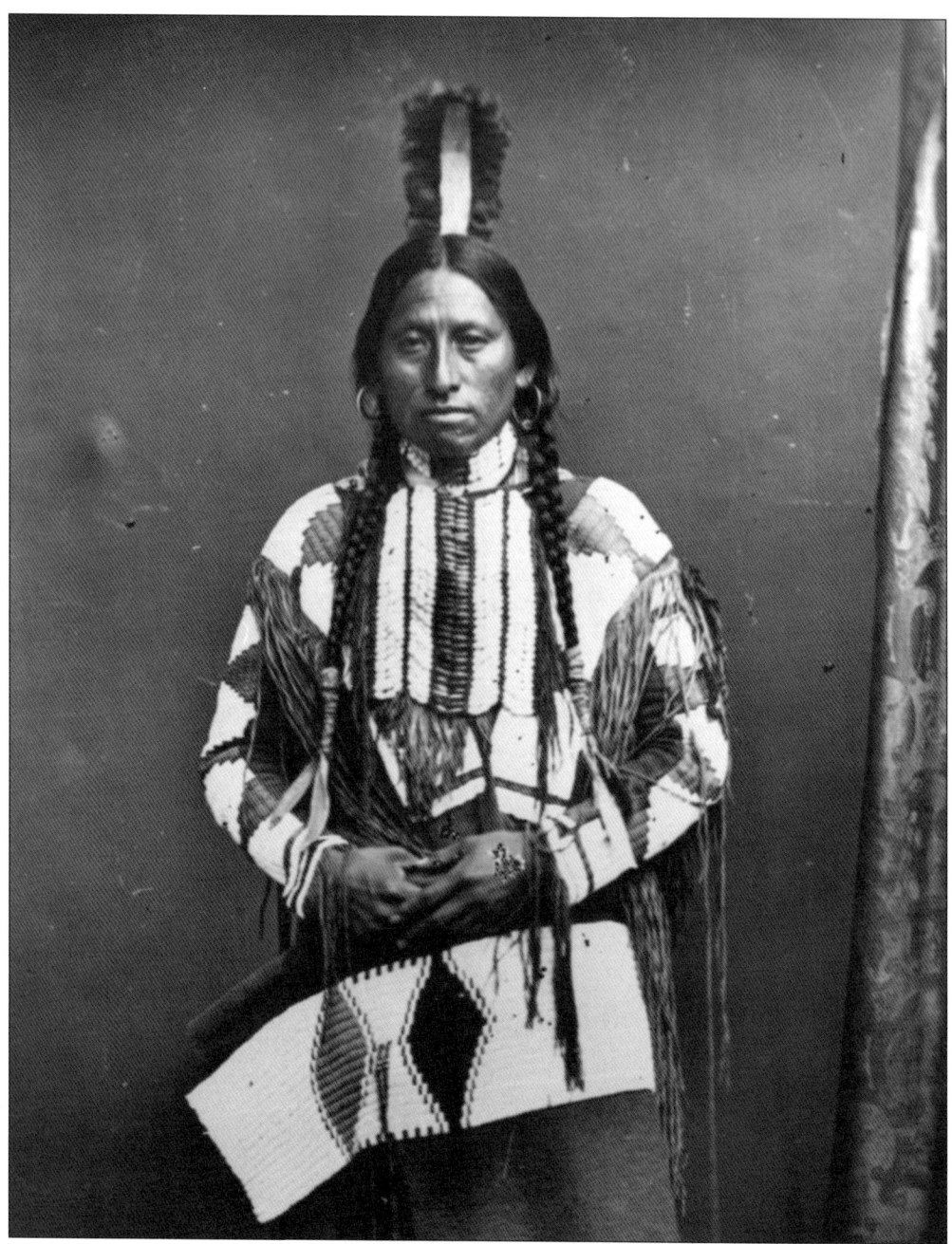

The intricate porcupine quillwork shirt and sash worn by this young Native American suggest that he is a Plains Indian visiting the Taos Pueblo for trade during the annual pow-wow held in Taos or another multitribal event. (Courtesy of Taos Historic Museums.)

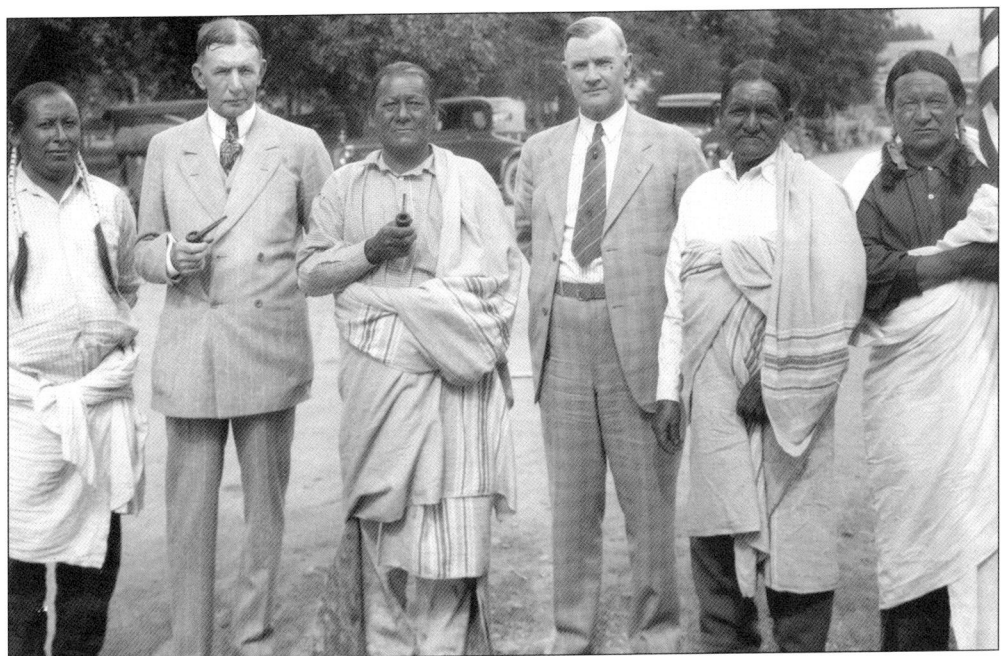

In the late 1920s, Vice Pres. Charles Gates Dawes, who held office from 1925 to 1929 under Pres. Calvin Coolidge, visited the Taos Pueblo. This photograph shows him meeting with Taos Pueblo Indian Council members. From left to right are Albert Martínez, Vice President Dawes, Juan de Jesús Concha, Alan Sells, Juan Archuleta, and an unidentified council member. (Courtesy of Taos Historic Museums.)

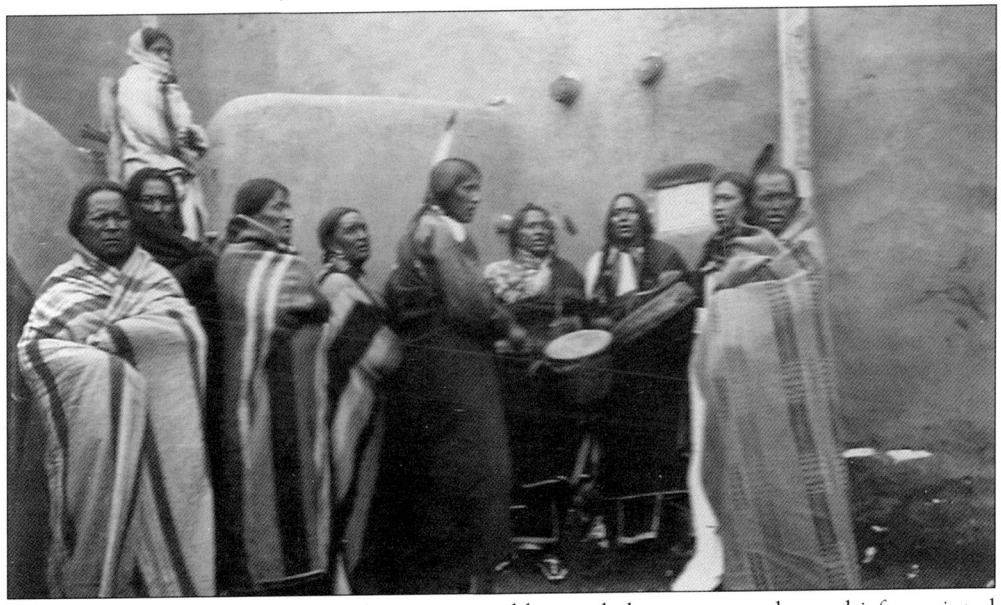

Historically, the Taos Pueblo has been governed by a tribal governor and war chief appointed annually by a group of male elders known as the tribal council. The governor's role is to address issues within the village and with the non-Pueblo world, while the war chief is concerned with protecting tribal land beyond the Pueblo walls. In this photograph, a group of tribal members gathers for a ceremony involving drums. (Courtesy of Taos Historic Museums.)

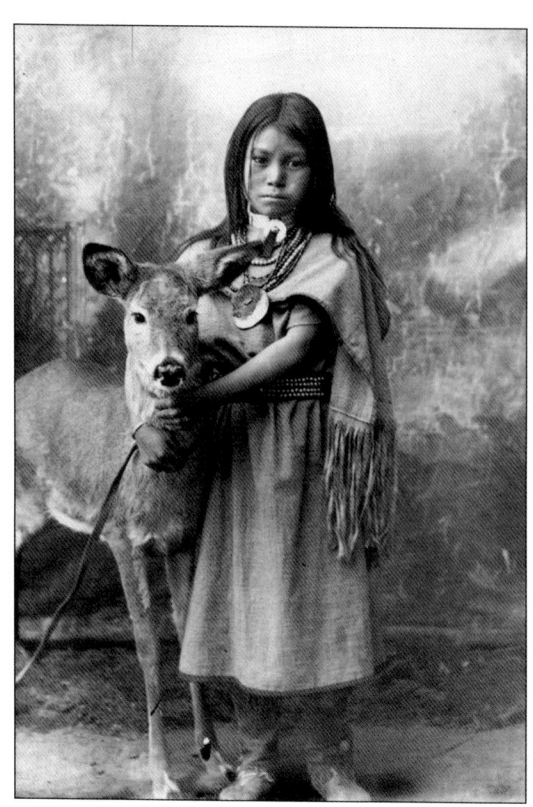

This beautiful Taos Pueblo girl, Crucita Mondragon Reyna, is posing with a fawn for Taos Society of Artists founder Bert G. Phillips. She was born in 1891 and lived for 84 years. In these images, she is wearing what appears to be an Apache dress. Crucita's son, Tony (opposite page), became a highly respected decorated war hero. (Courtesy of Taos Historic Museums.)

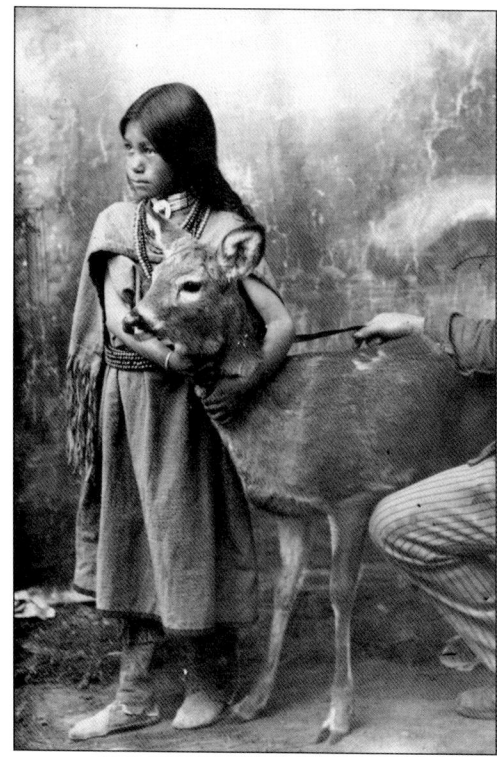

Born in 1915, Tony Reyna attended the Taos Day School and Santa Fe Indian School as a child. He graduated from Santa Fe High School in 1936. While serving his country in the Philippines in World War II, he was taken prisoner by the Japanese and sent, along with hundreds of other New Mexico soldiers, on what is now widely known as the Bataan Death March. For three and a half years, he was tortured and forced to bury hundreds of soldiers, including his best friend. Reyna is a well-respected local hero whose many accomplishments since the war include twice being named to the position of governor of Taos Pueblo. He and his wife, Annie Cota Reyna raised four children. Reyna is the last surviving Taos Pueblo soldier from the Bataan Death March. (Courtesy of the Reyna family.)

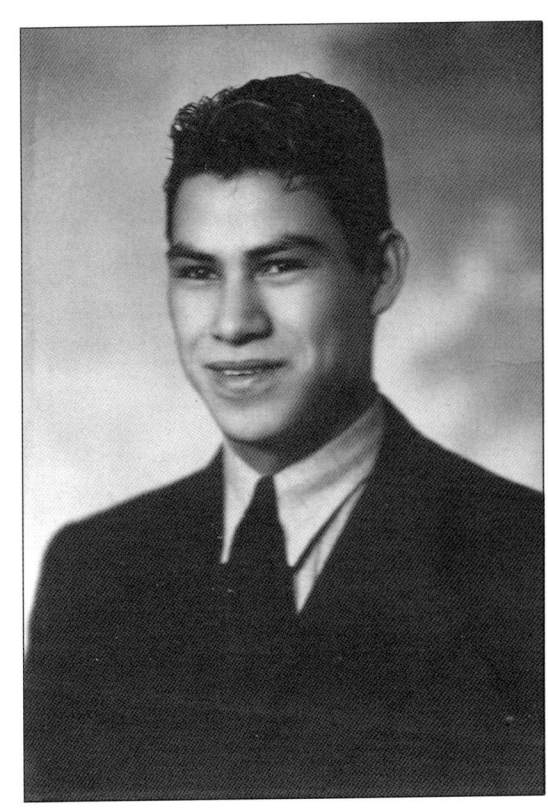

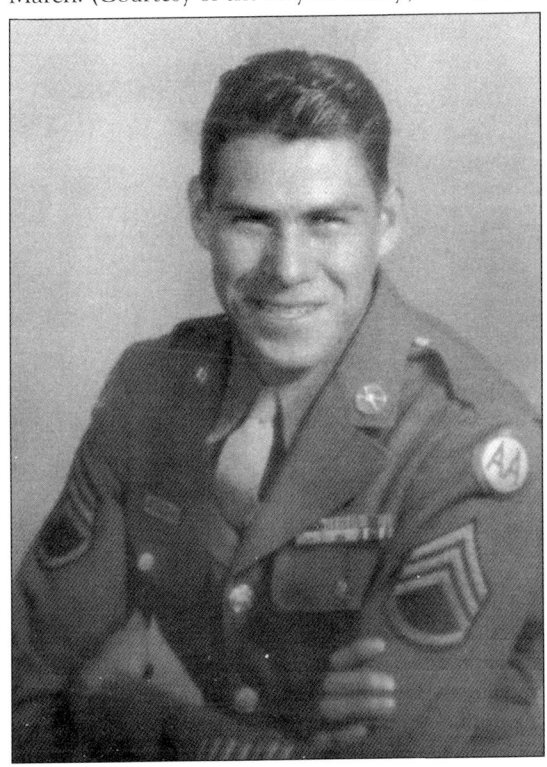

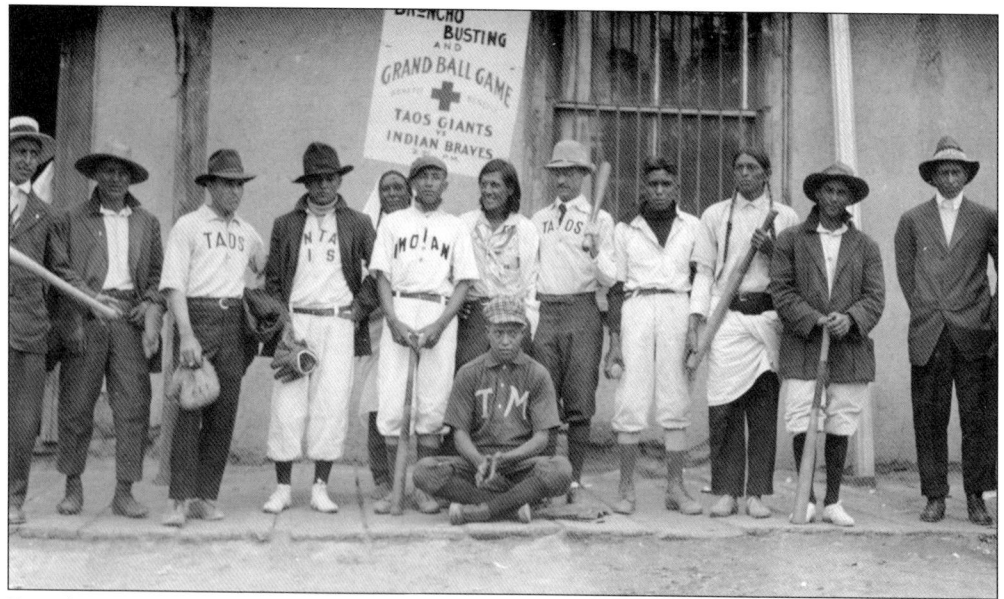

Founding Taos Society of Artists Ernest L. Blumenschein (near middle of image with a bat over his shoulder) stands with unidentified members of a local baseball team under a sign that reads, "Broncho Busting and Grand Ball Game Benefit, Taos Giants vs. Indian Braves." (Courtesy of Taos Historic Museums.)

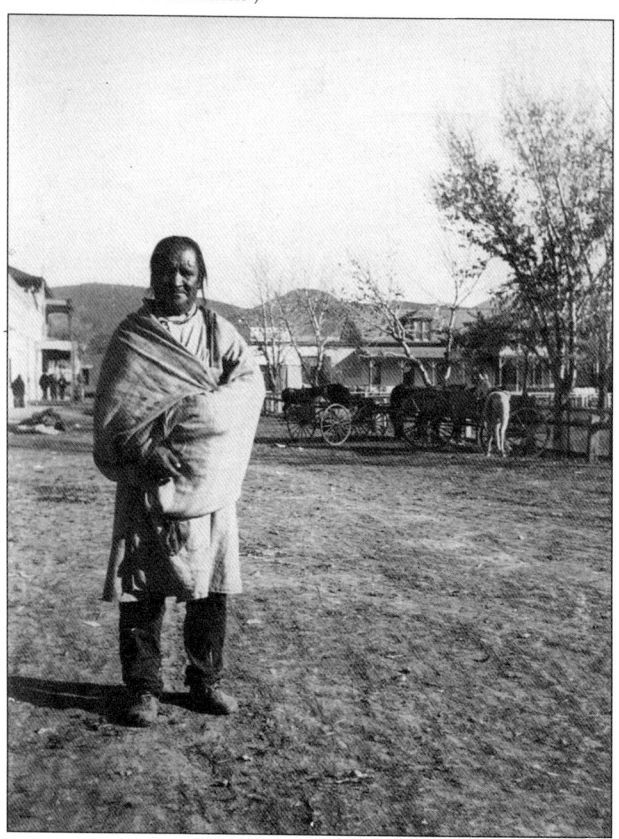

A Taos Pueblo man wrapped in a traditional blanket stands with his back to the old Taos Plaza. (Courtesy of Taos Historic Museums.)

Two

Historic Taos Plaza

Early Spanish settlers arrived in 1615 and later were forced to vacate the Taos Valley following the Pueblo Revolt of 1680. Many returned, and others migrated from Spain after the Spanish regained the territory in 1710. The king of Spain distributed what was called the Don Fernando Land Grant to 63 Spanish families in 1796, which led to the establishment of the Taos Plaza and surrounding neighborhoods. The threat of Indian raids by nomadic tribes dictated the fortress-like, thick-walled homes and business enterprises that made up the original plaza. Strong gates regulated the only means of entry and exit, and sentries guarded each corner. The interior of the plaza provided safe haven for livestock when needed, complete with a well for water. Several brutal battles occurred in and around the plaza in the 1847 rebellion against U.S. occupation, and a number of executions took place there.

In peaceful times, Taos Plaza was a place for community celebrations, fiestas, and church processions, and since Taos was a major crossroads for fur trading, the plaza was often filled with laden pack animals and lively mountain men. To accommodate the growing number of visitors, two hotels were built, the Don Fernando and the Columbian. A courthouse and jail were erected on the north side in 1830 and, eventually, saloons and gambling establishments replaced residences on the plaza.

Fire was a common threat to the plaza because of shared walls and proximity, and many buildings were lost to flames over the years. A particularly devastating blaze in the early 1930s destroyed the Don Fernando Hotel, a popular gathering place for local artists, and the Taos courthouse. In 1933 and 1934, several Taos artists, including Bert Phillips, Victor Higgins, Emil Bisttram, and Ward Lockwood were commissioned under the Works Progress Administration bill to create frescoes for the new courthouse built on the plaza in 1932 to replace the one lost to fire. While the county courthouse has since moved to another location, the frescoes remain intact in their original location on the plaza.

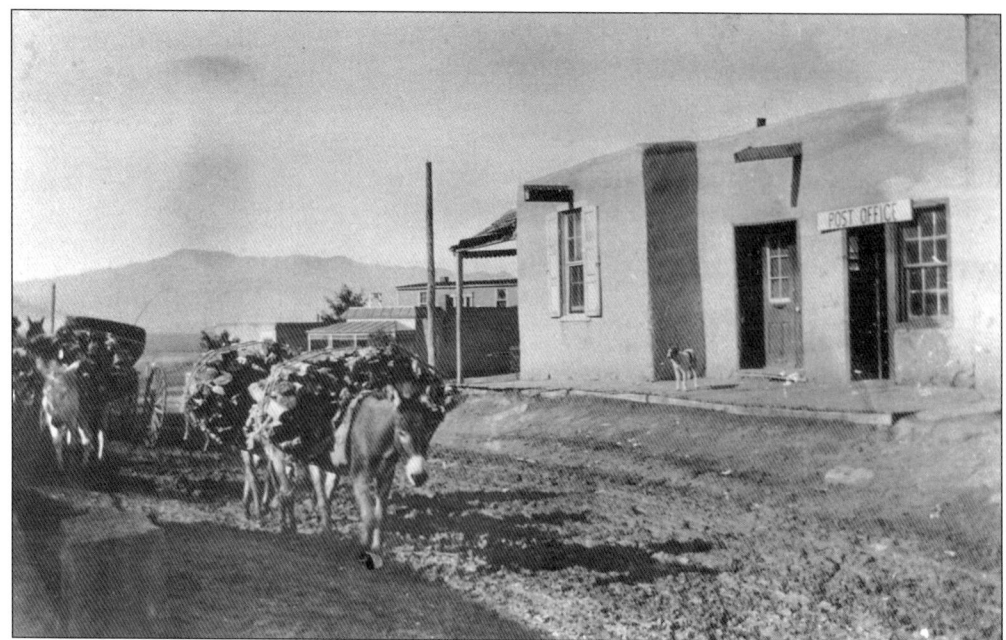

Three donkeys laden with firewood pass the old post office on their way to the plaza as a Taos dog looks on. Pack animals were a common sight on the plaza where the selling and trading of goods took place. (Courtesy of Taos Historic Museums.)

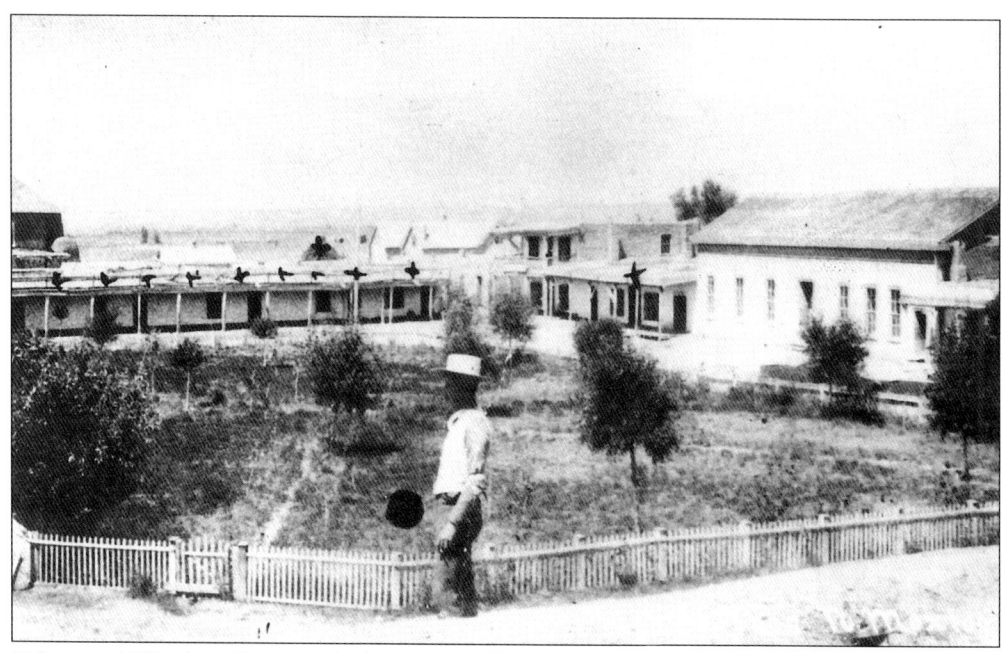

Taken in 1883, this photograph shows a small picket fence surrounding the square and rows of *portales* that were removed in 1887 during one of the many refurbishing efforts. The man is standing at the southeast corner, and the original Nuestra Señora de Guadalupe, or Our Lady of Guadalupe Church, built in 1833 can be seen at the far left of the photograph. (Courtesy of Taos Historic Museums.)

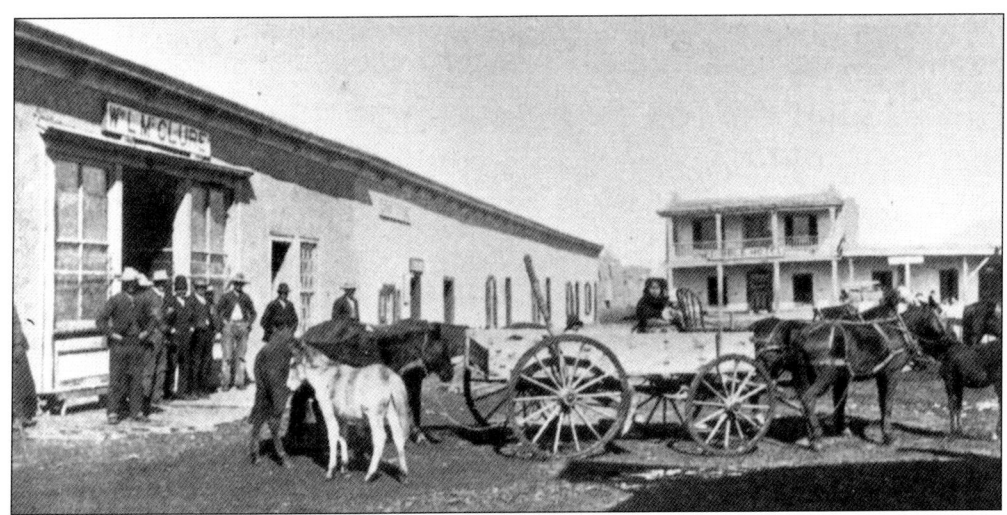

A horse-drawn wooden wagon sits in the center of the plaza in this 1883 photograph of the northwest corner. The Dibble Hotel, seen here, was established in 1867. (Courtesy of Taos Historic Museums.)

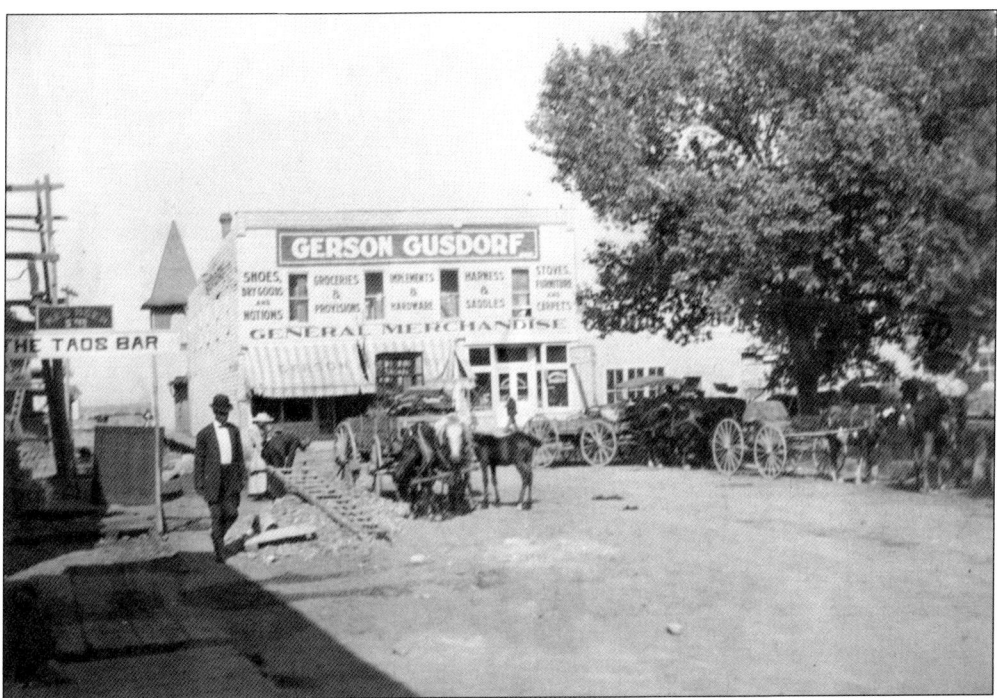

This general merchandise store carried a wide variety of items from shoes, dry goods, groceries, and provisions to saddles, stoves, furniture, and carpets. Alex Gusdorf was the first in the Taos area to operate a store, which he eventually sold to his younger brother, Gerston, and two other partners. Gerston went on to open his own store (seen here), while Alex served as president and chairman of the board of the First State Bank of Taos that opened in 1922. (Courtesy of Taos Historic Museums.)

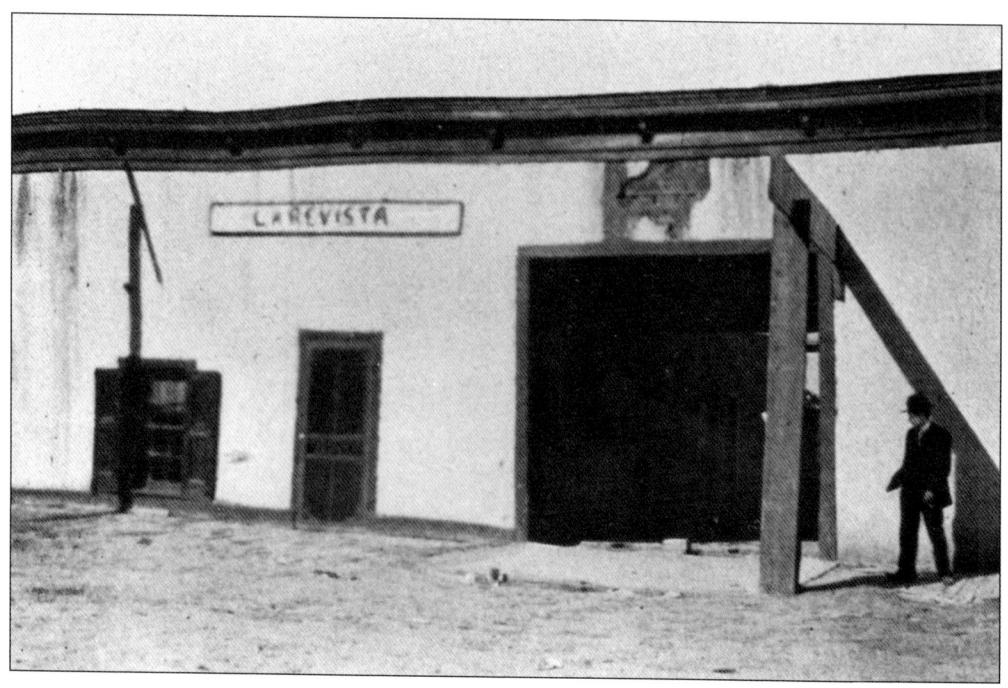

The Spanish-language *La Revista de Taos* was the first newspaper of the Taos Valley. It was established by Jose Montaner, born in Barcelona, Spain, in 1877, who arrived in Taos in 1901. An extremely enterprising man, Montaner eventually published an English-language paper called the *Taos Valley News* (below) as well. (See chapter six for additional information on Montaner's many impressive accomplishments.) (Both courtesy of Taos Historic Museums.)

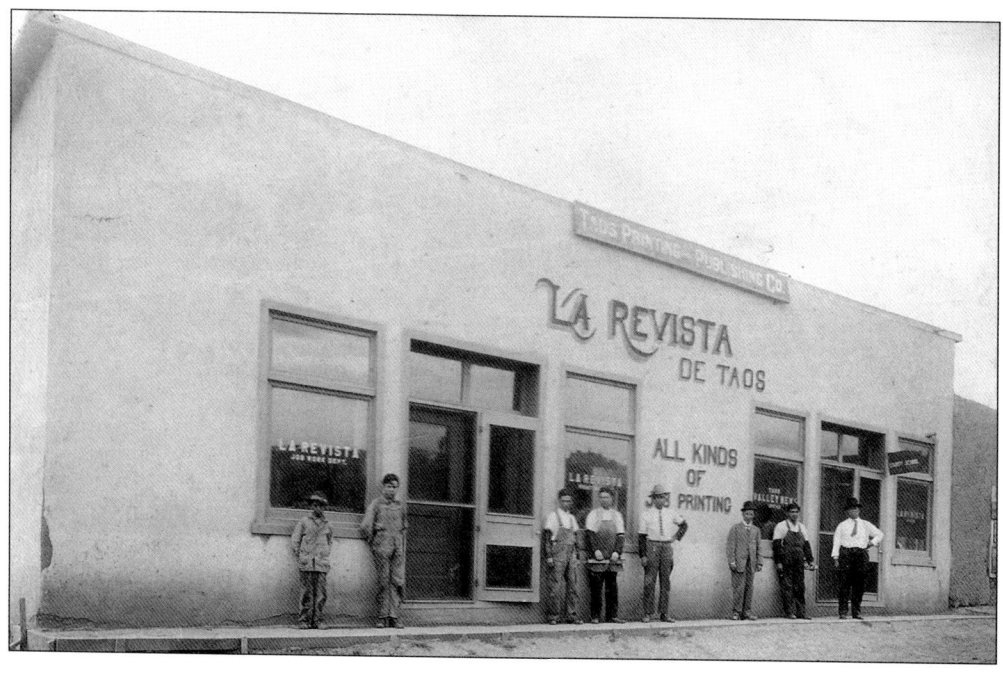

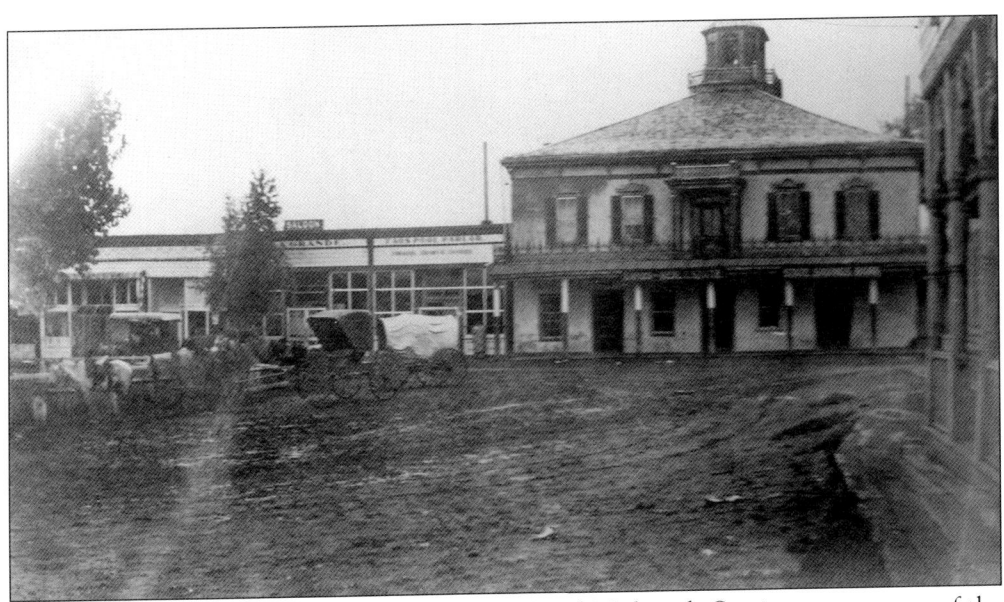

Juan de los Reyes Santistevan, son of José Maneul and Medina de Santistevan, was one of the first merchant bankers in Taos. He built this grand two-story residence on the northeast side of the plaza (shown here in 1916) that would later become the Taos Hotel. (Courtesy of Taos Historic Museums.)

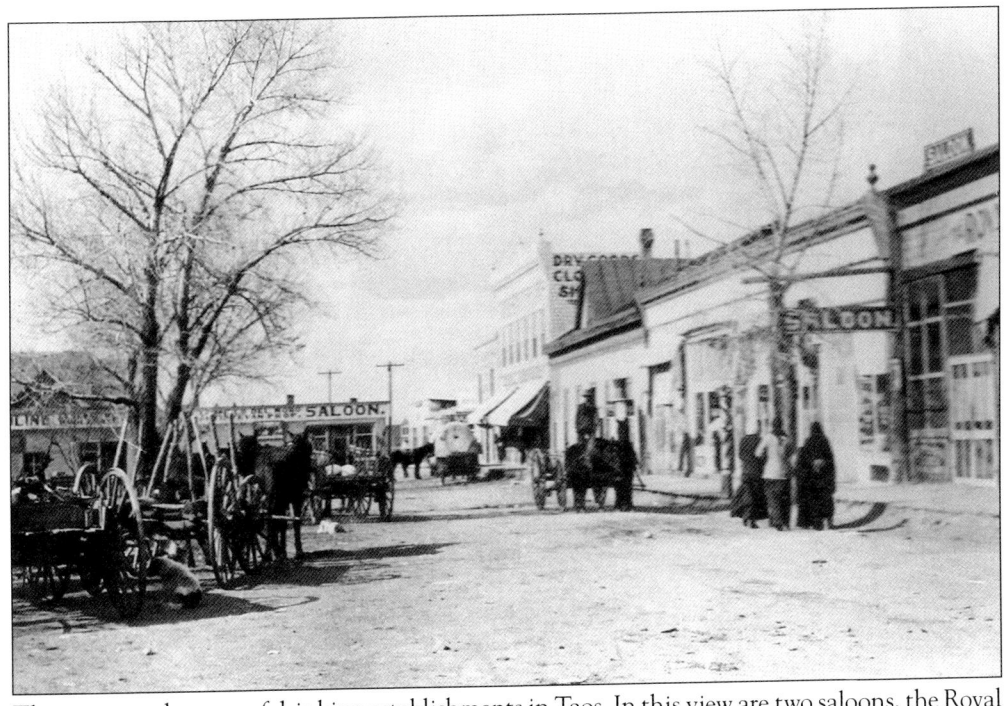

There was no shortage of drinking establishments in Taos. In this view are two saloons, the Royal Saloon and Taos Pool Parlor, on the right next to a barbershop. A dry goods establishment lies further down the row. (Courtesy of Taos Historic Museums.)

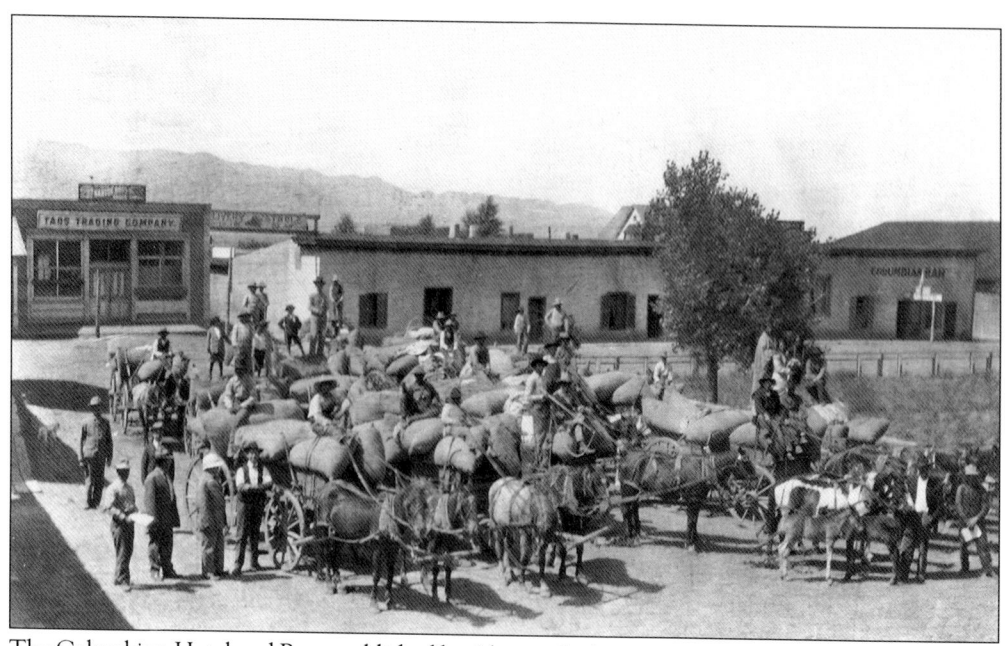

The Columbian Hotel and Bar, established by Aloysius Liebert in 1904, became a favorite gathering place among locals and visitors alike. In 1937, James and John Karavas changed the name to the La Fonda de Taos Hotel, which is still in operation today. (Courtesy of Taos Historic Museums.)

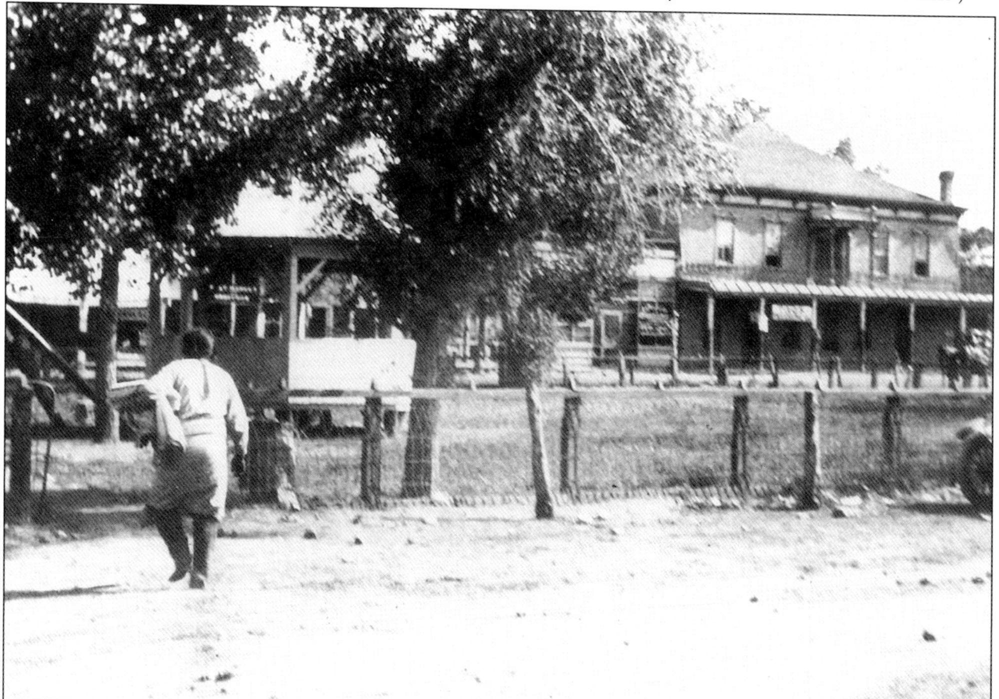

Taken in 1905, this view is of the northeast corner of the plaza. To the left, a Taos Pueblo man is walking toward the early bandstand, which has changed considerably since then. To the right is Juan de los Reyes Santistevan's home, which would later become the Taos Hotel. (Courtesy of Taos Historic Museums.)

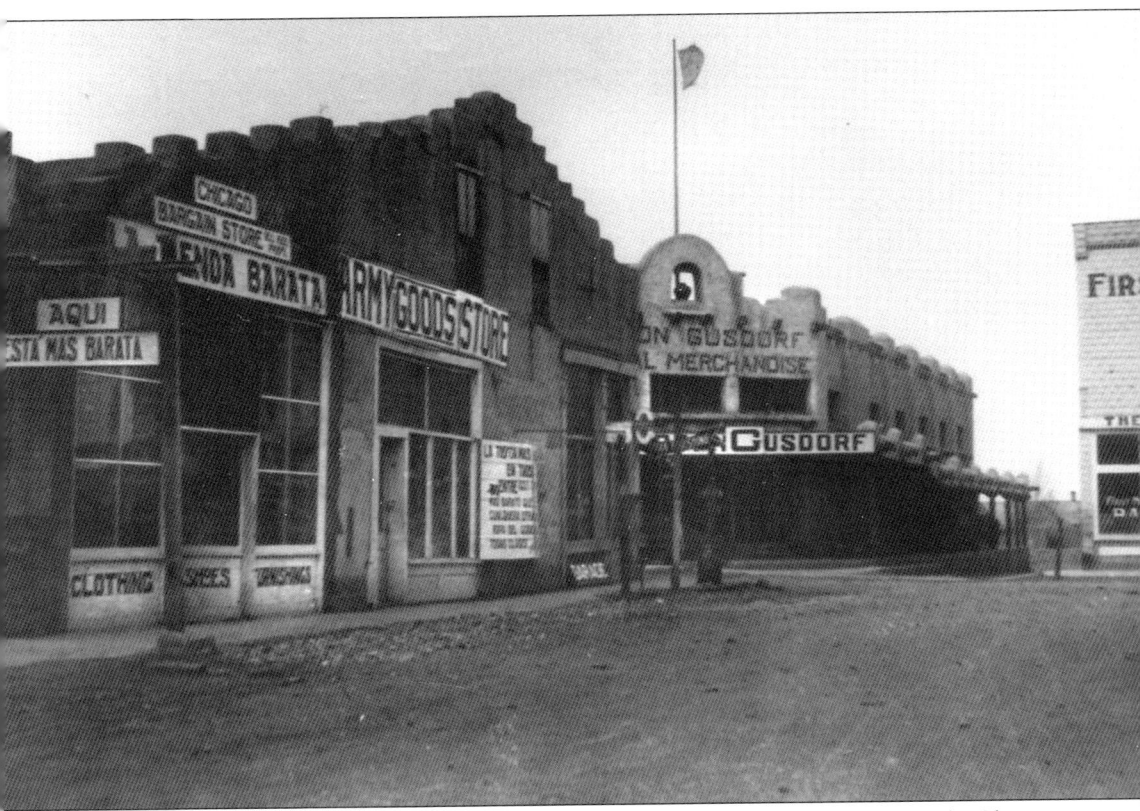

This rather bleak view of the plaza shows a number of business establishments, including the Chicago Bargain Store, Army Goods Store, and Gerston Gusdorf's General Merchandise Shop. In 1879, Gerston's older brother, Alex, had established a three-story general store and steam-operated flourmill on the plaza, which was destroyed by fire in 1895. (Courtesy of Taos Historic Museums.)

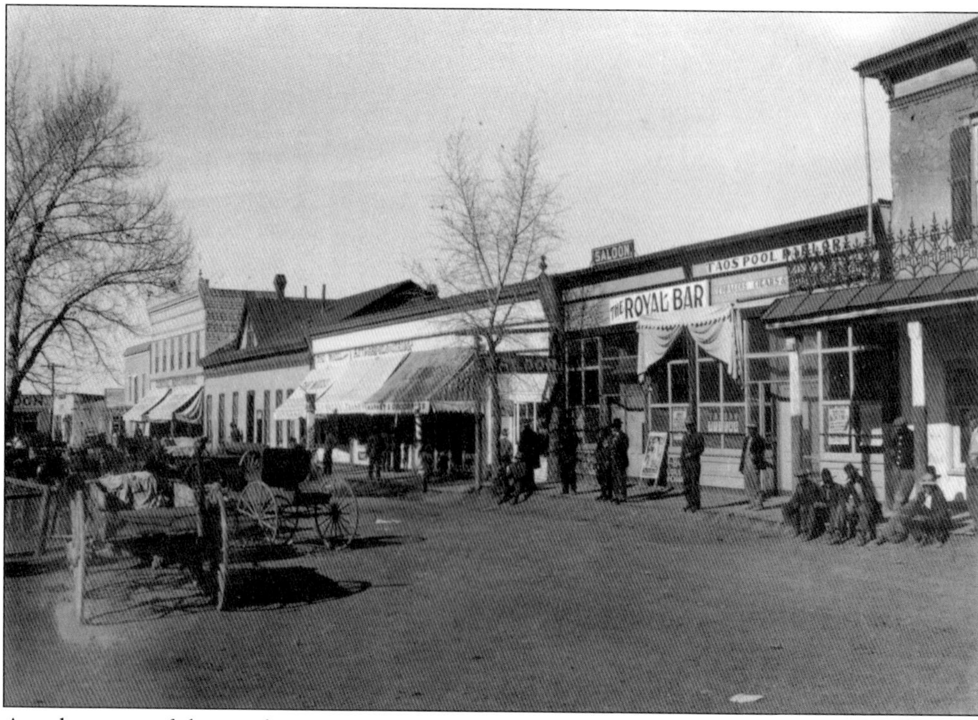

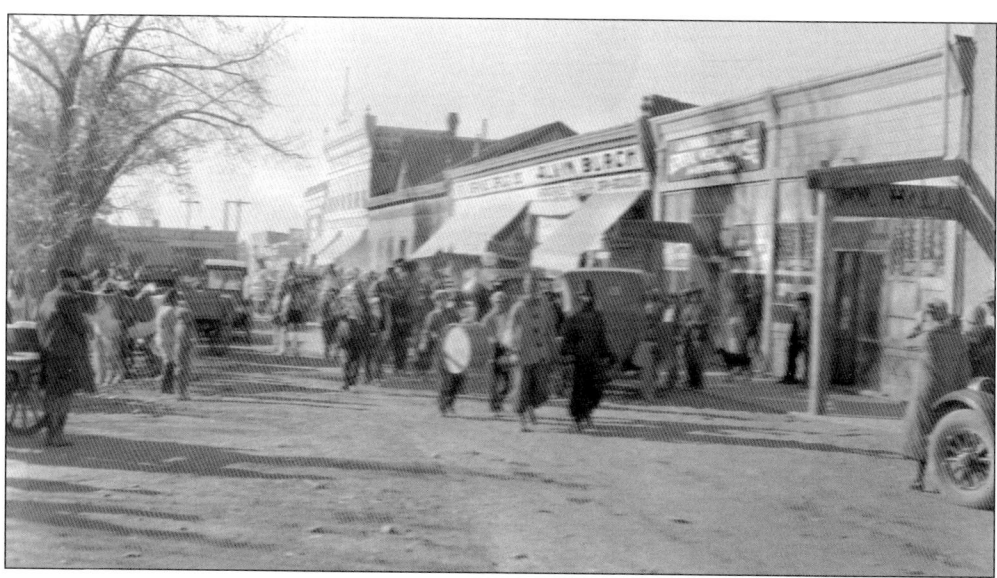

Another view of the northeast corner shows wagons lined up along the plaza while men sit and stand outside of the Royal Bar and Taos Pool Parlor. (Courtesy of Taos Historic Museums.)

The Taos Plaza was the community center for parades, fiestas, and religious processions. In this 1920s photograph, a parade makes its way toward the northeast corner of the plaza. (Courtesy of Taos Historic Museums.)

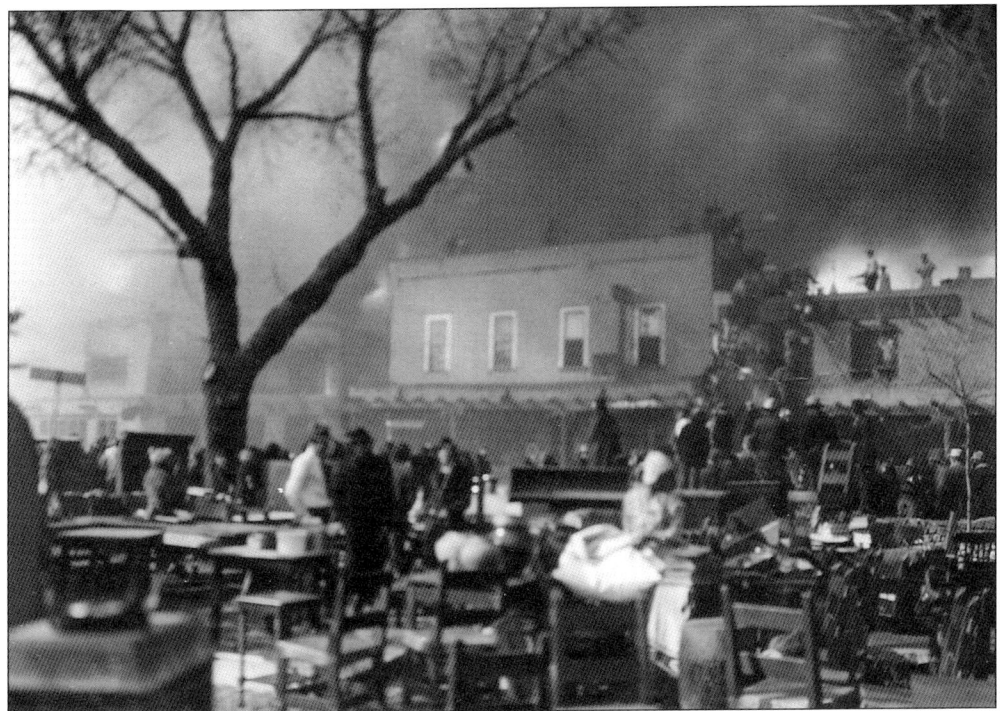

A devastating fire struck the Taos Plaza in 1933. Taos Society of Artists founder Ernest L. Blumenschein wrote on the back of the above photograph to his wife Mary and daughter Helen, "A sad x-mas without my dear girls. But hope it will be merry for you. Ernest 33. This photograph was taken in the fire. The "don" is no more." The Don Fernando Hotel was owned by Gerson Gusdorf from 1926 to 1933 and was a favorite gathering place for Blumenschein and other Taos artists. Since there were no art galleries in Taos at the time, Gerson allowed the artists to use the hotel as a gallery of sorts and a place where they could sell their work. Thanks to enough advance notice, most of the artwork and furniture was saved from this fire. (Courtesy of Taos Historic Museums.)

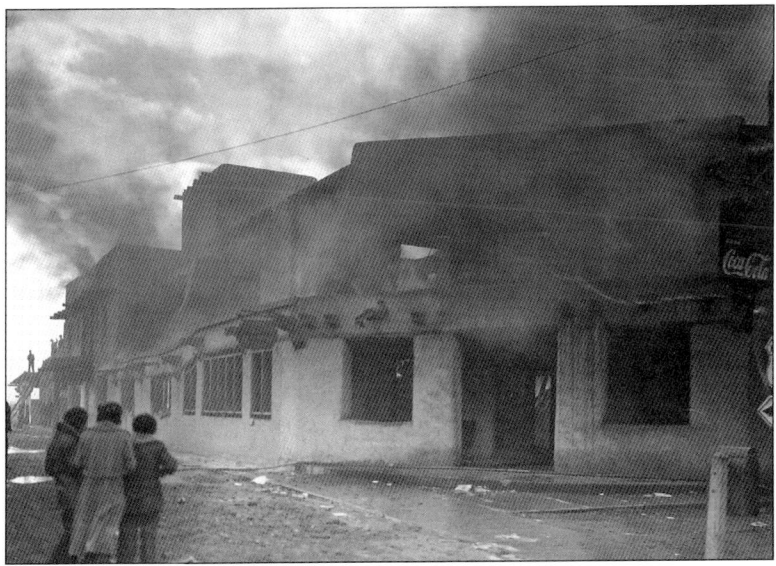

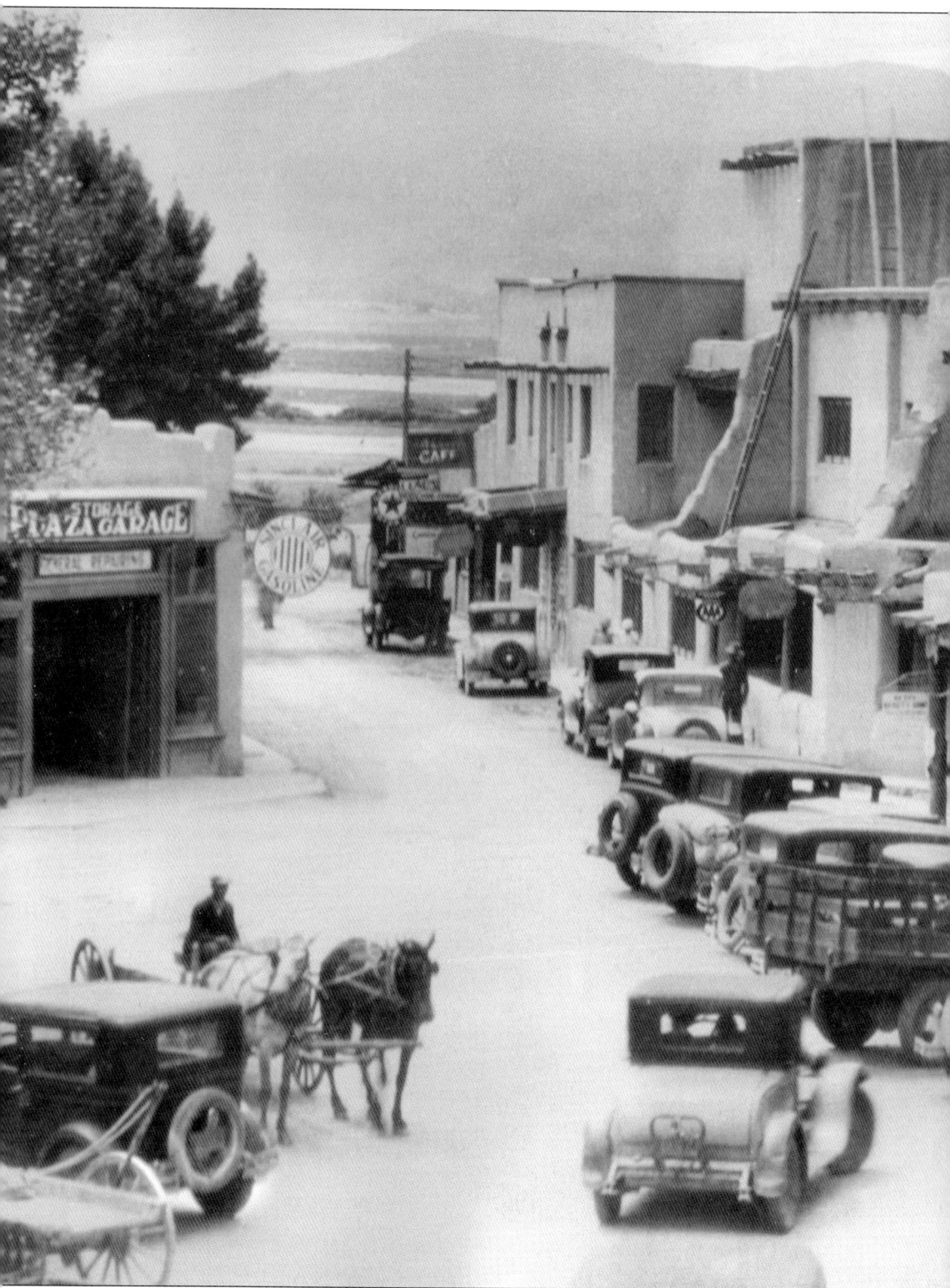

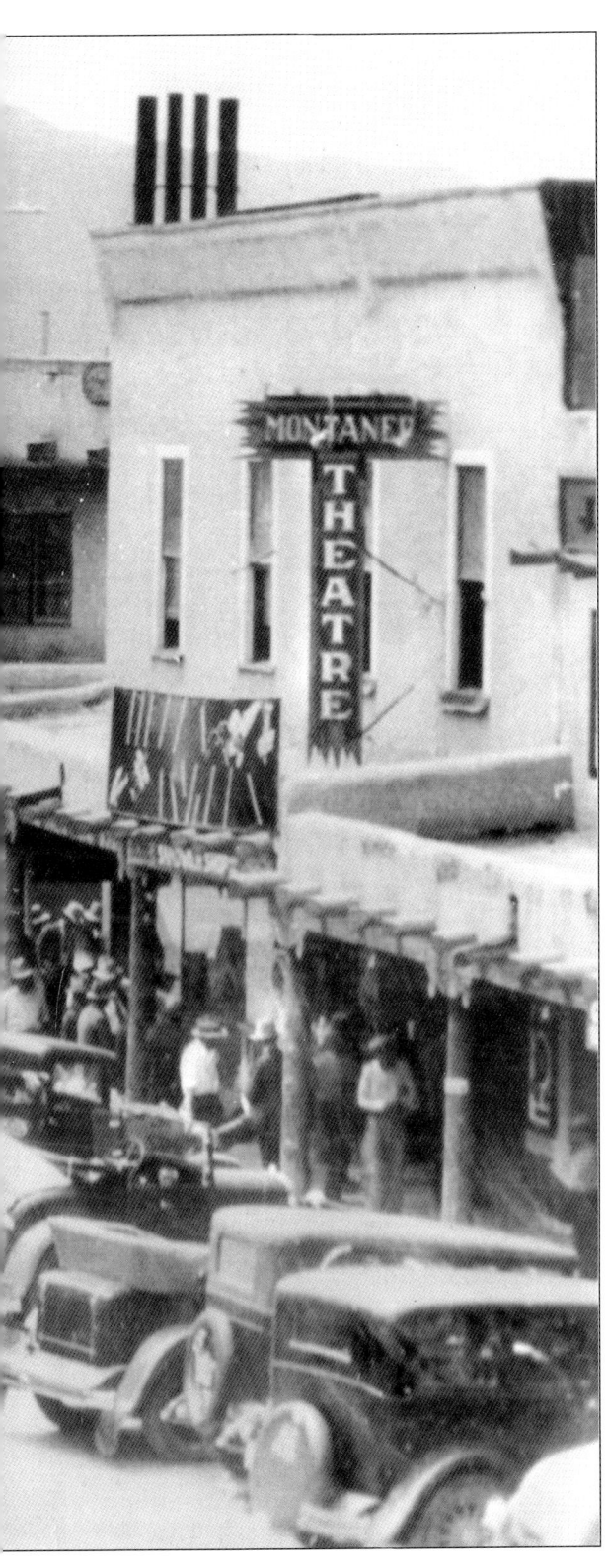

This wonderful view of the plaza was taken in the early 1930s. There are two gasoline stations and a parking garage. To the left is the Montaner Theater, established by José Montaner. (See chapter six.) (Courtesy of Annie Santistevan.)

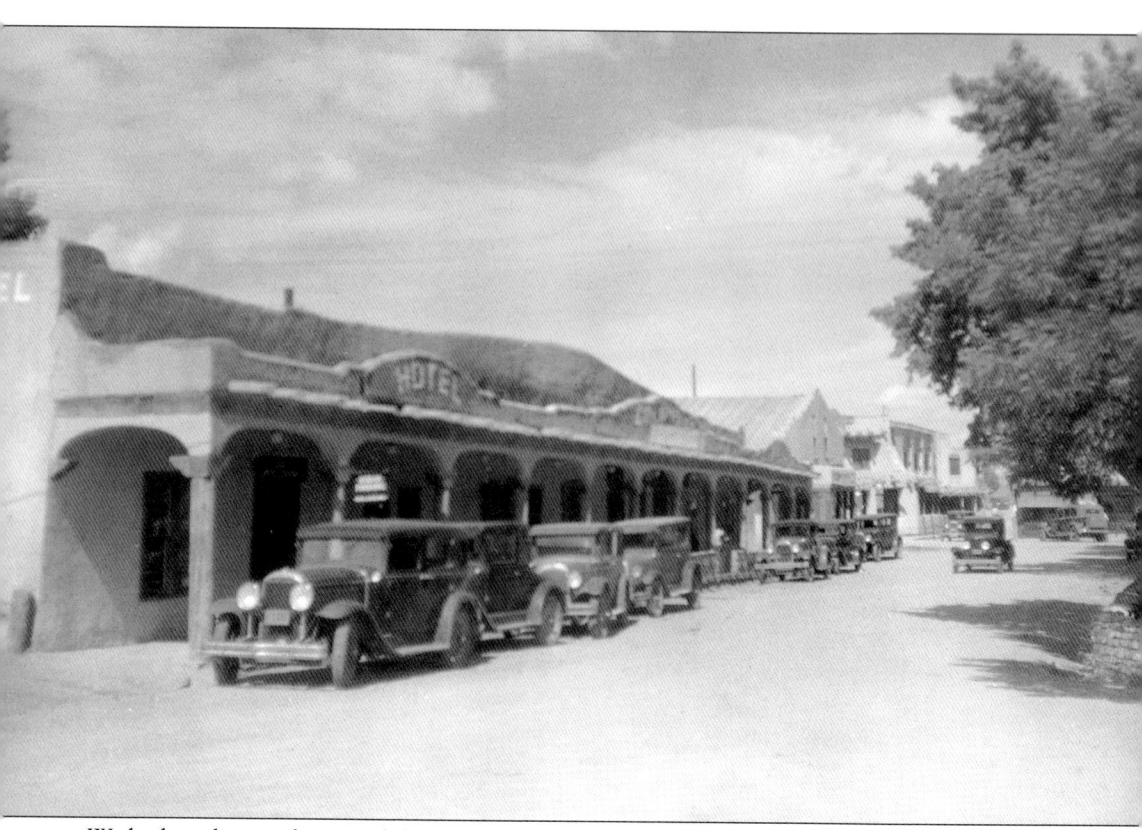
With the advent of automobiles came a more polished version of the plaza. The now paved street is lined with cars, and there is a conspicuous lack of horse and wagons. (Courtesy of Taos Historic Museums.)

Three

FIESTAS AND PARADES

With a unique mix of three cultures, the people of Taos enjoy a wide range of community events. Fiestas de Taos is an annual two-day religious celebration that has been a Taos tradition for more than a century. The first day of the fiesta honors Santiago de Compostela, the patron saint of Spain. In a show of respect, Taos men used to ride horseback around the plaza dressed in their finest clothes, or *en catrinado* (dressed to the nines) which usually consisted of a clean white shirt and jeans. The second day of fiesta weekend is devoted to St. Anne, known to be a model of virtue. Taos women would ride through the plaza in horse-drawn carriages dressed in fiesta skirts and lace mantillas. Adults attending fiesta festivities who were not wearing proper attire were subject to *desempeño* (paying the piper) by being sent to a makeshift jail where they would be put in front of a kangaroo court. To be released, offenders had to entertain the court with a song, dance, speech, or other form of entertainment. A tradition of choosing a fiesta queen and her court was established in the early 1940s and remains popular today. While initially a Catholic-Spanish celebration, the fiestas grew to include parades in which many other members of the Taos community took part. The following pages show residents of the Taos Pueblo participating in parades, including the Taos Society of Artists who often went to great lengths to design creative entries. During fiestas weekend, most businesses in Taos close, and the plaza is decorated with colorful banners and filled with food booths and other concession stands. Many other traditional American holidays are cause for parades in Taos as well, including Memorial Day, the Fourth of July, and homecoming weekend.

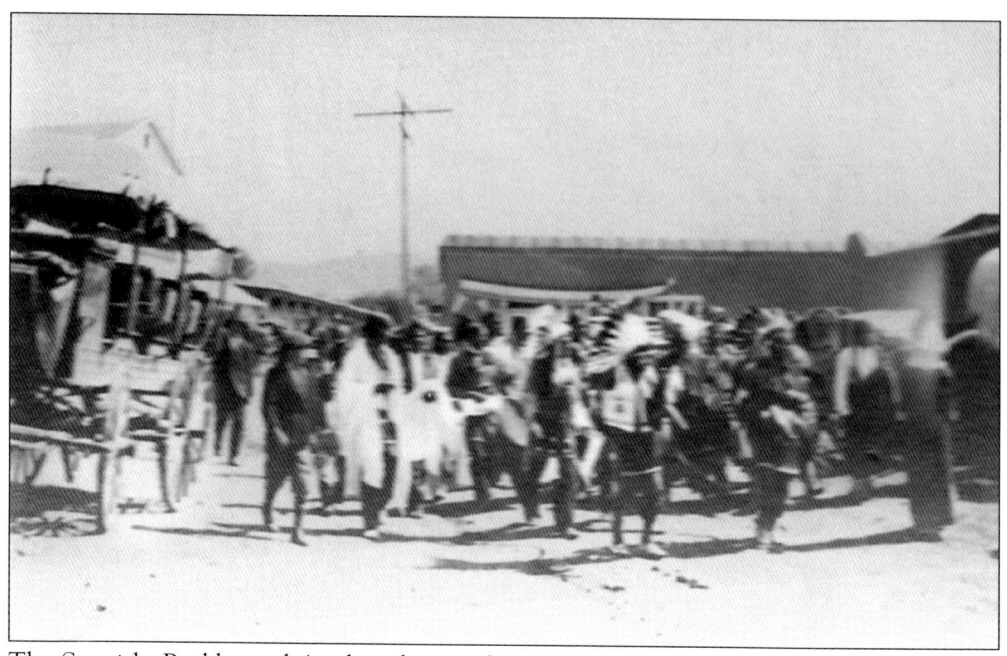

The Spanish, Pueblo, and Anglo cultures often joined in parades and celebrations. In this photograph, Pueblo Indians, two of whom are wearing Plains Indian-style headdresses, walk down a Taos street while spectators fall in line behind them. A stagecoach is visible in the left side of the image, with the Liebert home in the background. Aloysius Liebert established the popular Columbia Hotel and Bar on Taos Plaza. (Courtesy of Taos Historic Museums.)

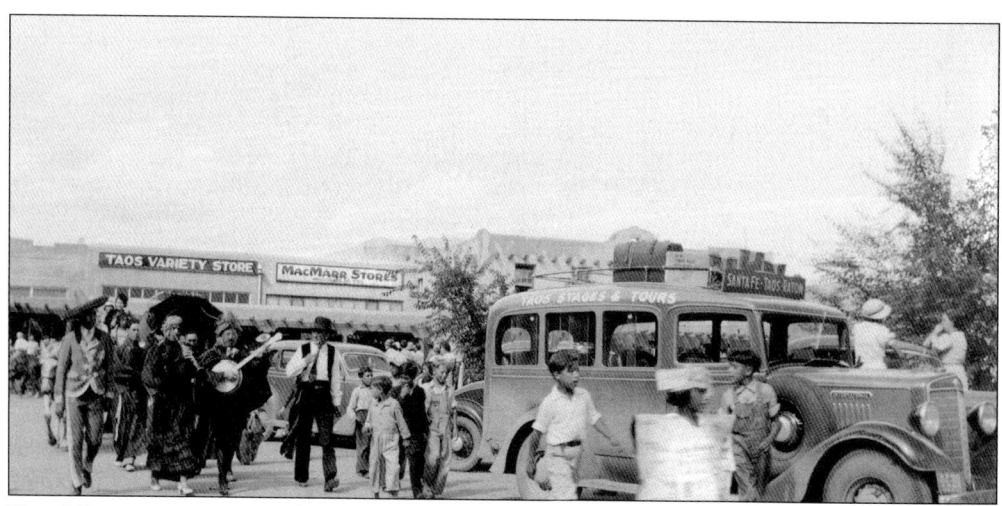

Taos folks participate in a Labor Day parade on Taos Plaza complete with musical accompaniment and a Taos Stages and Tours sedan. MacMarr and Taos Variety Stores can be seen in the background, and the old Taos County Courthouse is in the distance directly behind the tour sedan. (Courtesy of Taos Historic Museums.)

The caption on the back of this photograph reads, "John Dunn as Calliope driver with Captain Spotts." John Dunn was a legendary Taos rascal and entrepreneur who, among other things, owned a monopoly on transportation in and out of Taos for nearly 30 years. He built a toll bridge over the Rio Grande north of Taos and ran the only stagecoach/taxi service from Santa Fe to Taos until 1930. (See chapter six.) (Courtesy of Taos Historic Museums.)

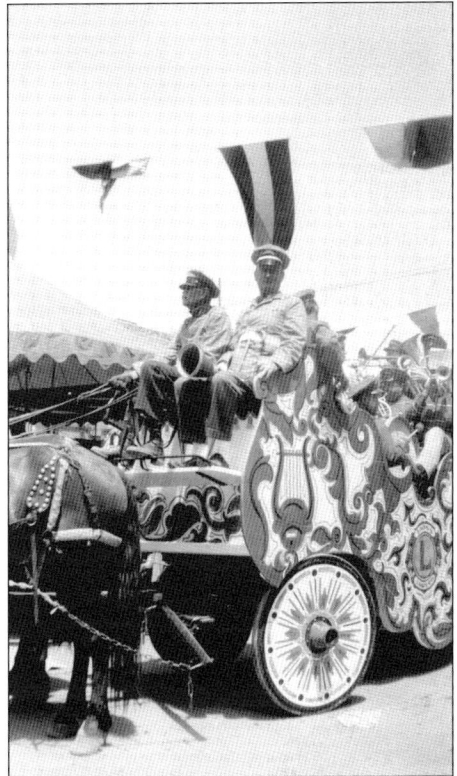

This photograph shows a group of Taos Pueblo Indians on foot taking part in the parade. Parades and fiestas were an opportunity for all Taos citizens to come together for celebrations. (Courtesy of Taos Historic Museums.)

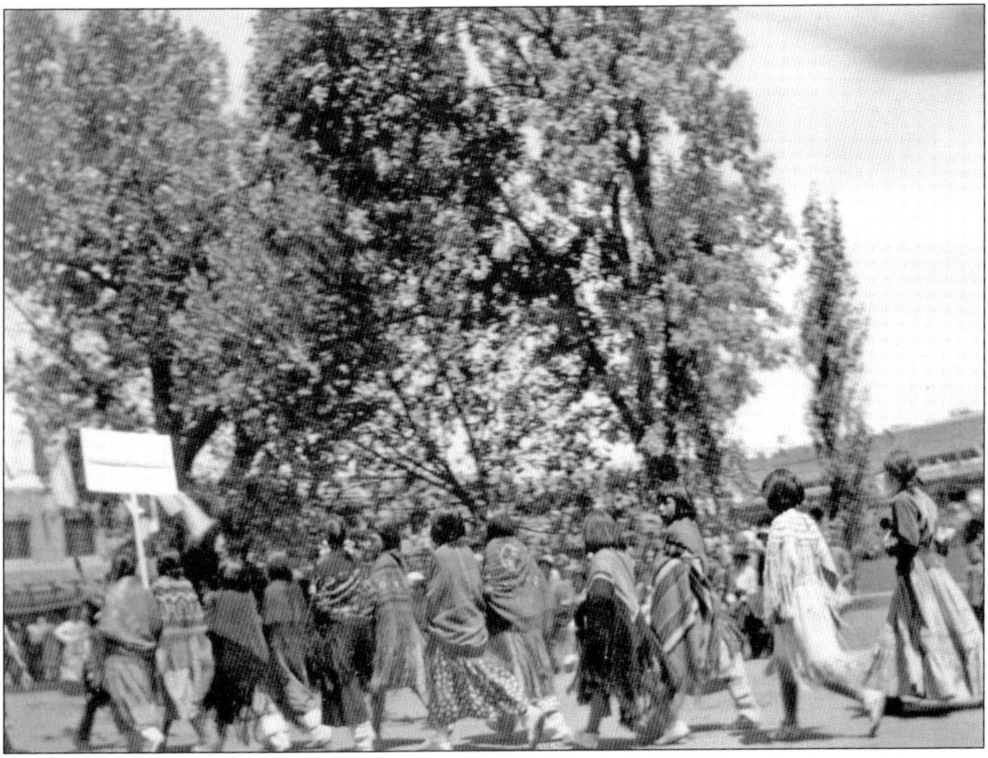

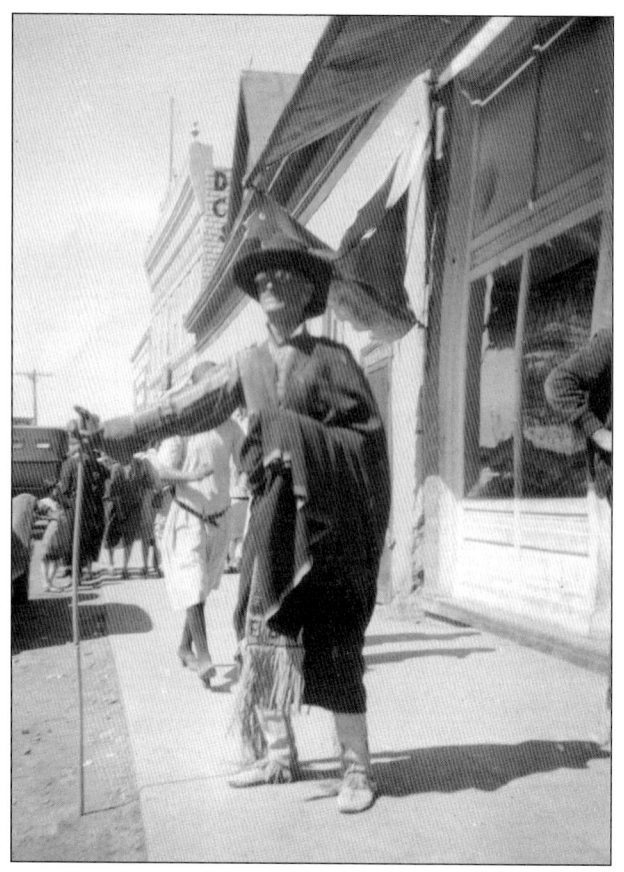

Many of the early Taos artists got swept up in the spirit of community parades. At left, artist Ernest. L. Blumenschein is on the plaza in an interesting parade costume. The photograph below shows Ernest L. Blumenschein and Bert G. Phillips on a 1940s San Geronimo float. The giant wagon wheel represents the legendary "broken wheel incident" that led to Blumenschein and Phillips settling in Taos and ultimately founding the Taos Society of Arts. (See chapter four.) (Courtesy of Taos Historic Museums.)

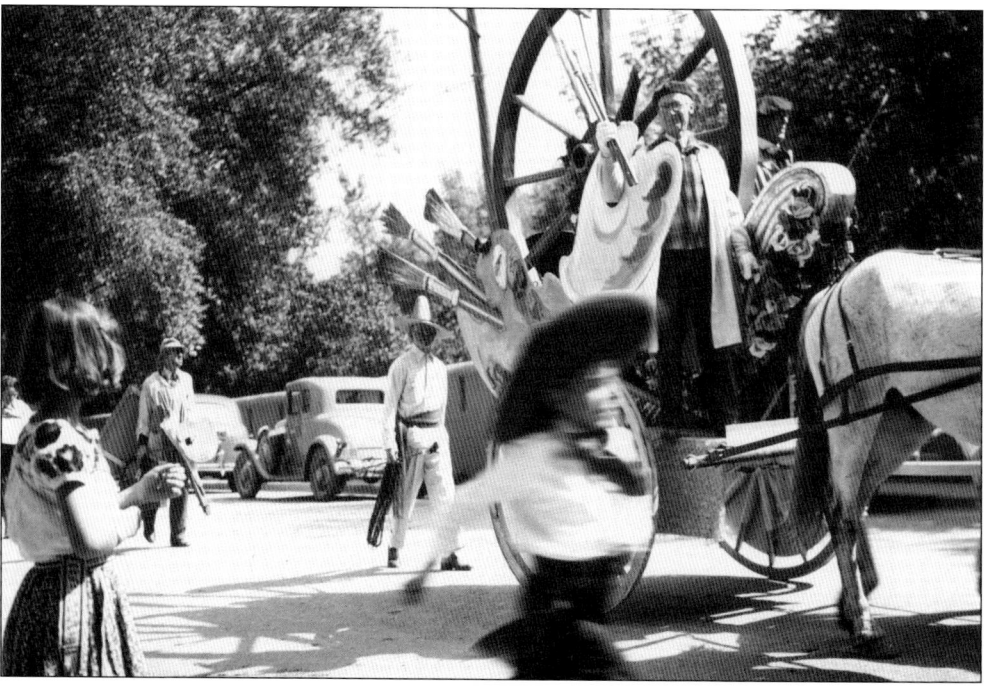

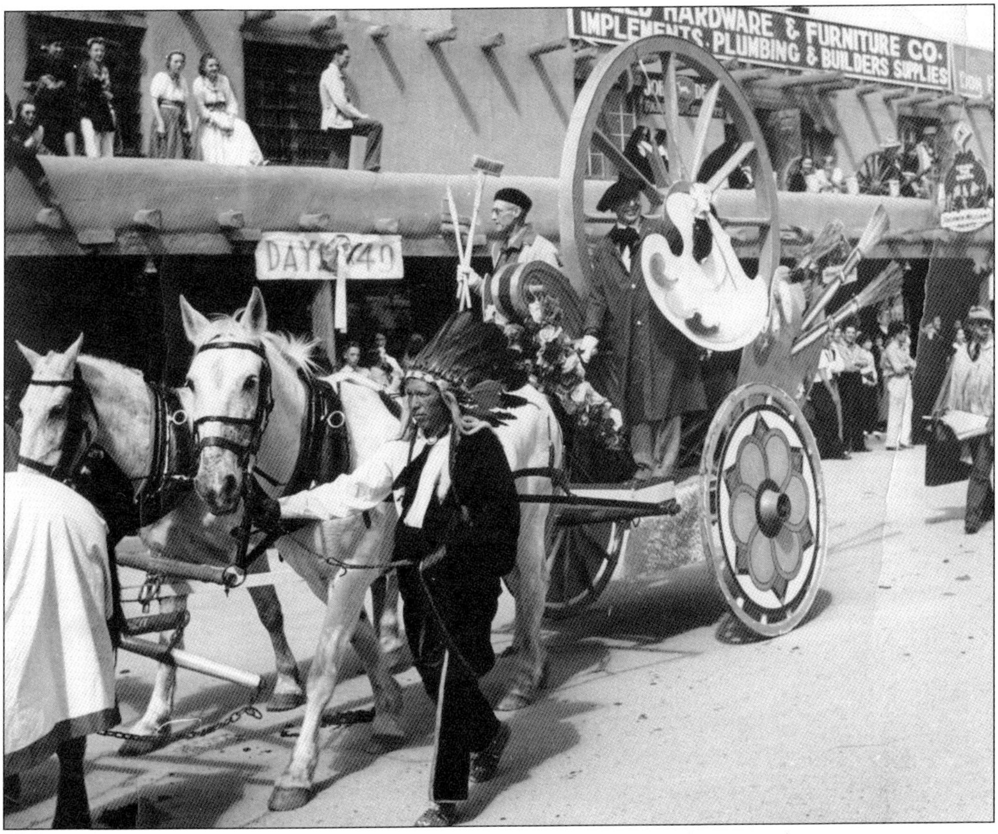

Here is another view of Blumenschein and Phillips wearing French berets and carrying giant artist palettes and brushes as their parade float passes Ilfeld's Hardware and Furniture Company on the west side of the plaza. They are being escorted by a Native American man wearing a Plains Indian headdress. (Courtesy of Taos Historic Museums.)

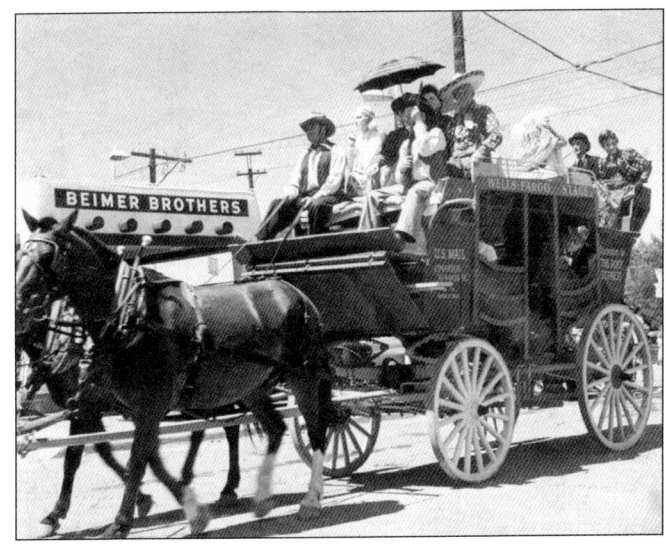

Riding in a horse-drawn Wells Fargo stagecoach, this Taos Society of Artists parade entry shows artist Rebecca Salsbury James (white hair) riding up front as the float passes Beimer Brothers store on the plaza. After the festivities, the stagecoach was permanently parked in front of Jack Denver's Restaurant on South Santa Fe Road (across from the present day Taos County Courthouse) where it remained for many years as a local landmark. (Courtesy of Taos Historic Museums.)

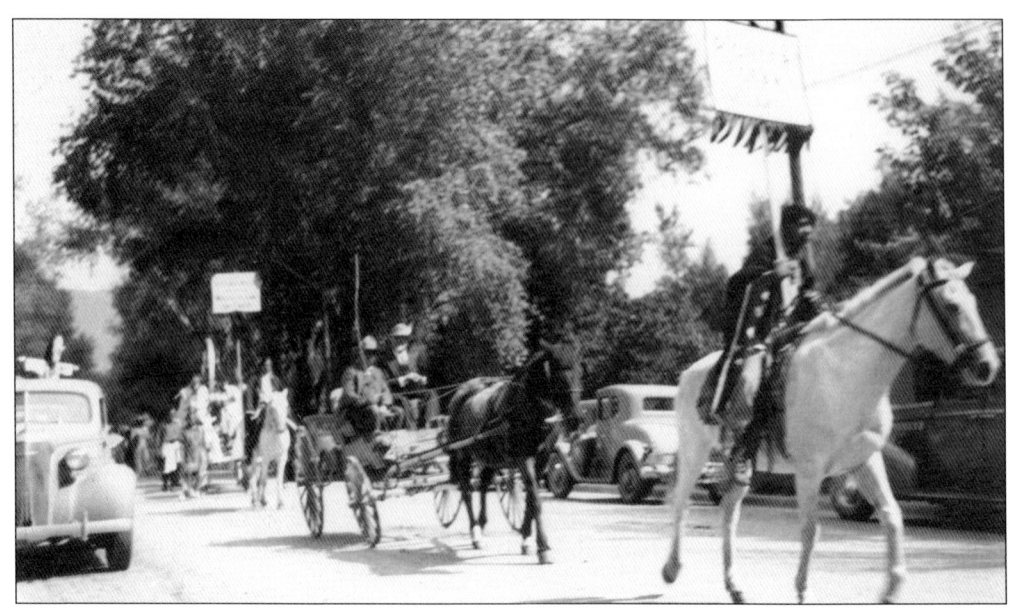

These photographs illustrate the spirit of Taos parades that include participants from each of the Taos area cultures. Above, Taos Pueblo men on horseback ride between men in suits in a horse-drawn wagon along the tree-lined street leading to Taos Plaza. Below, local families wait to enter the parade in a line of covered wagons reenacting the long wagon trains that arrived in 1824 after the opening of the Santa Fe Trail. (Courtesy of Taos Historic Museums.)

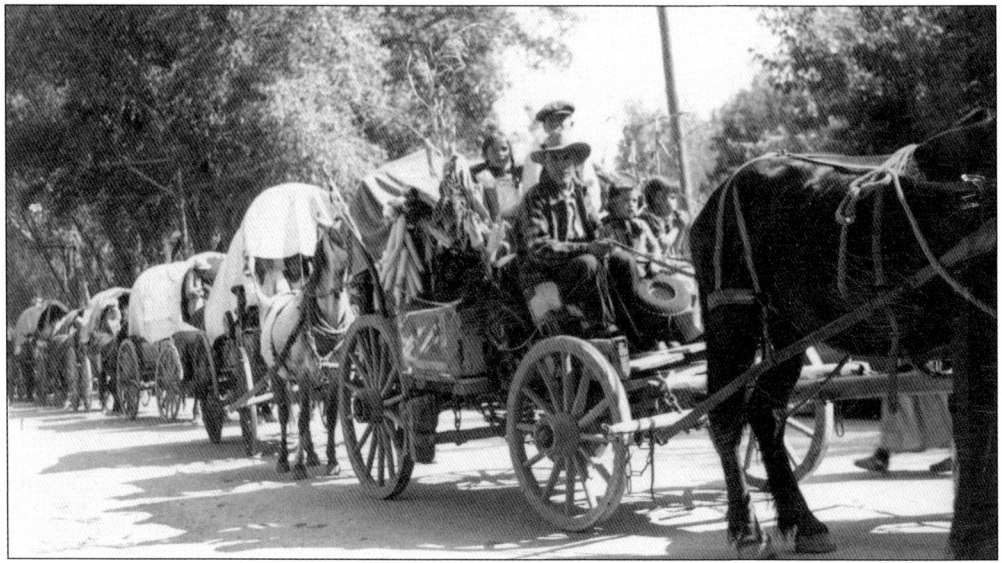

Taos Society of Artists founder Ernest L. Blumenschein and Mary Green Blumenschein's daughter Helen is dressed as a clown in the photograph at right. Helen moved to Taos with her parents at age 10 and attended the Sisters of Loretto Catholic School. She would later become a lieutenant in the Women's Army Corps during World War II and gained recognition as an artist in her own right and as an art historian. The somber procession below representing Taos artists is walking past "Doc" Martin's office, now known as the Taos Inn. Artist Rebecca Salsbury James is second in line, wearing a long dark dress and stylish shoes. (See more on Rebecca Salsbury James in chapter five.) A banner on the donkey reads, "How to paint Injuns." (Courtesy of Taos Historic Museums.)

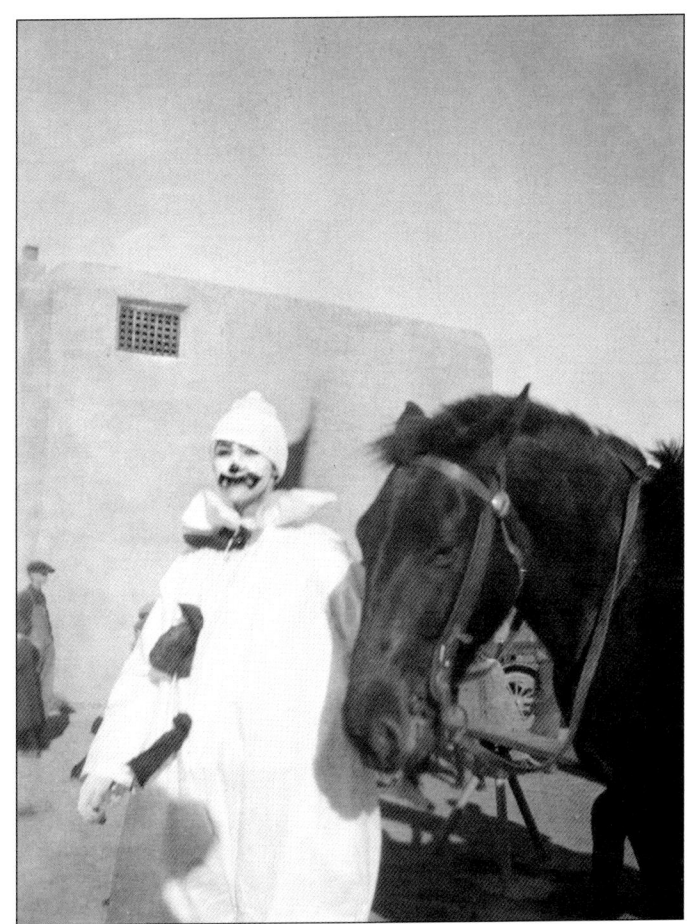

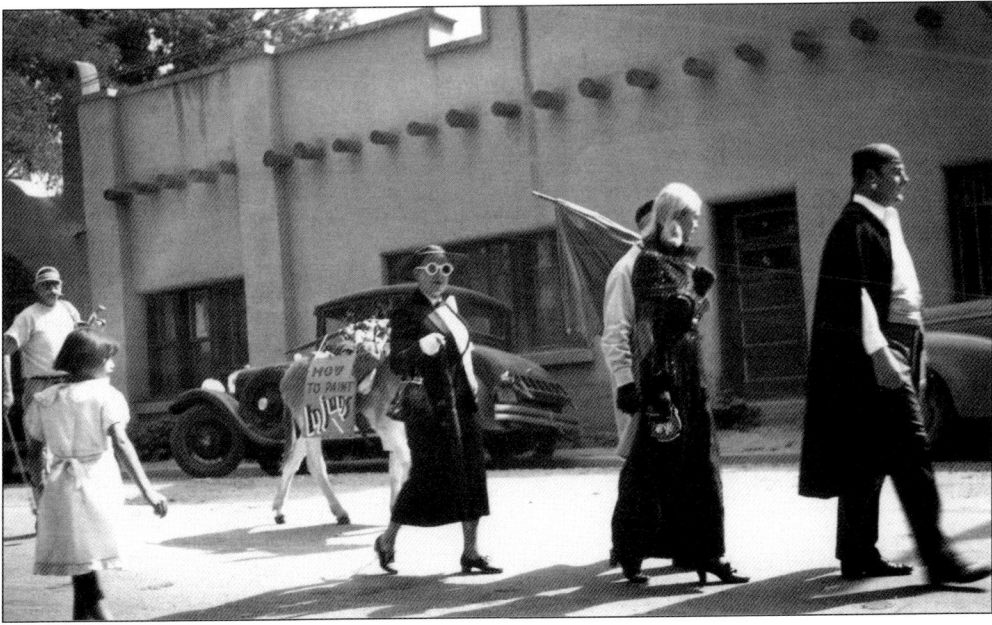

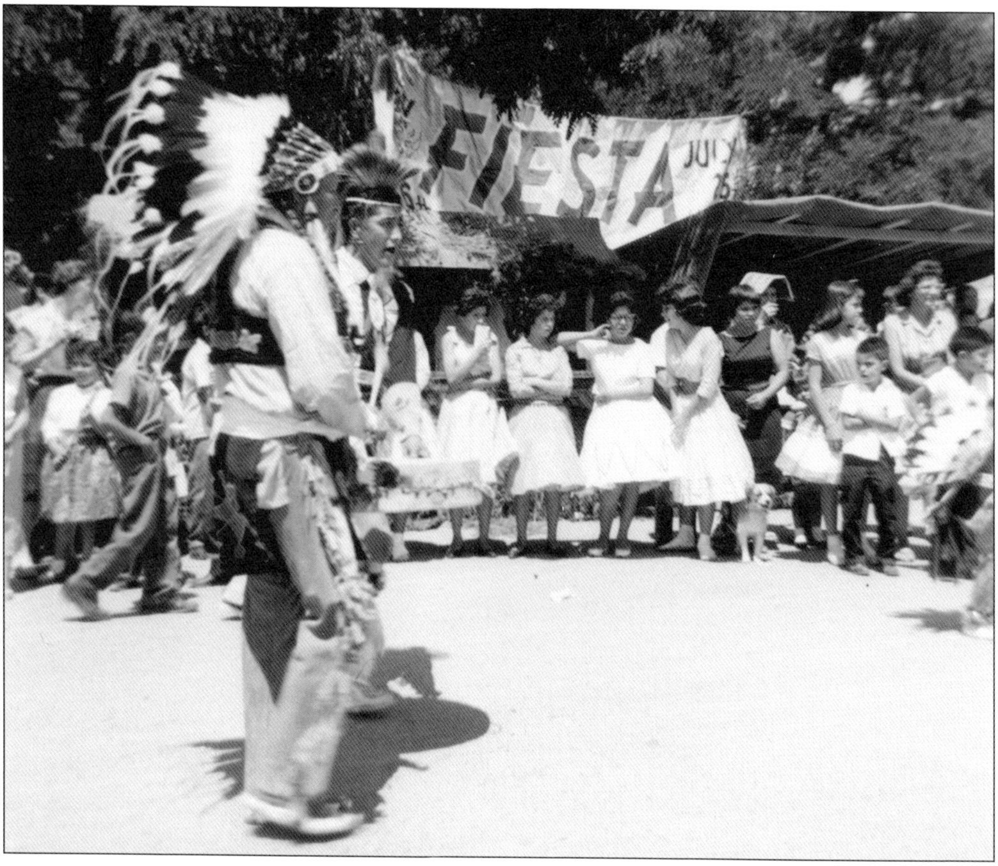

At a July 25 fiesta, bystanders line the street as two Indians pass by wearing Plains Indian headdresses. (Courtesy of Taos Historic Museums.)

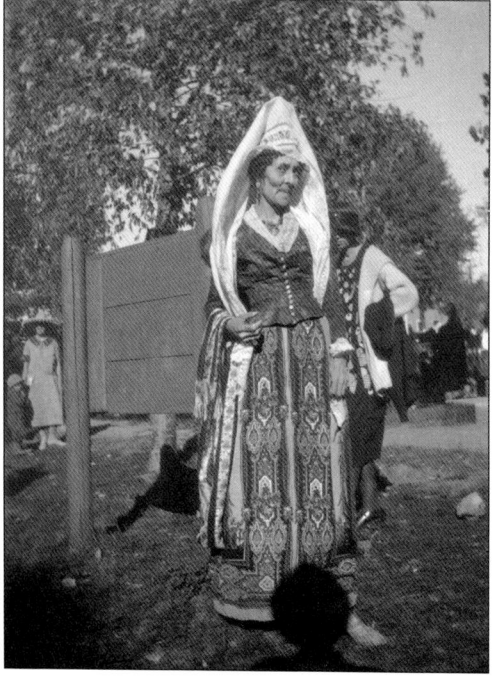

Fully decked out in celebration garb, this unidentified woman smiles coyly for the camera. (Courtesy of Taos Historic Museums.)

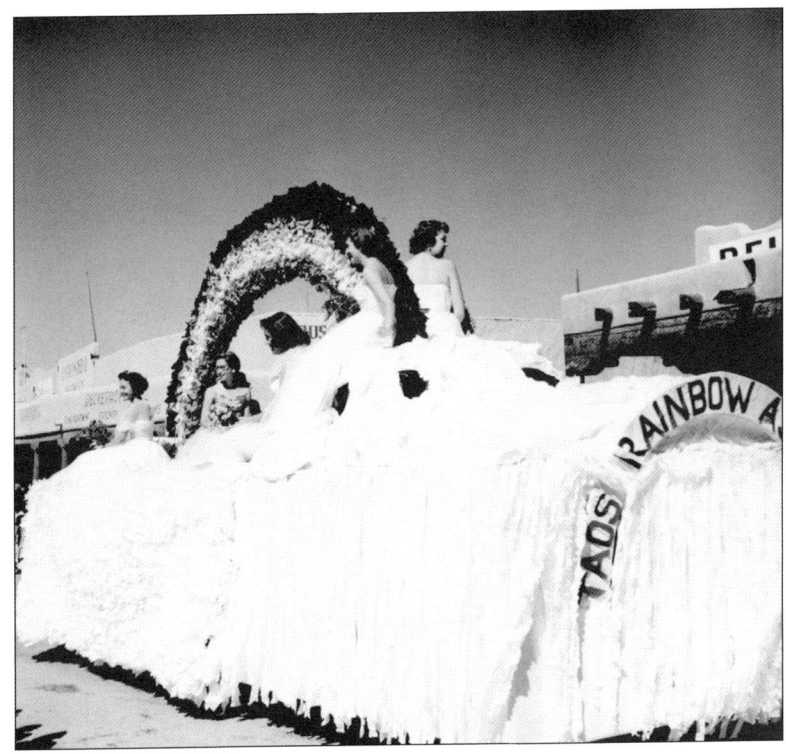

Several young Taos women wearing fancy dresses pass by the Beimer Brothers store on the Taos plaza in this elaborate Rainbow Girls Fiestas float. (Courtesy of Taos Historic Museums.)

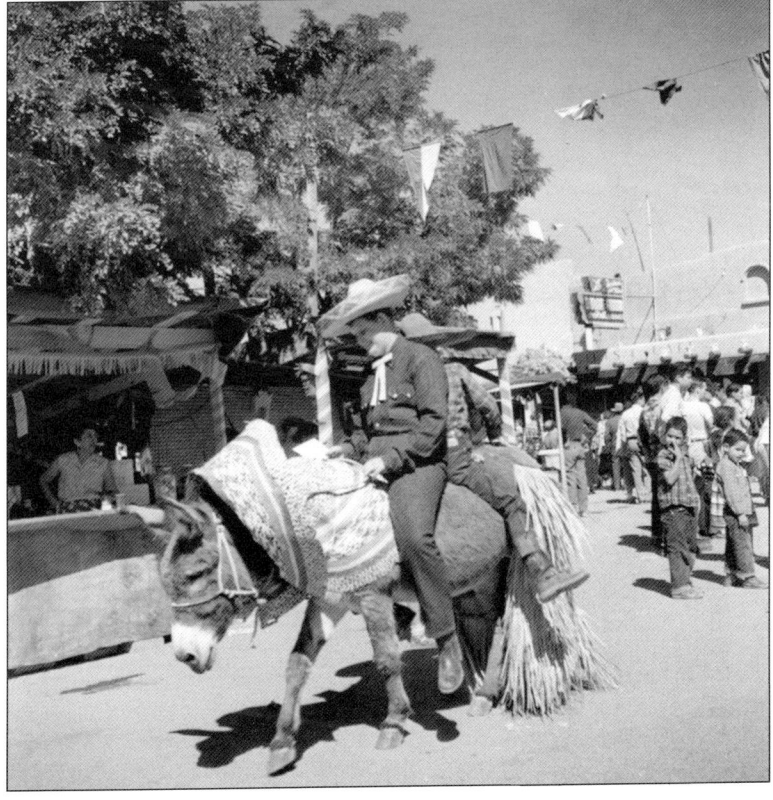

Two boys, one facing front and one facing back, ride a decorated burro past food concession stands that line the interior of the Taos Plaza. Festive fiesta flags crisscross the plaza as crowds in the back enjoy the festivities. (Courtesy of Taos Historic Museums.)

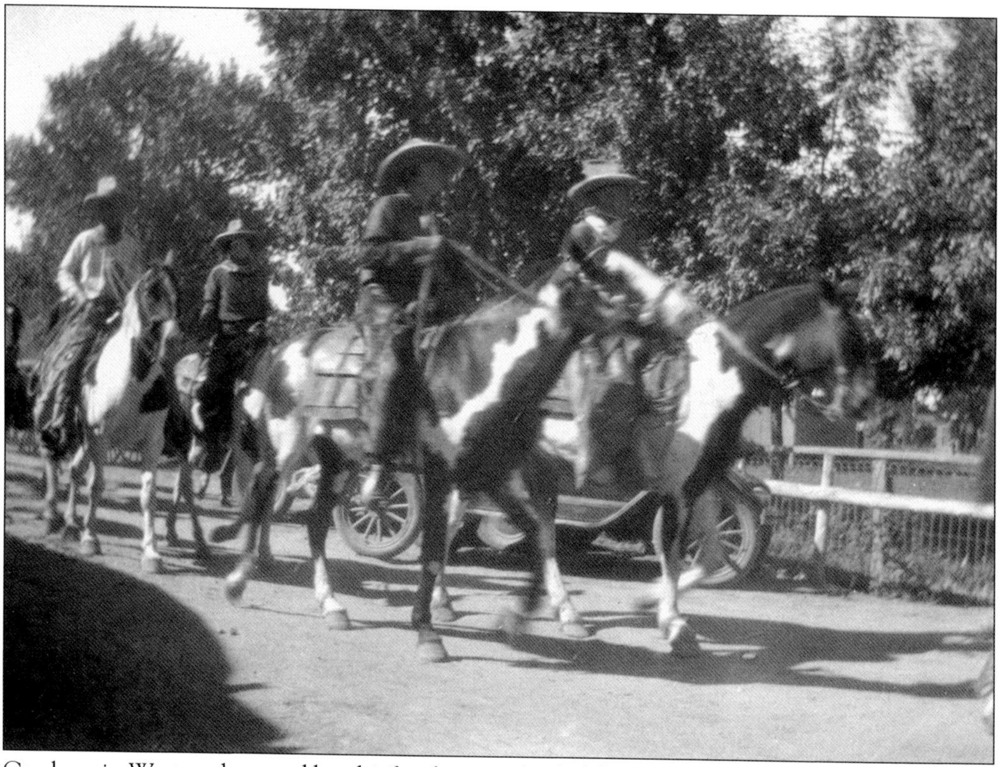

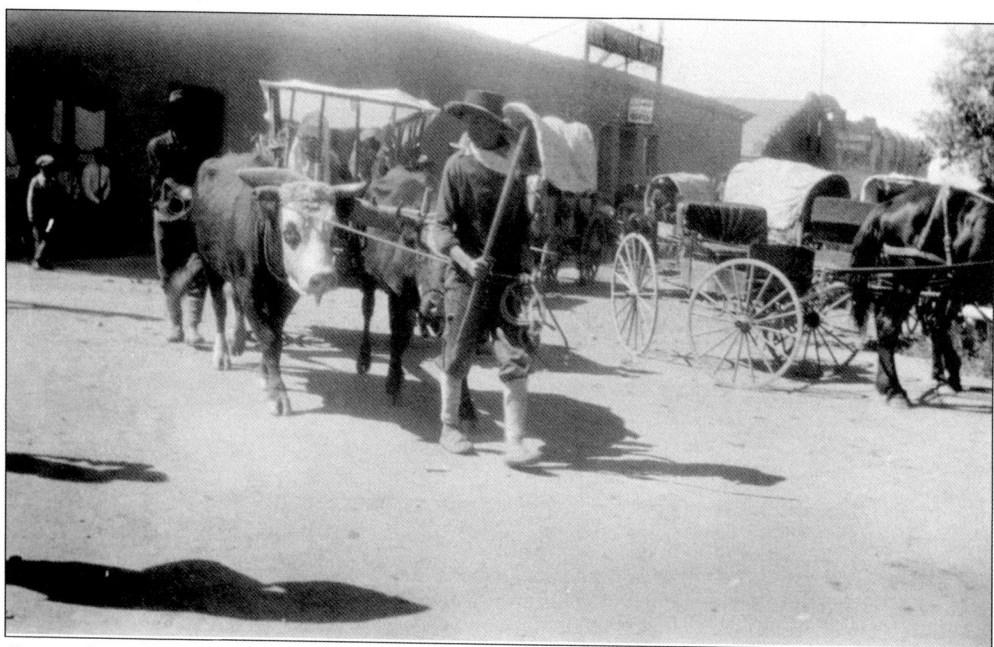

Cowboys in Western hats and kerchiefs ride pinto (piebald) horses in a parade. (Courtesy of Taos Historic Museums.)

Covered wagons pulled by work animals represent the arrival of wagon trains from the east by way of the old Santa Fe Trail. The popular Columbian Bar, which would later become the La Fonda, is seen in the background. (Courtesy of Taos Historic Museums.)

Taken by John Goldmark in 1951, the photograph at right shows the fiesta queen and her royal court in full fiesta finery. Wearing her mother's lace mantilla and holding an ostrich feather fan, fiesta queen Cecelia Martinez is seated between Martha Saavadra and Marianne DesGeorges. While the fiestas have been celebrated for over 100 years, the tradition of naming a fiesta queen dates back to the early 1940s. In the photograph below, fiesta queen Cecelia Martinez and her court ride in the fiesta parade. (Courtesy of Martinez y Montaner/Martinez y Salazar.)

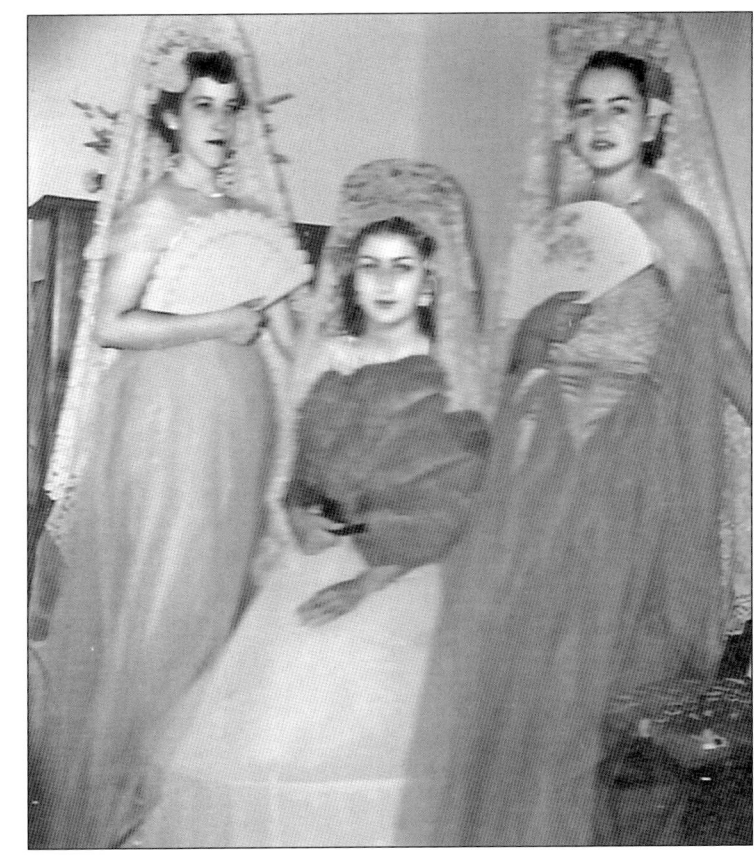

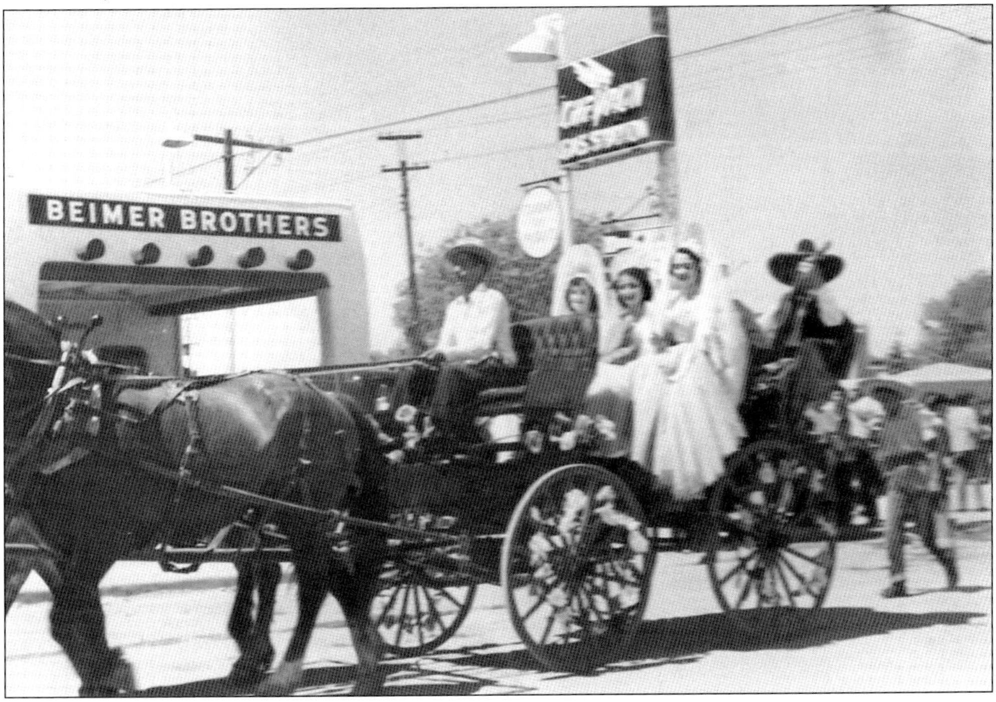

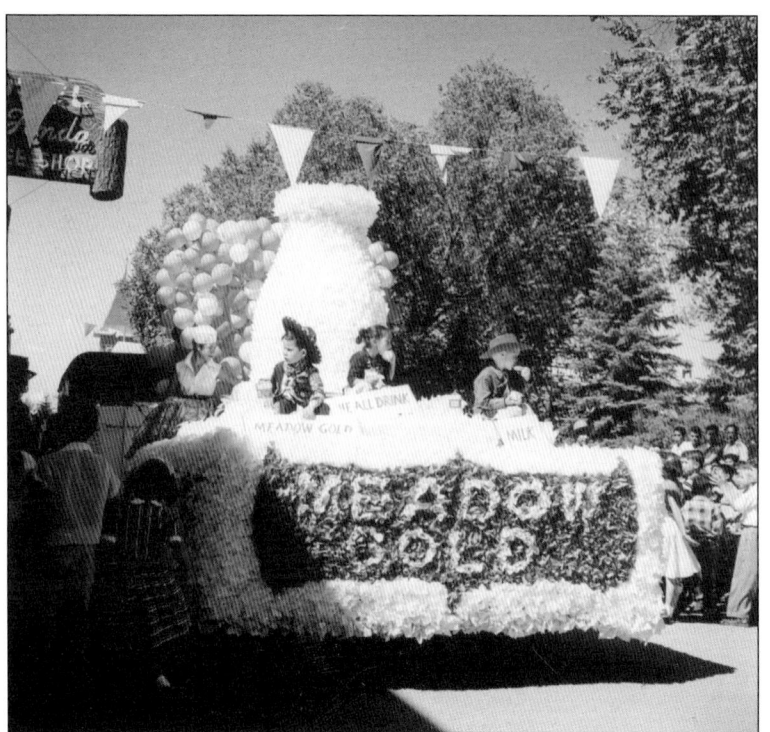

This elaborate fiesta parade entry is courtesy of Meadow Gold Milk, complete with a giant milk bottle and balloons. The children riding the float have signs that read, "We all drink Meadow Gold." (Courtesy of Taos Historic Museums.)

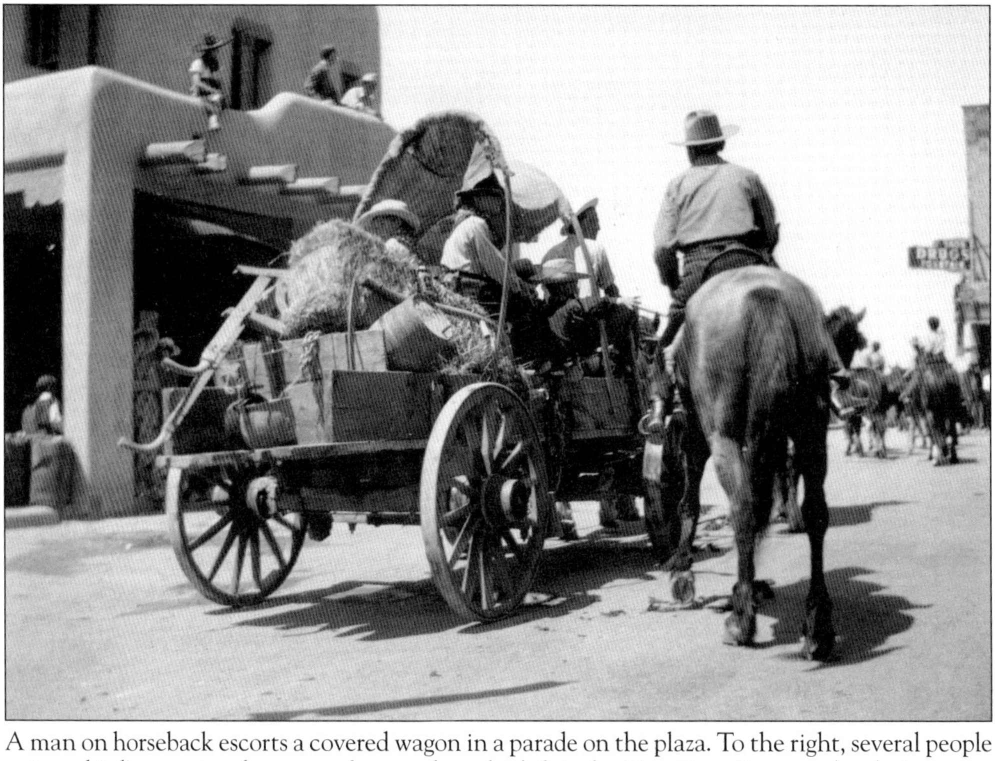

A man on horseback escorts a covered wagon in a parade on the plaza. To the right, several people enjoy a bird's-eye view from a rooftop, and on the left is the Taos Drug Store and soda fountain. (Courtesy of Taos Historic Museums.)

Led by Rowena Meyers with son Ouray Meyers in a papoose on her back, children and grownups decked out in Indian and Western garb parade past a crowd in the plaza. A passenger-filled fire truck rounds the corner behind them. The old Conoco gas station is seen to the top left of the photograph. (Courtesy of Taos Historic Museums.)

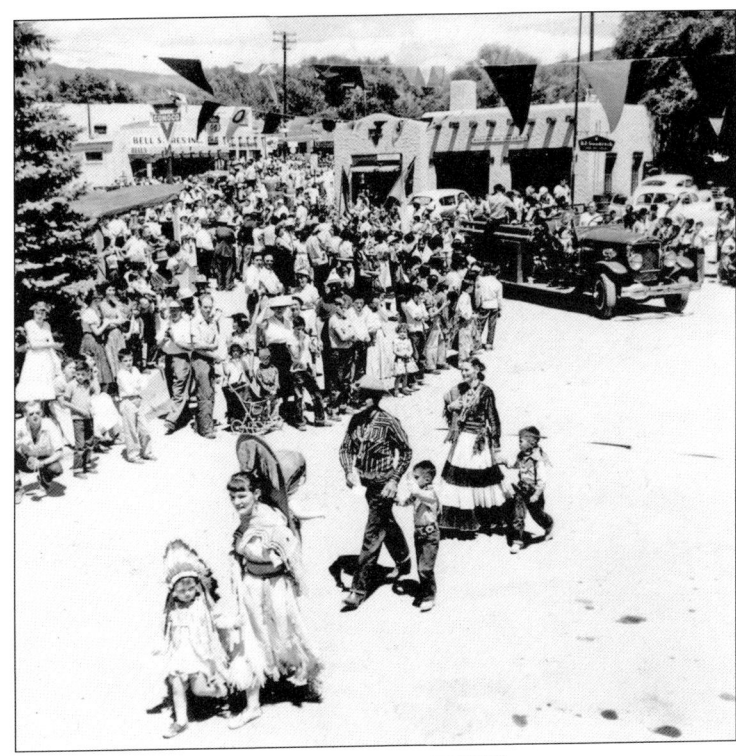

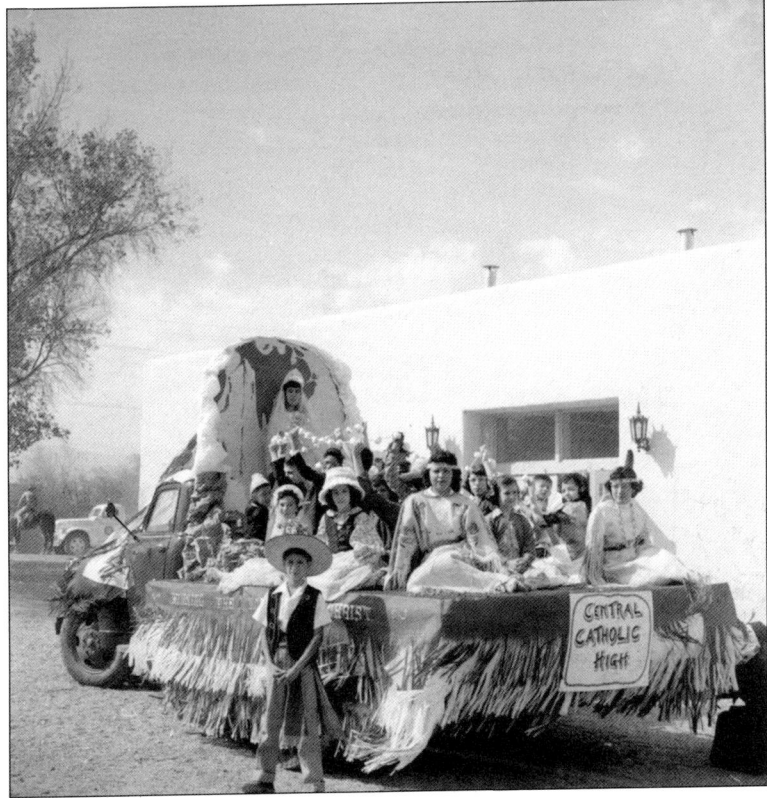

This parade entry representing Central Catholic High School is packed with costumed children sitting on top of an old flatbed truck. (Courtesy of Taos Historic Museums.)

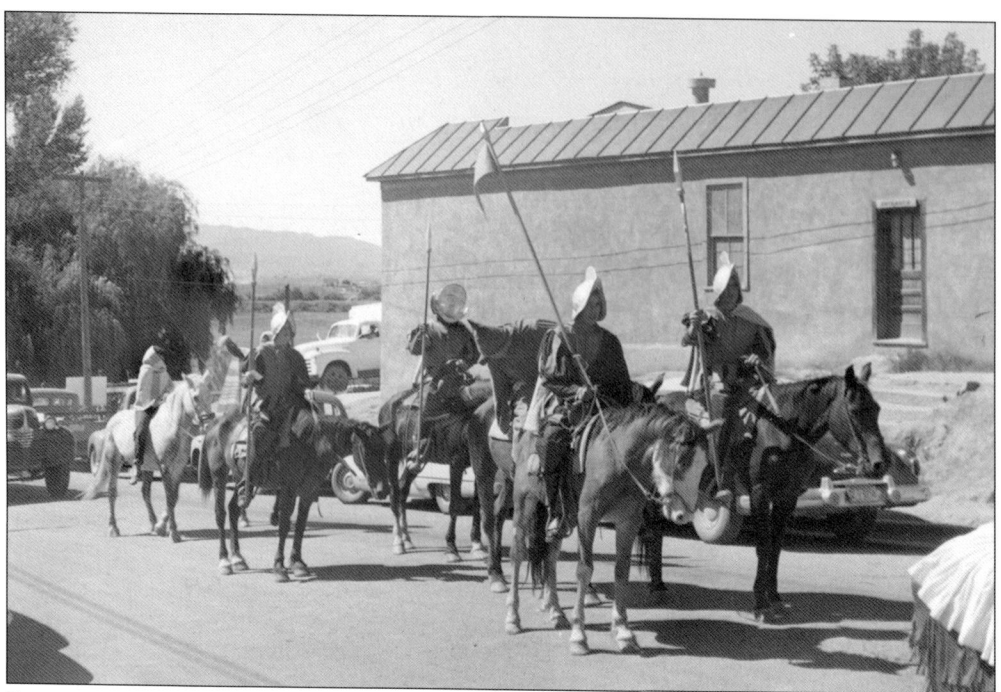
Four young men on horseback dressed as Spanish conquistadors pay homage to their ancestors in this fiesta parade. (Courtesy of Taos Historic Museums.)

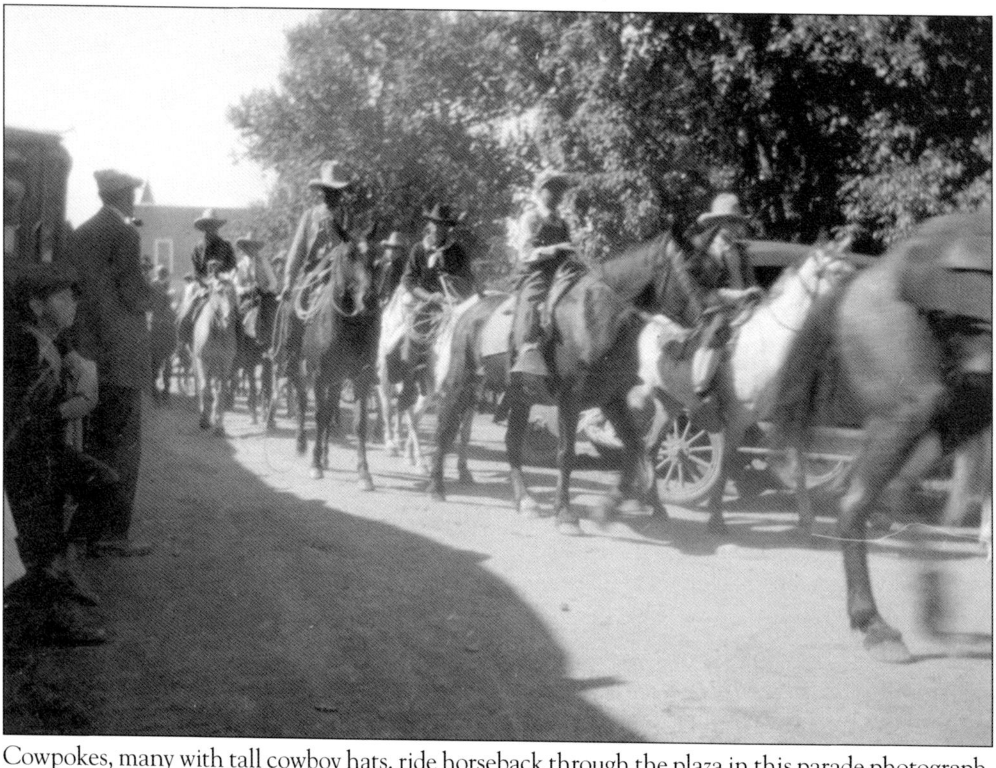

Cowpokes, many with tall cowboy hats, ride horseback through the plaza in this parade photograph. (Courtesy of Taos Historic Museums.)

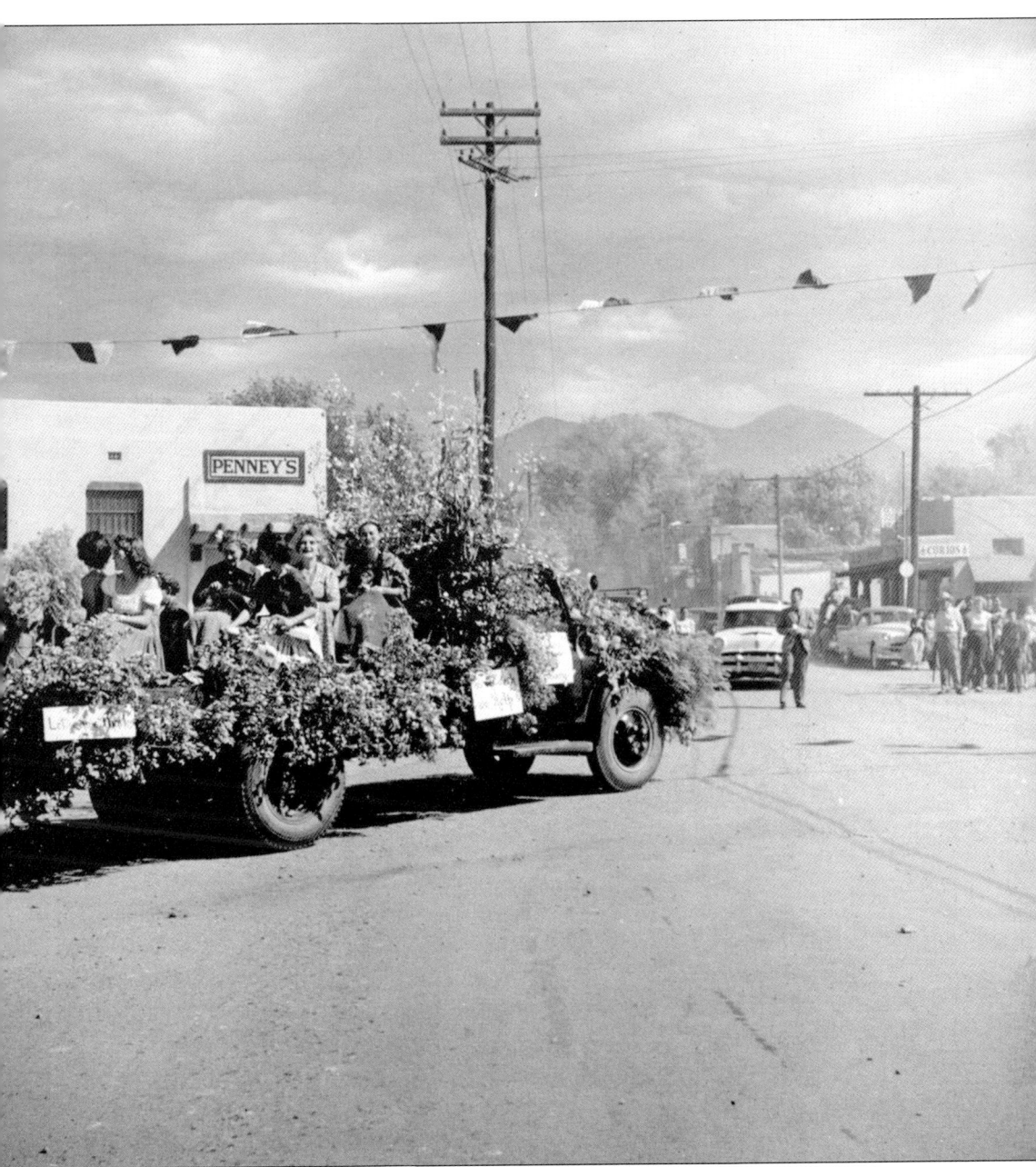

A group of well-dressed women ride on the back of a flatbed truck as it makes its way past Penney's Department Store on the plaza. Parade-goers line the street in anticipation. (Courtesy of Taos Historic Museums.)

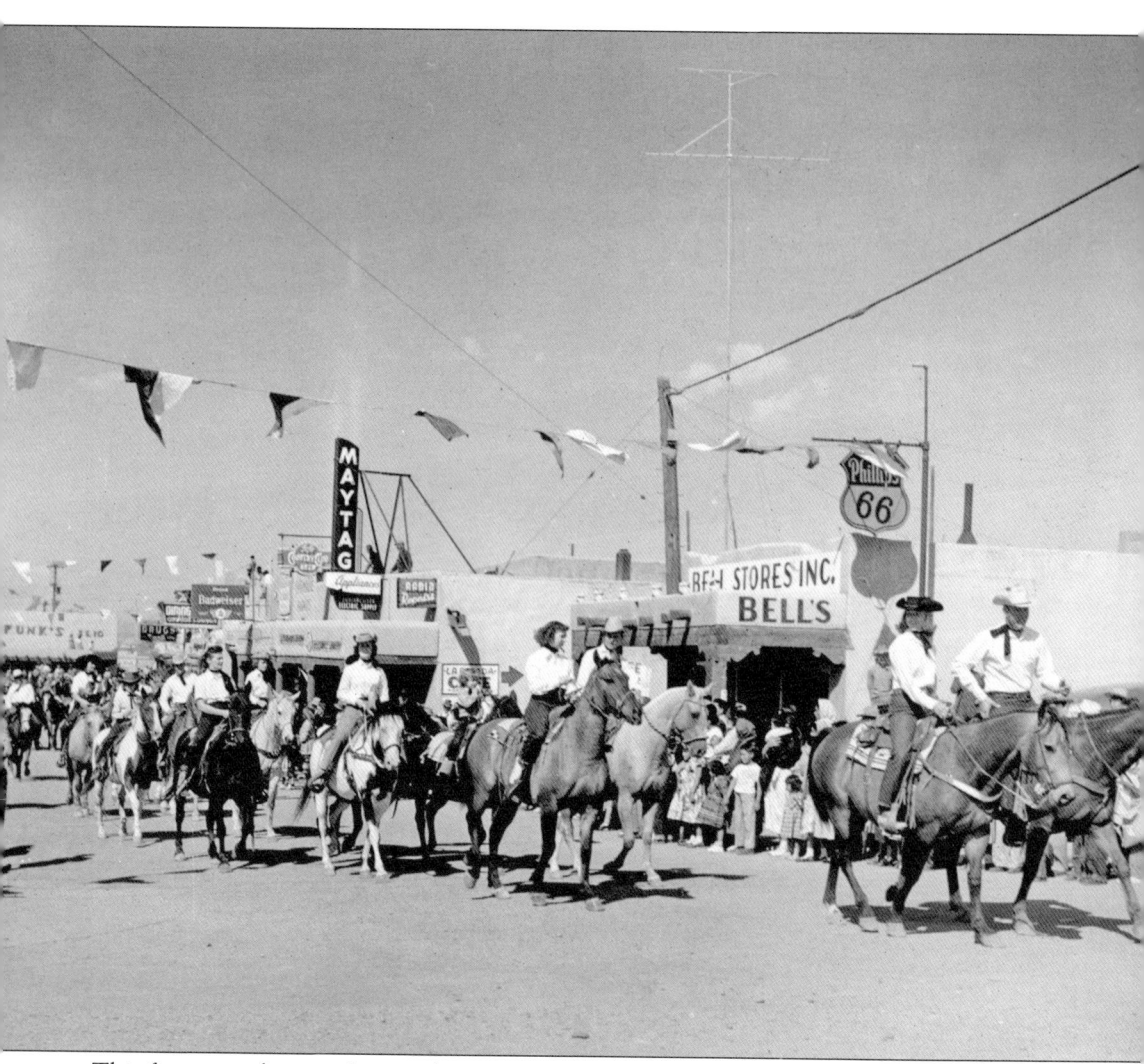

This fiesta parade view shows a thriving Taos Plaza with commerce including a Phillips 66 gas station, Bell's Stores, a radio repair shop, a Maytag appliance store, a bar, and the Taos Drug Store, as horsemen and horsewoman ride past. (Courtesy of Taos Historic Museums.)

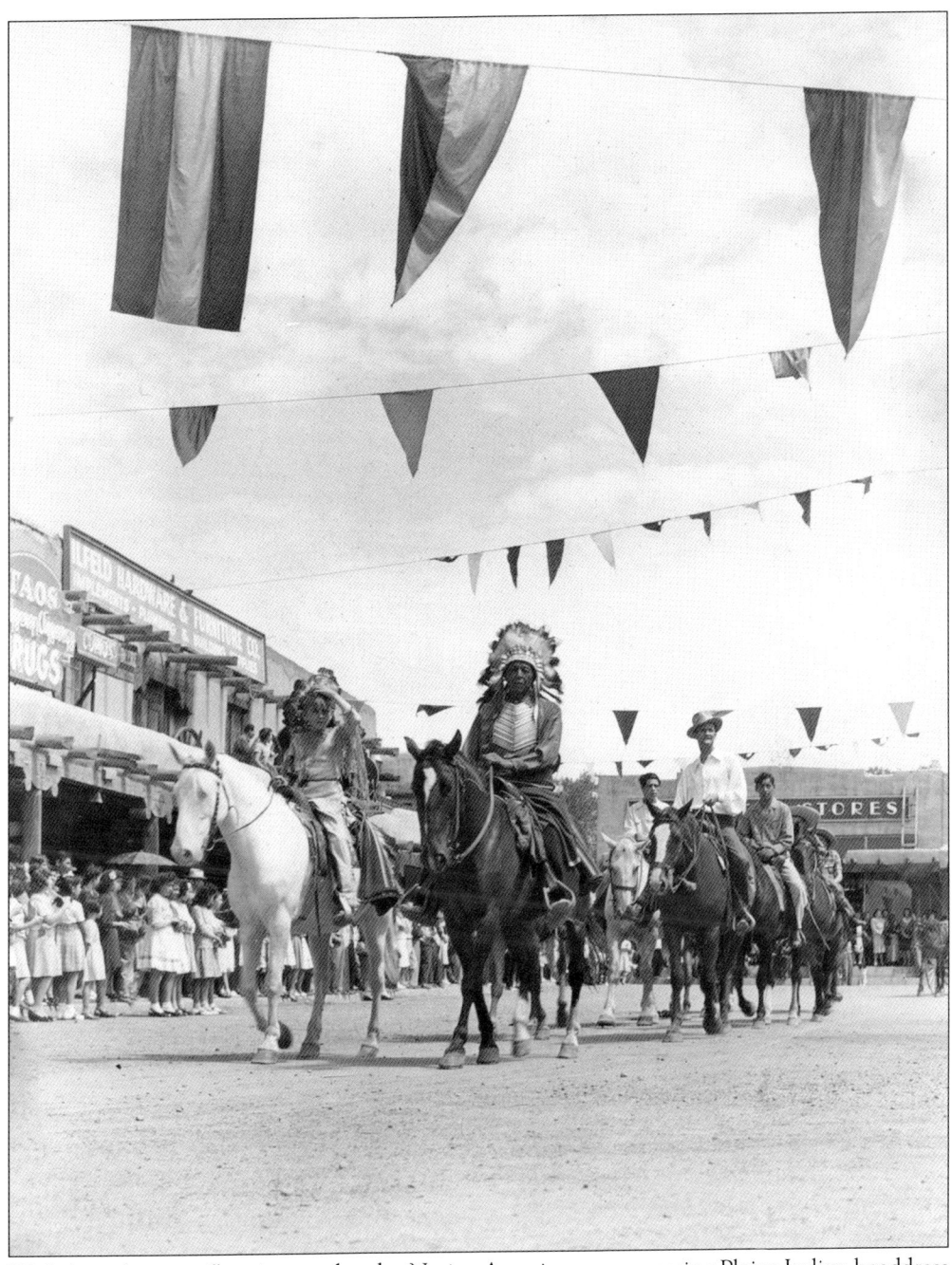
With fiesta banners flapping overhead, a Native American man wearing Plains Indian headdress leads a group of men on horseback past Ilfeld's Hardware and Furniture Store and the Taos Drug Store on the plaza. (Courtesy of Taos Historic Museums.)

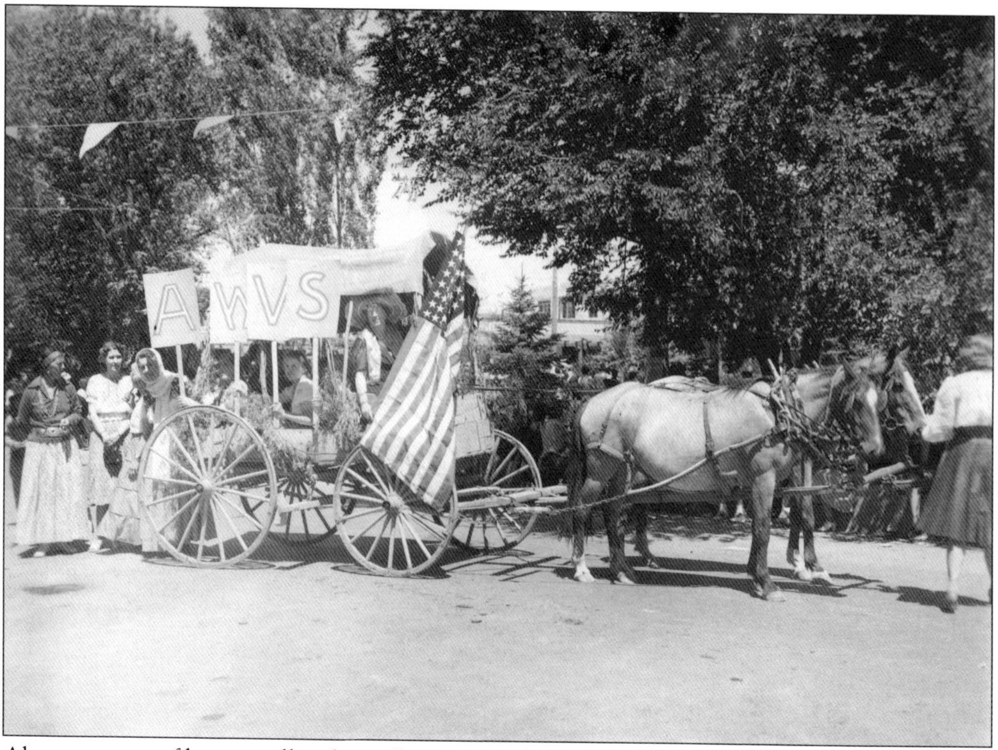

Above, a team of horses pulls a fiesta float entry of women riding in an old wooden wagon. The American flag waves proudly. Below, costumed men and women pose in front of the wagon, with scenes of the plaza behind them. (Courtesy of Taos Historic Museums.)

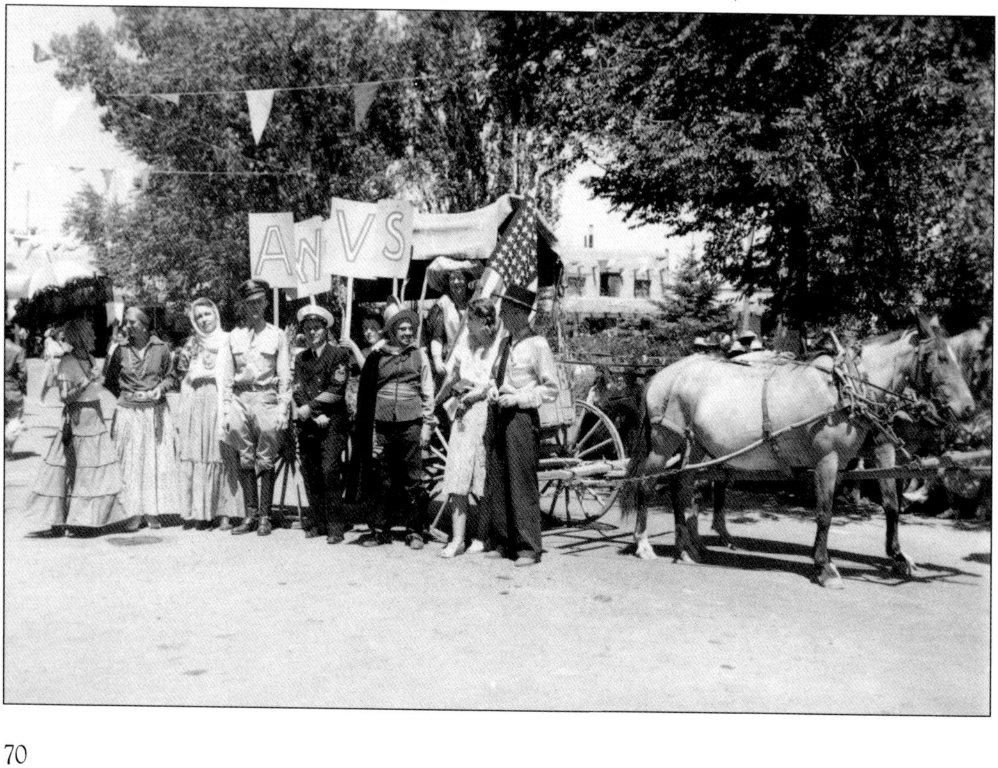

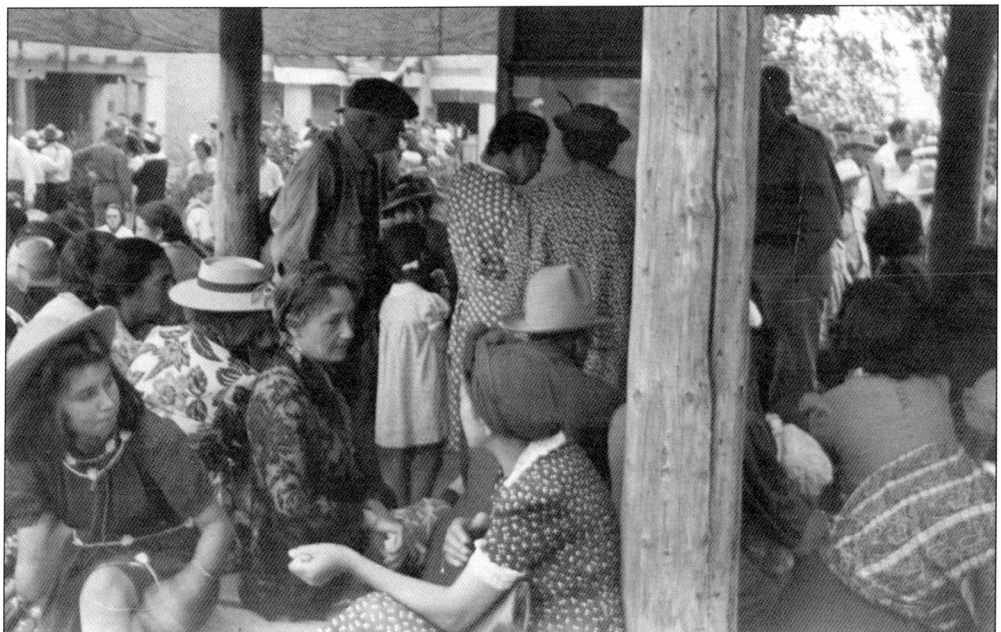

This photograph shows locals gathered in the bandstand/pavilion at the center of Taos Plaza for a fiesta celebration. Maggie Gusdorf (wearing a dark-colored lace blouse) faces a friend wearing a flower print dress trimmed in white. A police station and restrooms were located beneath the platform. (Courtesy of Taos Historic Museums.)

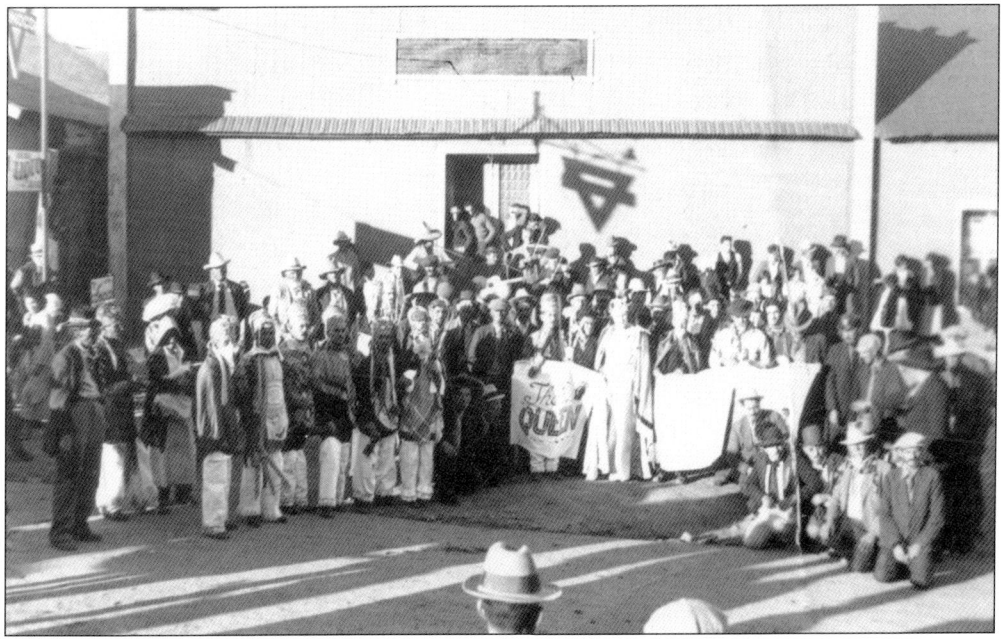

At a midwinter celebration, a crowd gathers for a group photograph in front of the Conoco gas station owned by a Mr. Farrell. This was the former site of the hanging tree, which ceased to be used for executions after 1912. In the front left are six members of the Los Matachinos Dance Troup. The monarch can be seen in the back wearing a crown. (Courtesy of Taos Historic Museums.)

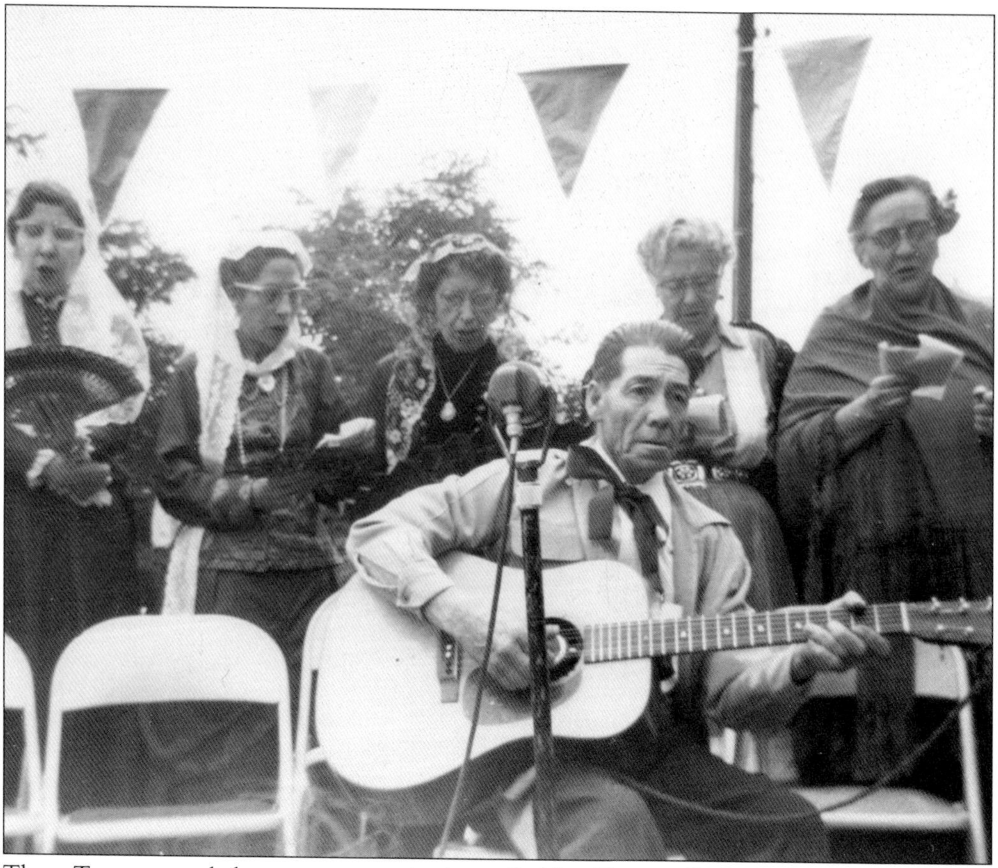

These Taos women belong to an organization called Las Taseñas Dedicated to the Learning of Proper English. Guadalupe Vaughn (front right) was a local teacher and president of the Taos Historical Society who became head of the New Mexico State Historical Society. The gentleman on guitar is believed to be Nat Flores. (Courtesy of Taos Historic Museums.)

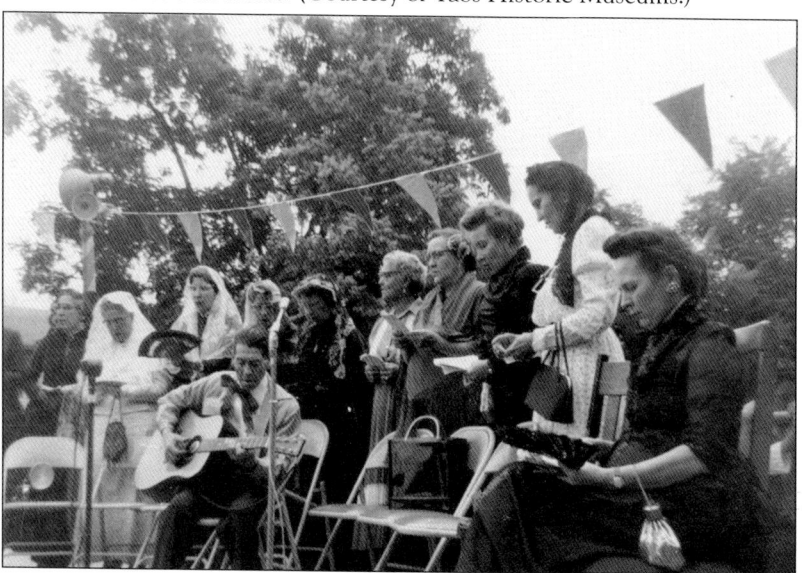

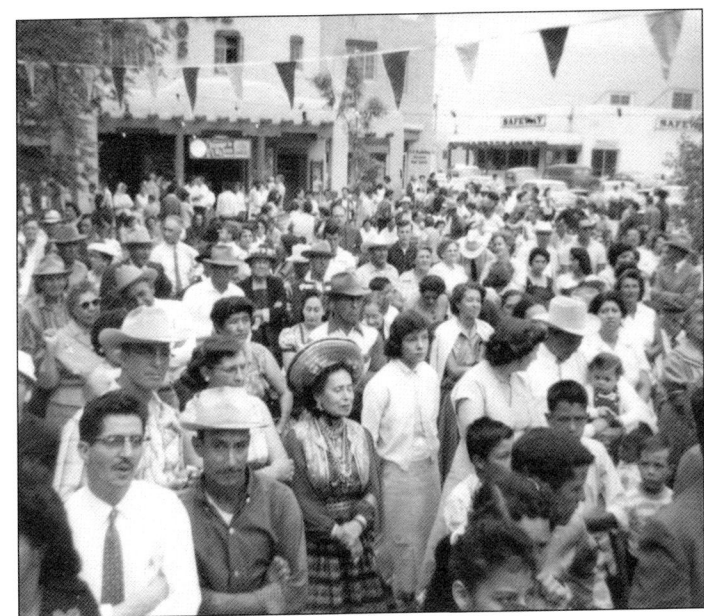

Crowds of people gather on the plaza to celebrate St. Anne's Day in 1959. The man at the far left wearing a white shirt and tie is former Taos County treasurer Leo Martinez. Nearby wearing a wide-brimmed straw hat is Greek immigrant Noula Karavas, whose son Saki owned the LaFonda Hotel for many years. In the right foreground are members of the Torres family including mother Irene, father Fermin, and children Larry, Bernice and Phil. (Courtesy of Taos Historic Museums.)

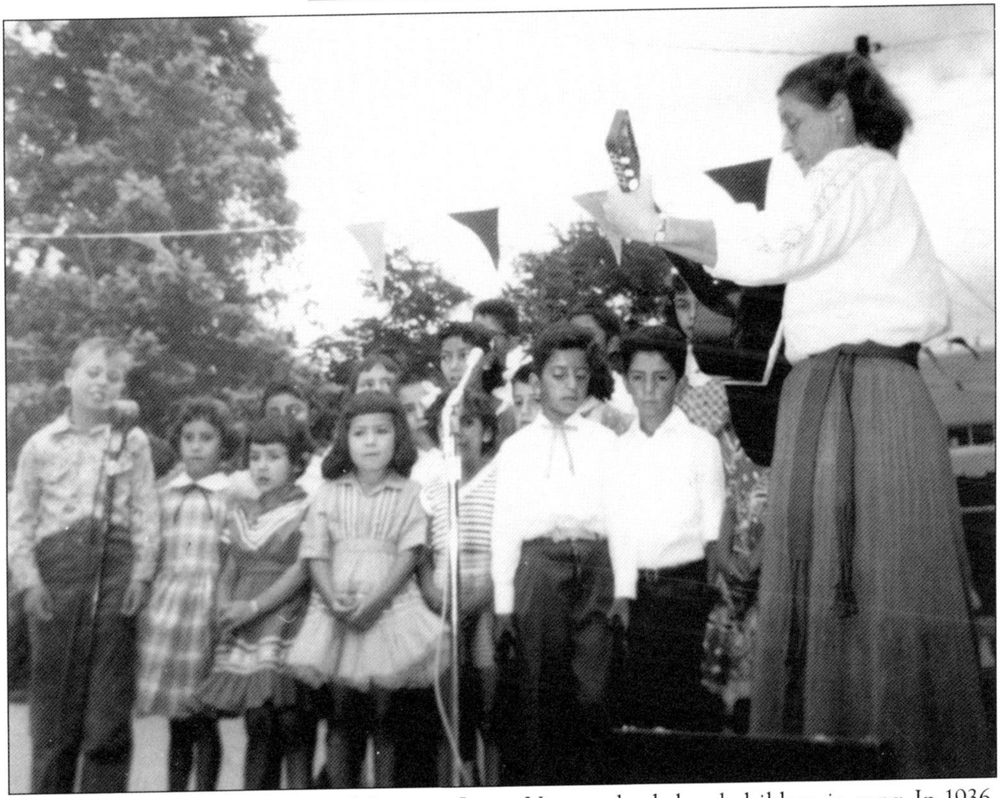

During a 1959 St. Anne's Day celebration, Jenny Vincent leads local children in song. In 1936, Jenny and her first husband moved to northern New Mexico at the invitation of Frieda Lawrence. A talented folk musician, Jenny has performed with Pete Seeger, Woody Guthrie, Earl Robinson, and Malvina Reynolds, all of whom, like Jenny, have used music to fight for civil liberties and human rights. (Courtesy of Taos Historic Museums.)

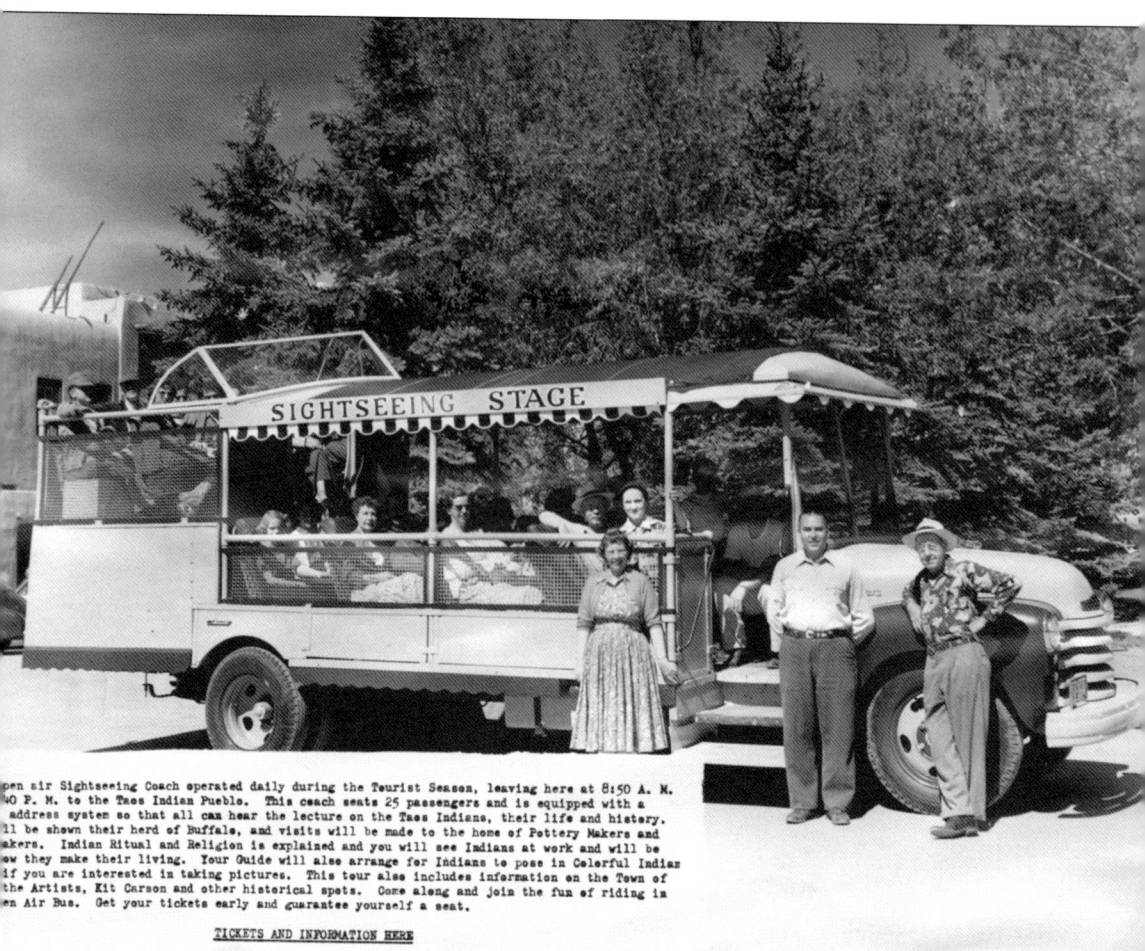

Pictured here is a sightseeing stage on the Taos Plaza. The text that accompanies the original photograph boasts of a public address system so tourists can "hear lectures on the Taos Indians, their life and history." It promises, "You will be shown their herd of buffalo, visit homes of pottery makers and drum makers" and that the "tour guide will also arrange for Indians to pose in colorful Indian dress if you are interested in taking pictures." (Courtesy of Taos Historic Museums.)

Four

TAOS SOCIETY OF ARTISTS

Artist Ernest L. Blumenschein first heard of Taos from Henry Sharp when he was a young art student studying in Paris. Sharp had spent time in what he described as an Indian village and urged Blumenschein to paint the West before it was gone. After returning to the states in 1898, Blumenschein convinced his friend artist Bert Phillips to accompany him on a sketching trip through the West. In Denver, they purchased two broncos and a wagon, proceeded to fill it with camping and painting supplies, and headed south with the intention of reaching Mexico. After several weeks of camping and painting, one of the wagon wheels collapsed, leaving them stranded just north of Taos. They flipped a $3 gold coin, and Blumenschein was chosen to carry the wheel to the nearest town for repair. He was so enamored with what he saw in the Taos Valley that within days, he and Phillips sold the wagon and broncos and decided that Taos would be their future home. Thus was the beginning of the Taos art colony. Before long, other artists joined them, and in 1915 a group of six established the Taos Society of Artists whose primary goal was to gain public recognition of the work of its members through traveling exhibitions. The six founding members included Blumenschein, Phillips, E. Irving Couse, Oscar Berninghaus, Herbert Dunton, and Joseph H. Sharp, with the later addition of Walter Ufer, Victor Higgins, E. Martin Hennings, and Kenneth M. Adams. In March 1927, the group agreed it was time to disband. However, the Taos Society of Artists influence was far-reaching. The group was instrumental in establishing Taos as a serious art colony—a reputation it still enjoys to this day.

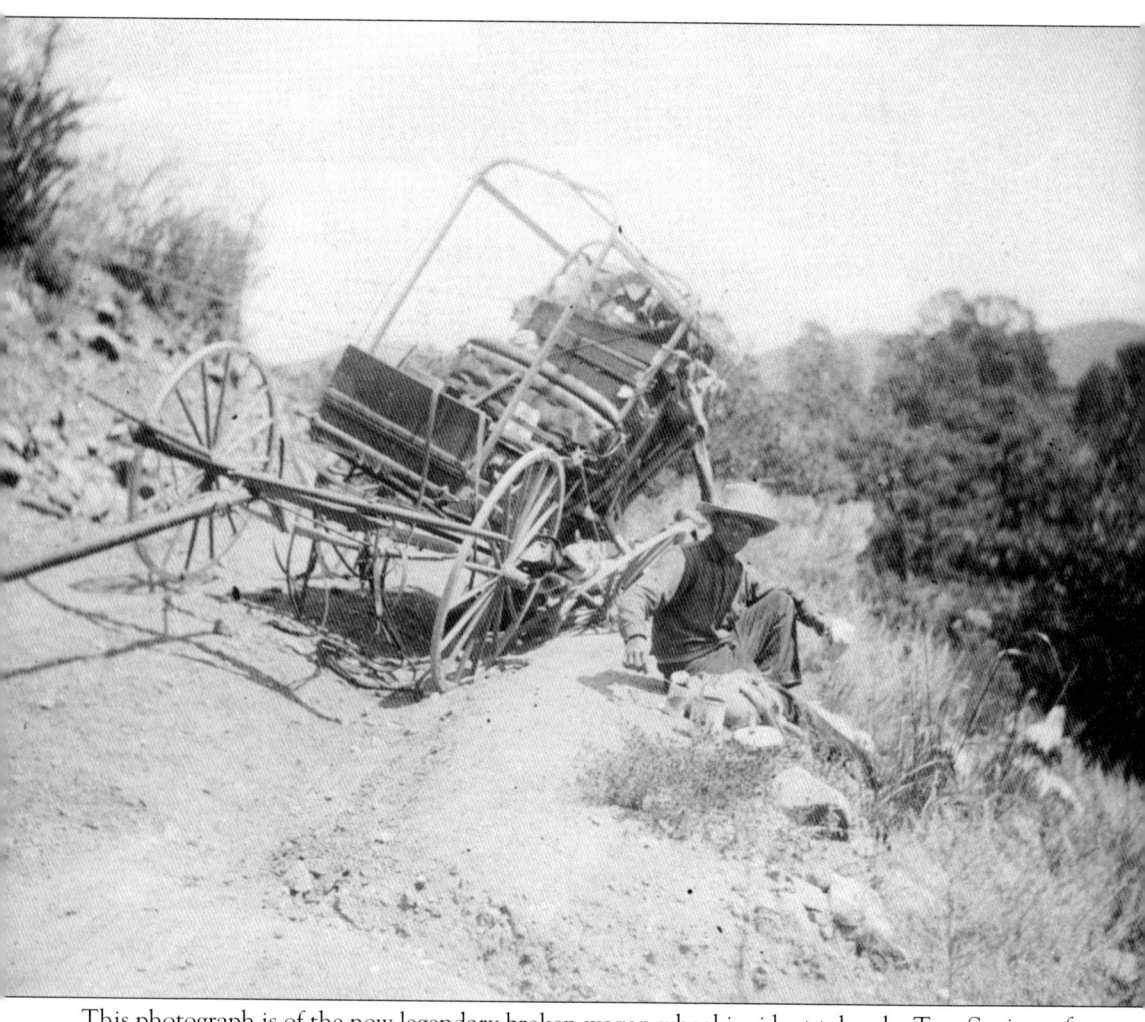

This photograph is of the now-legendary broken wagon wheel incident taken by Taos Society of Artists founder Bert Phillips in 1898. Ernest Blumenschein sits next to the wagon preparing to eat lunch. This accident ultimately led to the establishment of the Taos art colony. (Courtesy of Taos Historic Museums.)

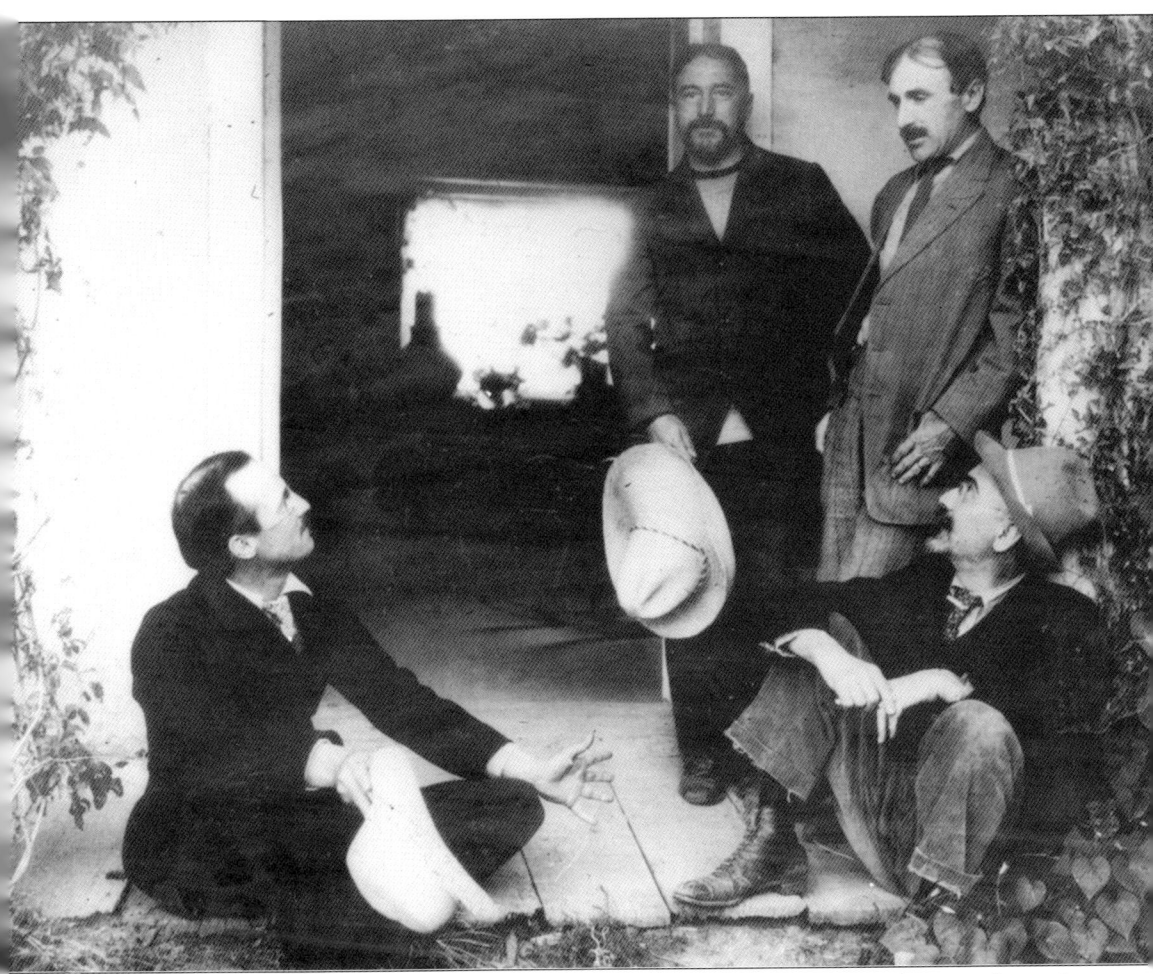

Taken outside of the Couse residence, this photograph shows four of the founding members of the Taos Society of Artists. Seated are Joseph Henry Sharp (left) and Ernest Blumenschein, and standing E. Irving Couse (left) and Bert Phillips. (Courtesy of Taos Historic Museums.)

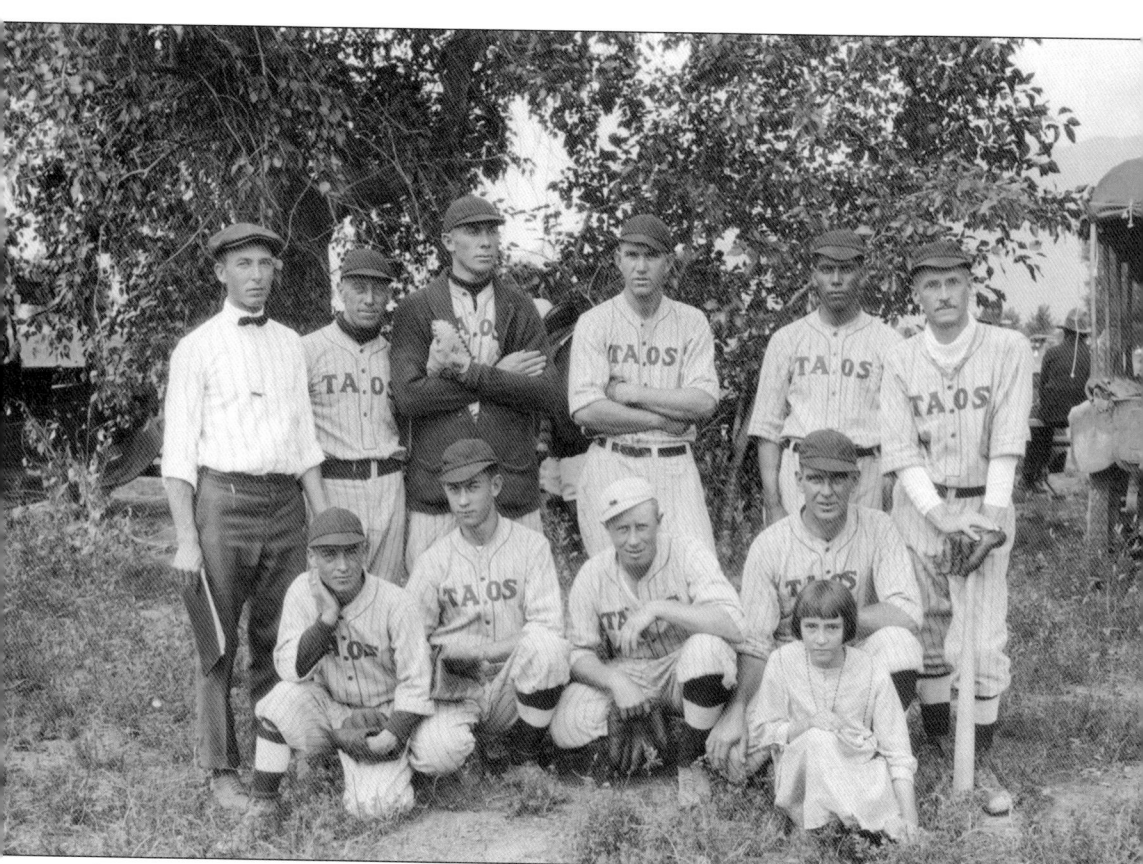

Sports were an important part of Ernest Blumenschein's life. He was an avid tennis player until age 75 and was very active in local Taos baseball, which he played until he was in his 50s. This photograph is of Blumenschein and his Taos baseball team. His daughter Helen, a notorious tomboy, is seated in the front. (Courtesy of Taos Historic Museums.)

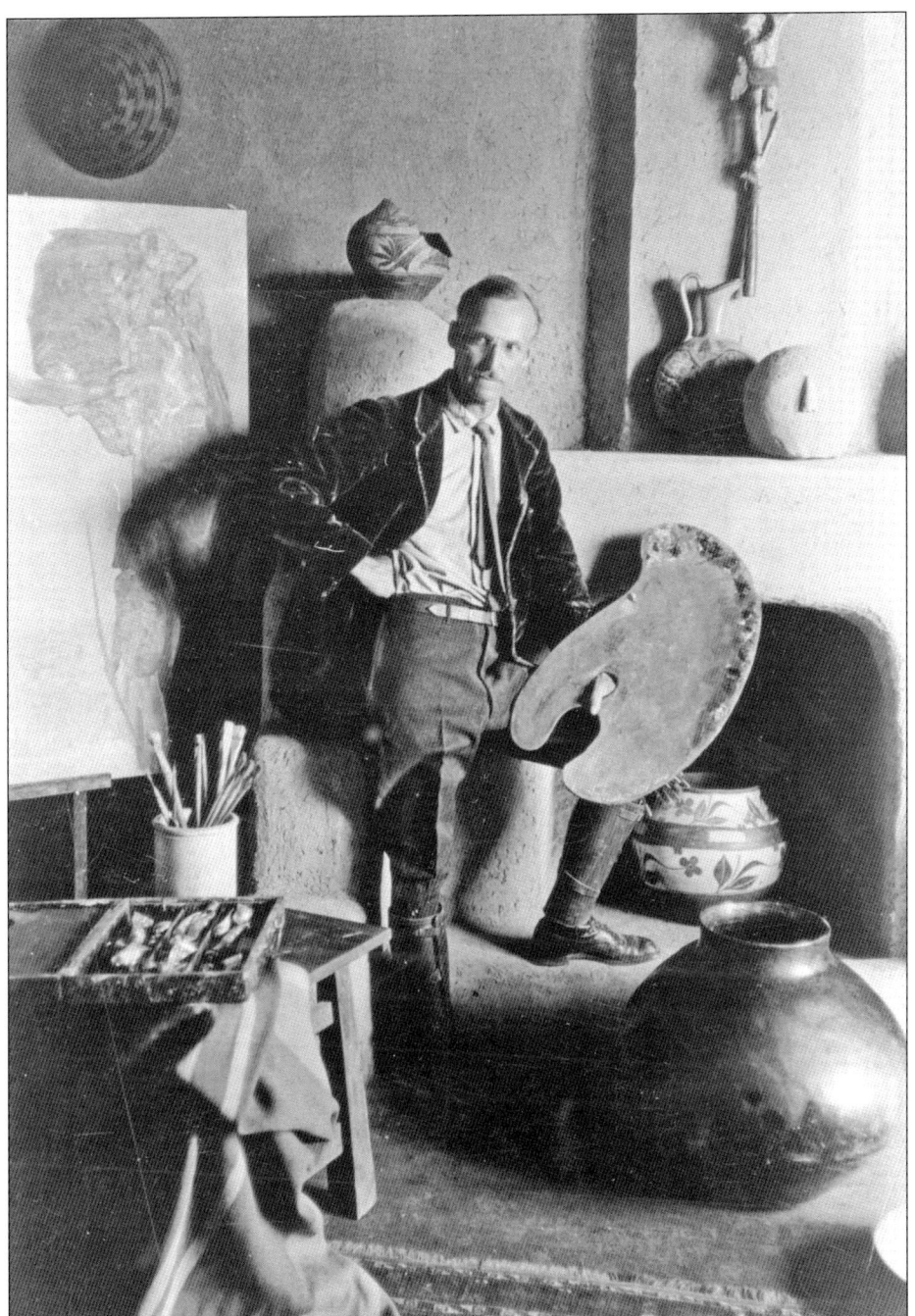

This photograph of Blumenschein was taken in his Taos studio on Ledoux Street. Ernest L. Blumenschein was born in Pittsburgh on May 26, 1874, to Leonora Chapin, who was a direct descendant of Heber Allen, brother of revolutionary war hero Ethan Allen, and W. L. Blumenschein, an accomplished musician who was a conductor, teacher, and composer of more than 150 choral pieces. As a young man, Ernest spent two years at the Arts League of New York before going to Paris to study at Académie Julian. In Paris, he met Mary Shepard Greene, an accomplished artist in her own right. They were married in 1905. (Courtesy of Taos Historic Museums.)

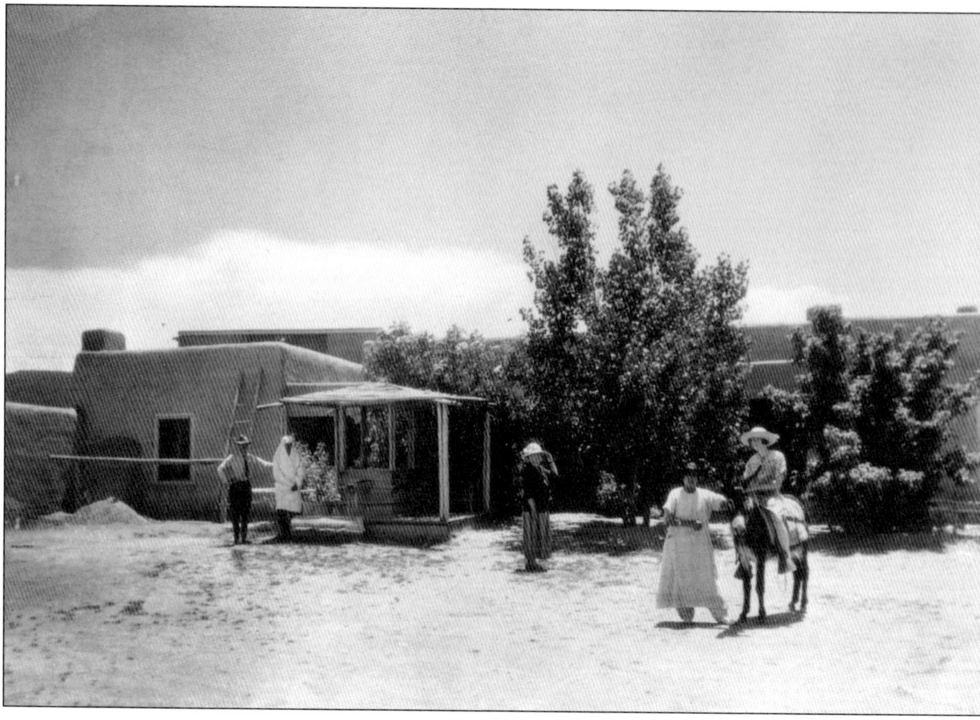

The Blumenscheins set up housekeeping on Ledoux Street in Taos. The photograph above shows a girl on a burro outside of their residence, and below is a view of the home's interior. The property is now an historic museum. (Courtesy of Taos Historic Museums.)

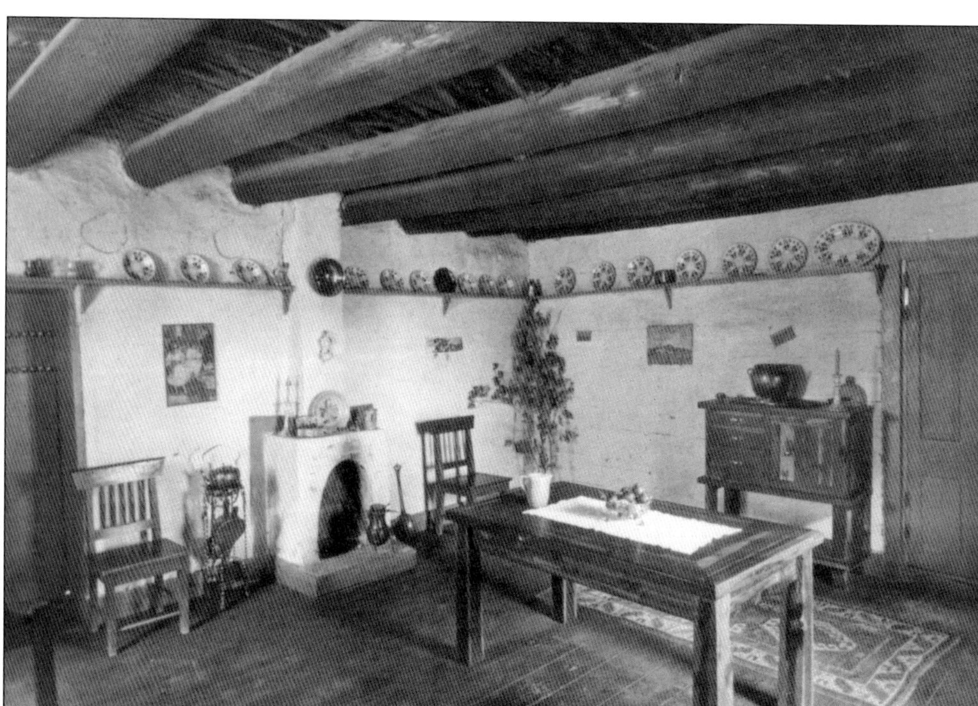

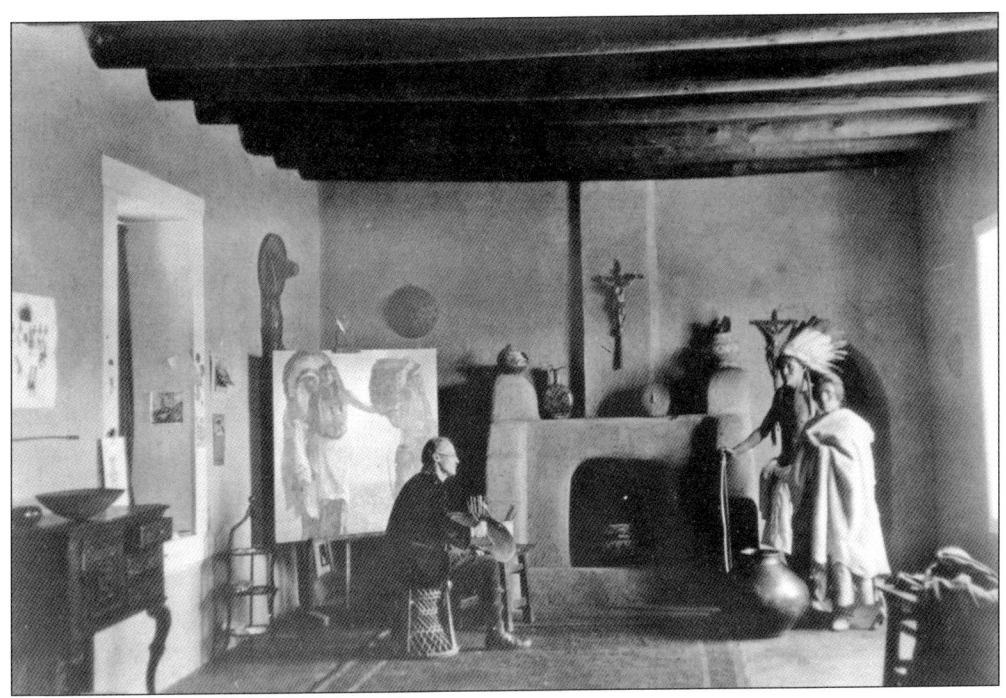

The image above shows Blumenschein in his studio with a Taos Pueblo model. Below is a photograph of Blumenschein on horseback. (Courtesy of Taos Historic Museums)

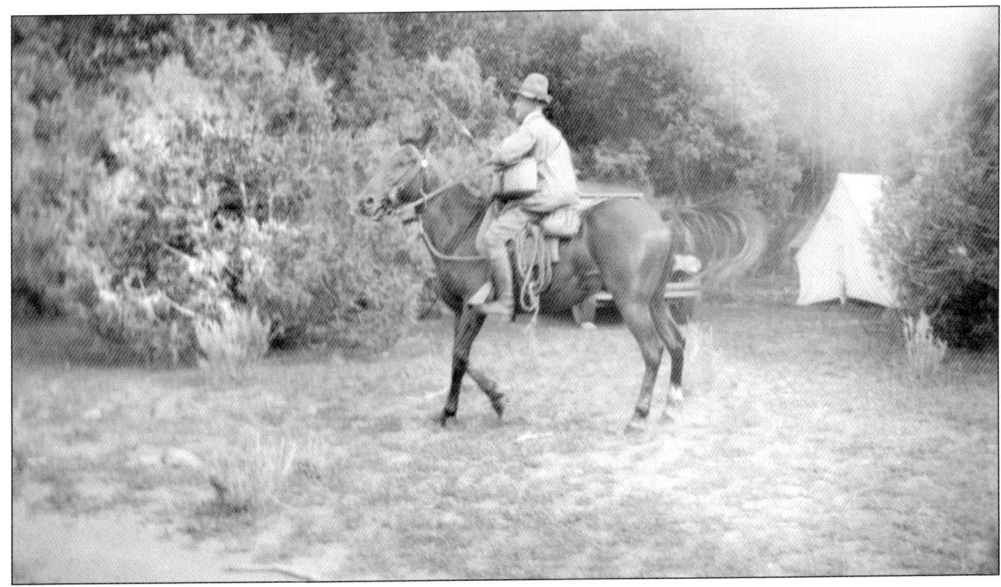

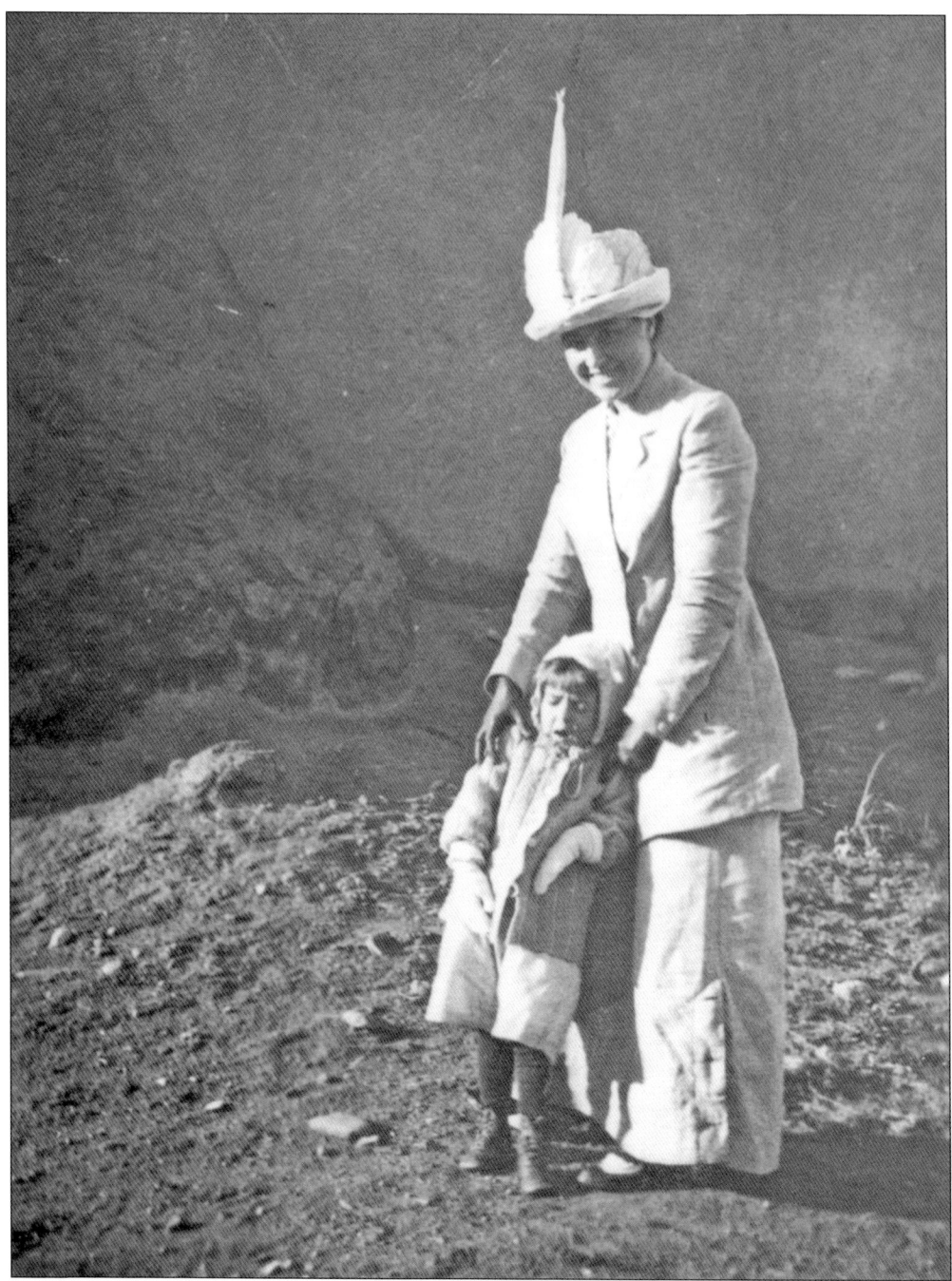

This is a 1913 photograph of Mary Shepard Greene Blumenschein and her daughter Helen. Helen was born in Brooklyn in 1910 and moved to Taos with her parents at age 10. (Courtesy of Taos Historic Museums.)

While lesser known than Ernest, Mary Blumenschein was a talented, award-winning artist. She was well respected in European circles when the couple met, having won medals in the prestigious Paris Salon in 1900 and 1902. Some believe her best work was done after she was married and had moved back to the United States. Her paintings are in the permanent collection of the Brooklyn Museum, among others. The photograph at right shows Mary in her studio on Ledoux Street, and she is with two of her beloved dogs below. (Courtesy of Taos Historic Museums.)

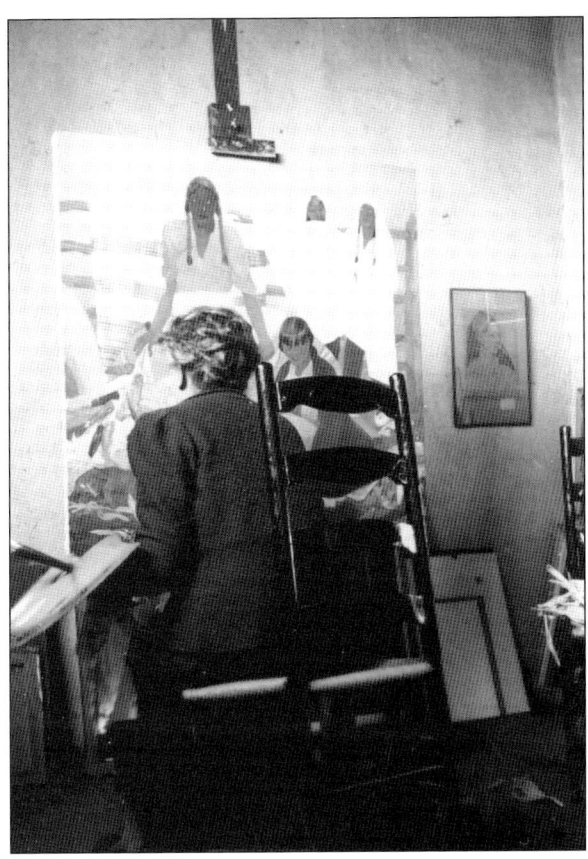

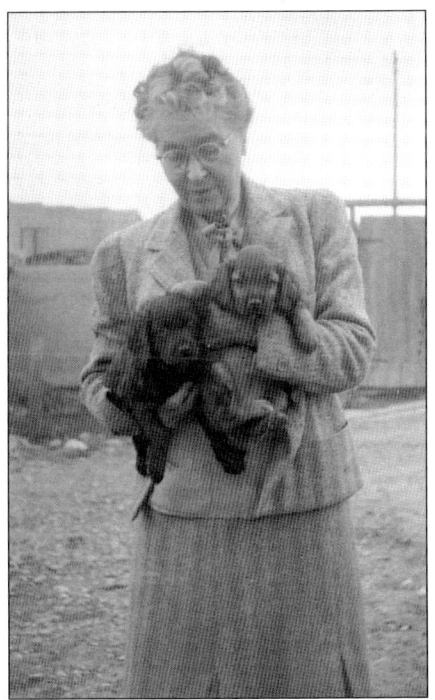

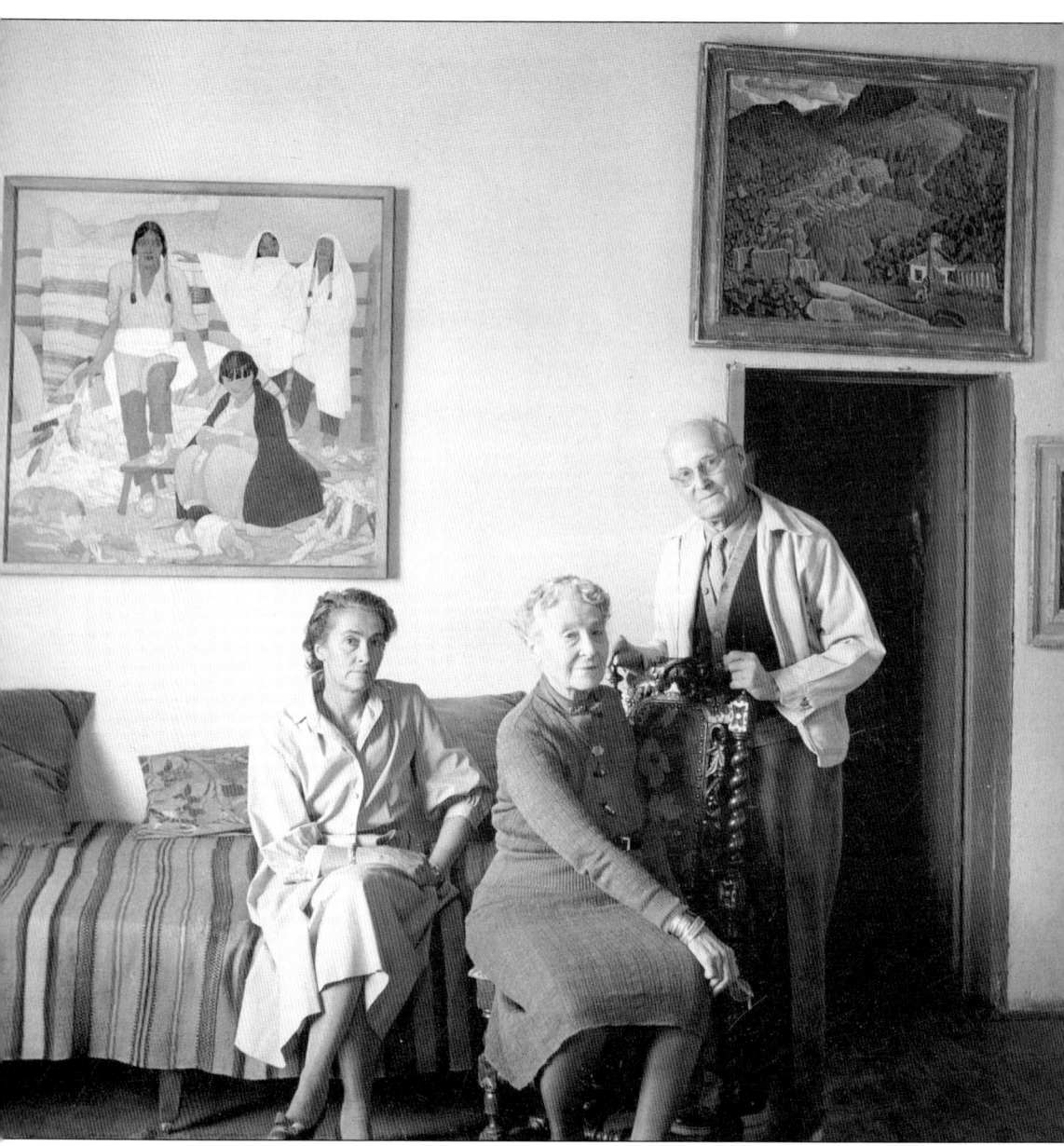

This photograph taken in 1957 shows Helen Blumenschein, who served as a lieutenant in the Women's Army Corps during World War II and became a respected artist and historian, with parents Mary and Ernest in their home on Ledoux Street. (Courtesy of Taos Historic Museums)

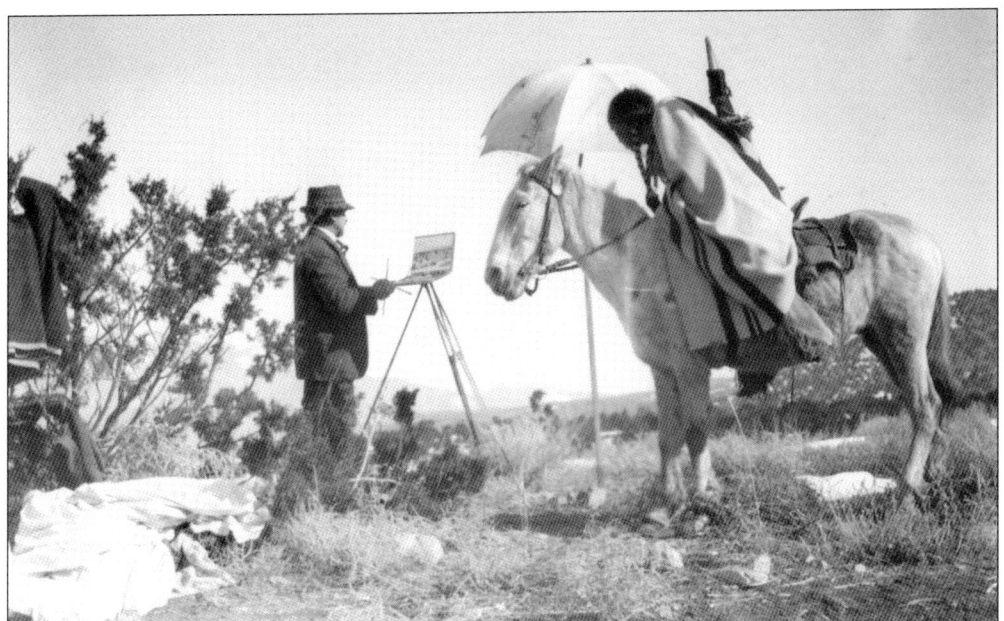

Taos Society of Artists founder Bert Geer Phillips's love of Native American culture began as a boy, when he read endless accounts on the life of Kit Carson and American Indian tribes. While he was sharing a New York City studio with Ernest Blumenshein, the two painted from photographs and from Indian and cowboy models but found these paintings lacked an authenticity they later found in abundance in Taos. Phillips is painting a Native American man on horseback above and below a Pueblo man posed against an adobe wall. (Courtesy of Taos Historic Museums.)

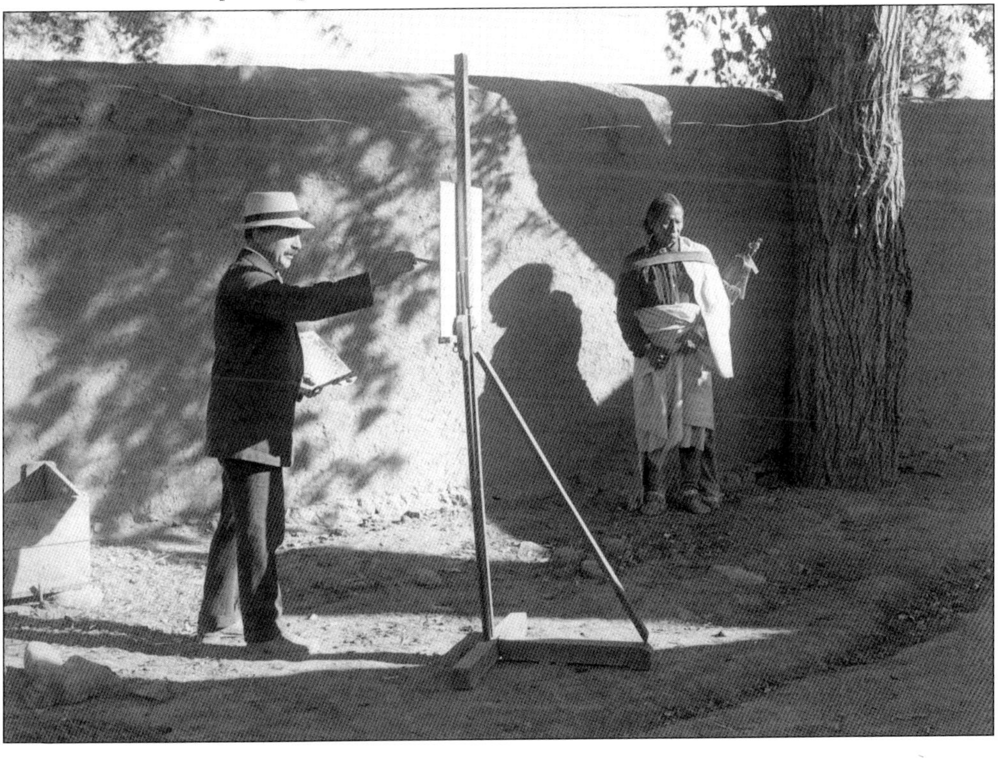

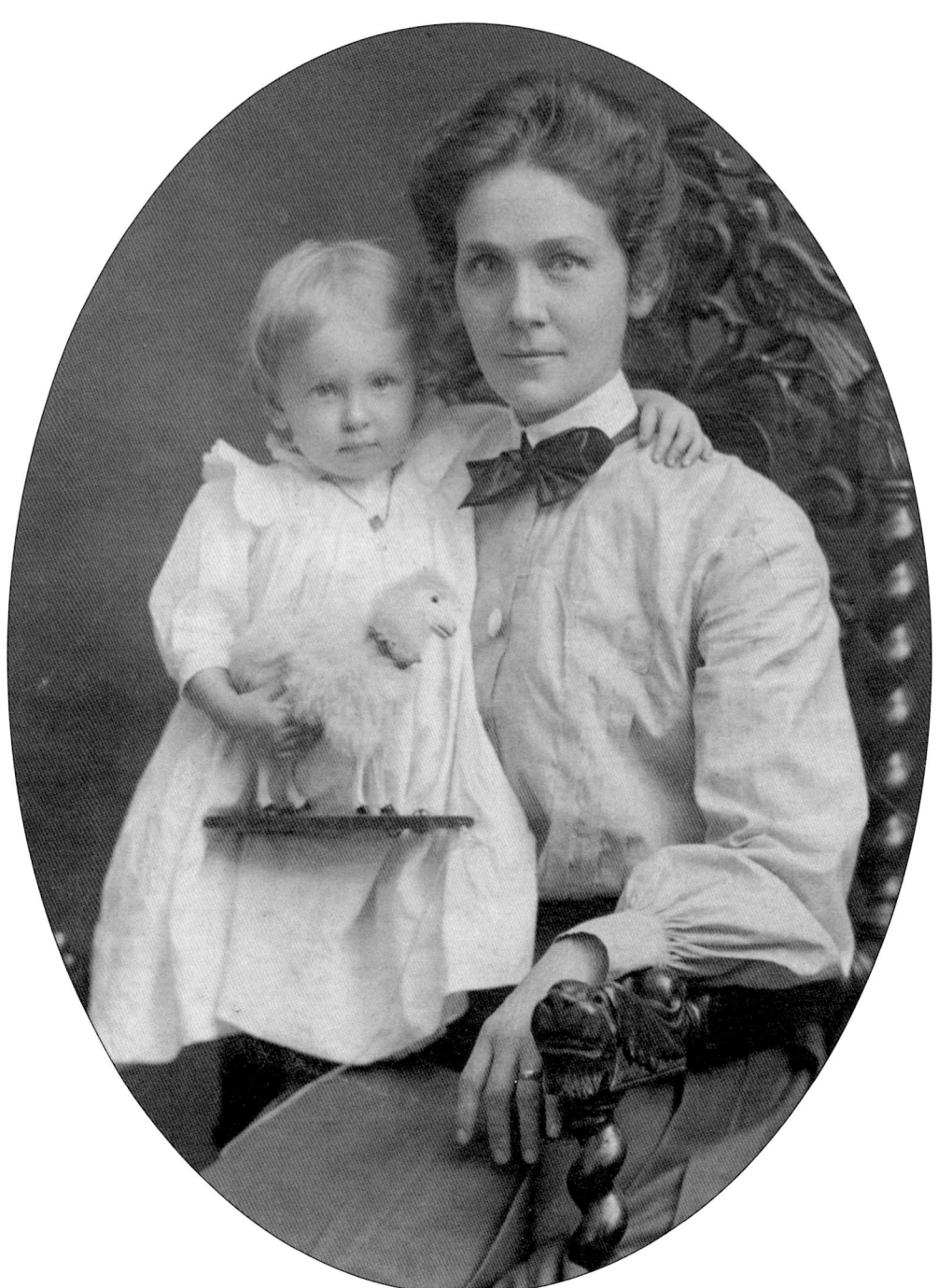

Taken in 1905, this is a portrait of Bert Phillips's wife, Rose, with daughter Margaret. Rose Martin was raised in Shippenberg, Pennsylvania. She traveled to Taos to visit her brother, T. P. Martin, a popular Taos doctor affectionately known as Doc Martin, and there she met her lifelong partner, Bert. They were married in 1899 and raised two children, Margaret (above) and Ralph. It was during a gathering at T. P. "Doc" Martin's home in 1915 that the Society of Artists was founded. (Courtesy of Taos Historic Museums.)

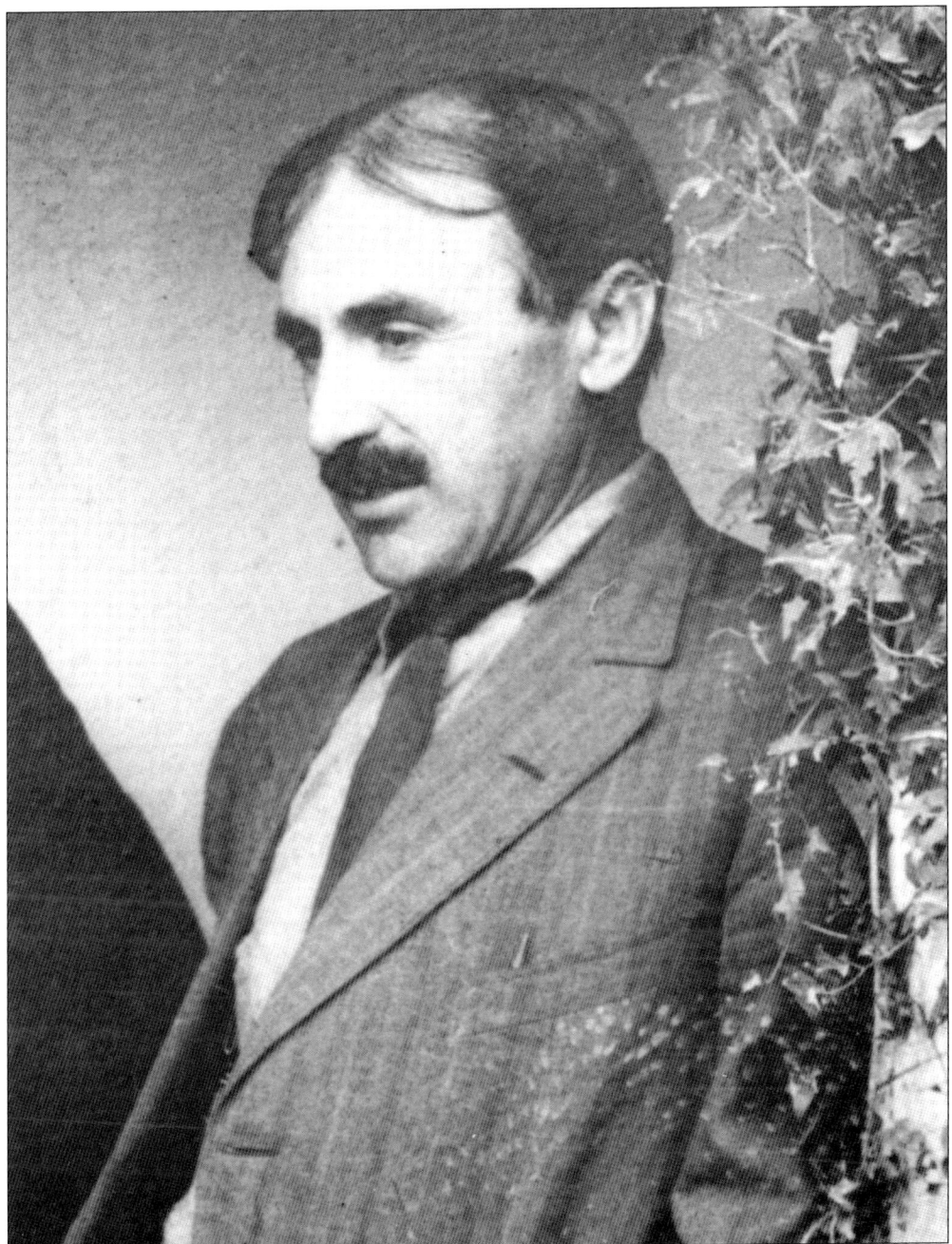

Bert Geer Phillips was born in 1868 in Hudson, New York, to William and Elizabeth (Jessup) Phillips. He began drawing as a youth and won first prize at a county fair for watercolors. As a young man, Phillips studied at the New York Arts League and National Academy of Design. After graduating in 1889, he set up a studio in New York City where he stayed for several years. In 1894, he sailed to England to live for a few months before moving on to Paris. Once he and Blumenschein happened on Taos following the broken-wheel incident, Phillips knew he had found his home. He and Rose enjoyed a long and happy marriage and, except for winter trips to California, Phillips lived in Taos for the rest of his days. (Courtesy of Taos Historic Museums.)

Joseph Henry Sharp was born in Bridgeport, Ohio, in 1859 to William Henry and Ann (Raynes) Sharp. He suffered from deafness from age 10 and had lost his father when he was a young boy. Sharp was born with a natural artistic talent that he developed at the University of Cincinnati's McMicken School of Design and then at the Cincinnati Art Academy while working to pay his tuition. In the early 1880s, he began traveling to Europe, but it was not until 1883 on a trip to Santa Fe that Sharp's destiny unfolded. His first wife died in Taos in 1913, and he later married her sister, Louise Byram, with whom he traveled extensively. The couple split their time between residences in Taos and Pasadena. Sharp lived to be 93 years old and by all accounts was deeply loved by those who knew him. (Courtesy of Taos Historic Museums.)

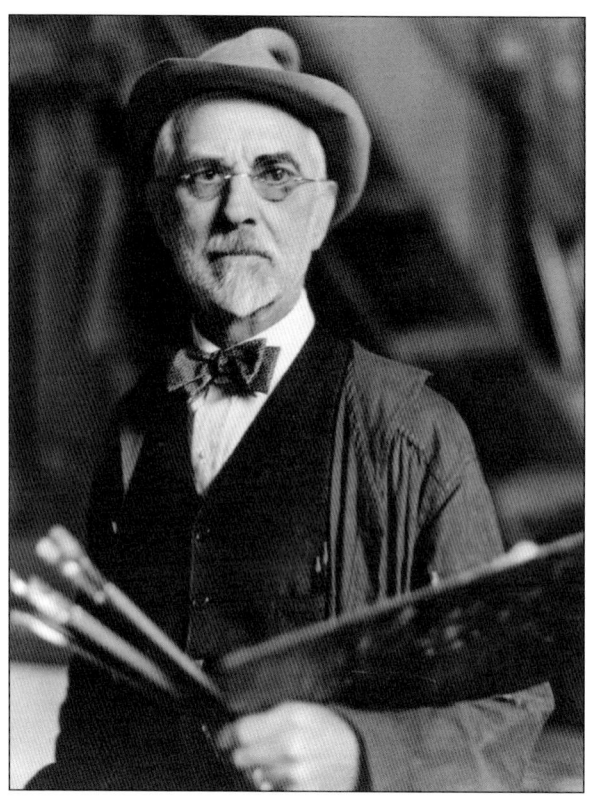

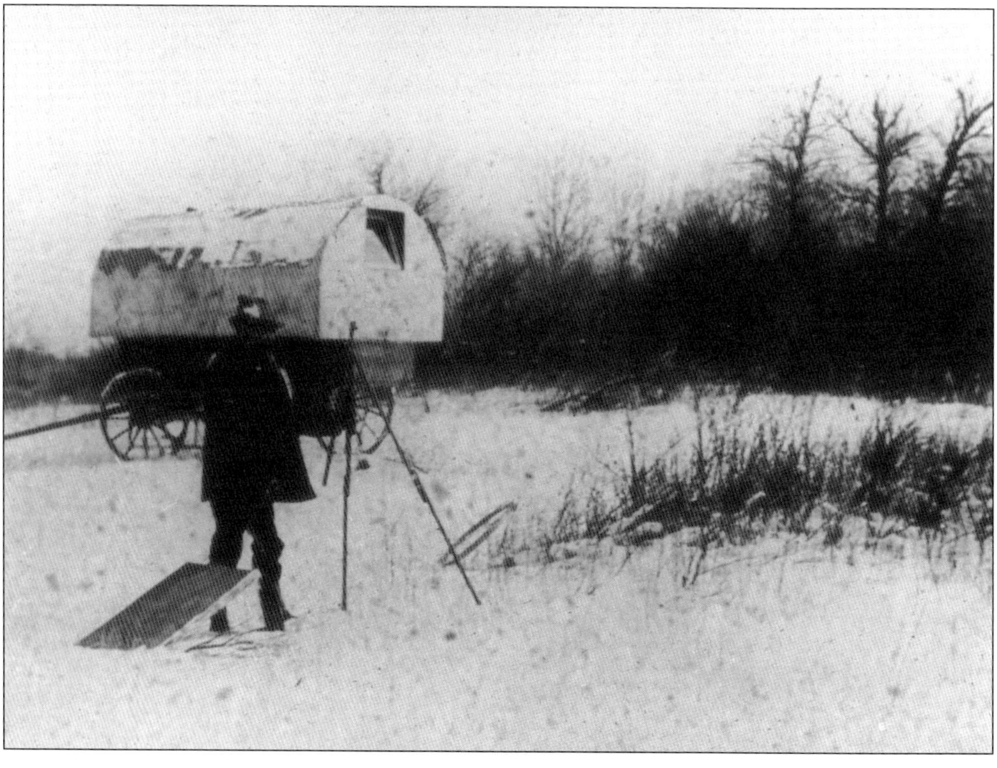

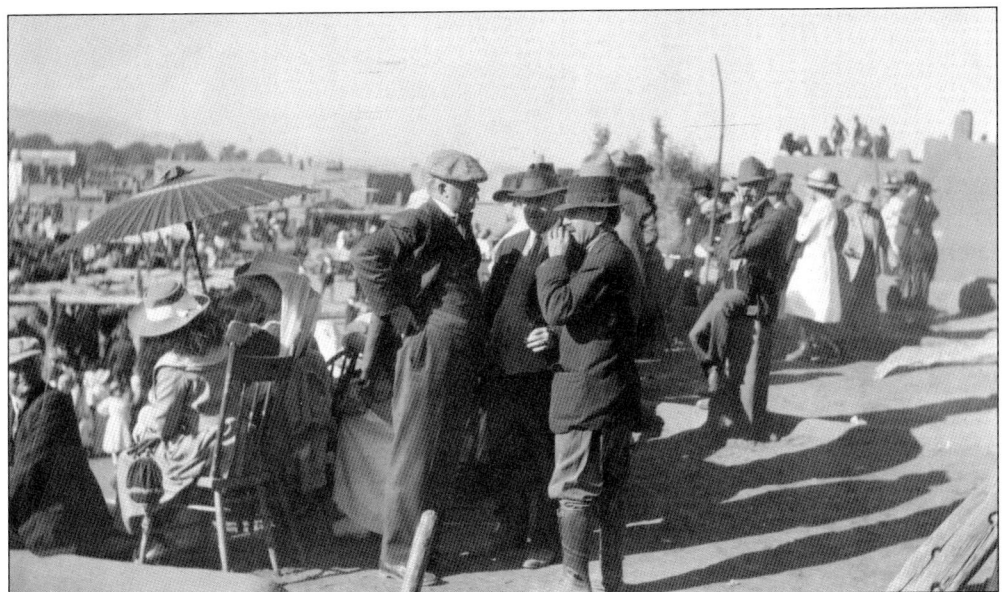

This photograph of a Taos gathering shows Phillips (front center wearing riding boots) in conversation with two unidentified men, while Sharp, leaning on a post, watches nearby. (Courtesy of Taos Historic Museums.)

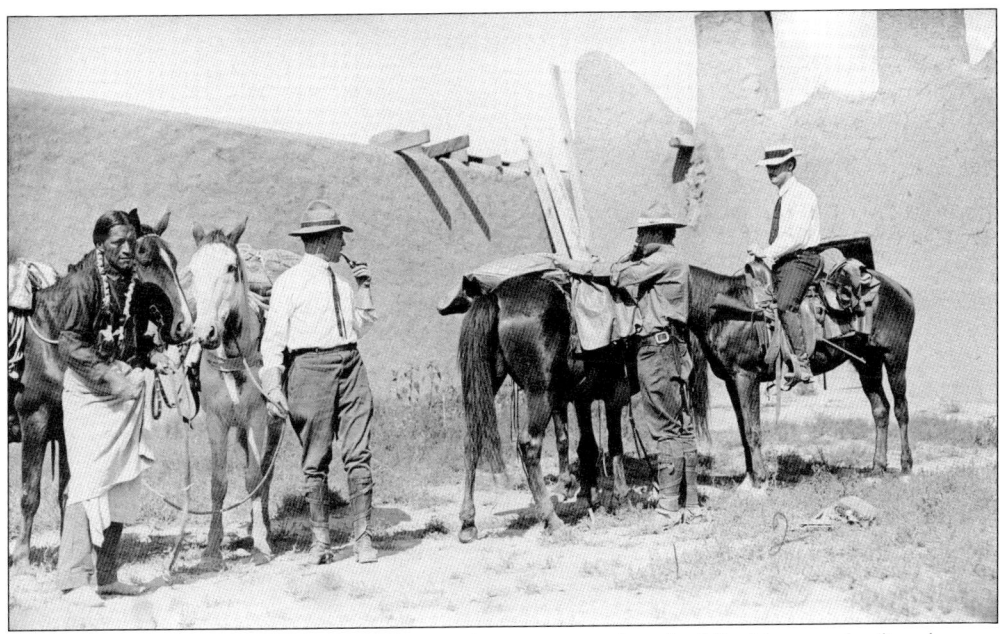

Preparing for a camping trip from left to right are an unidentified Pueblo man leading horses, Lou Wyle, E. Irving Couse's son Kibbey, and Ernest L. Blumenschein. The Couse residence appears in the background to the left, and adjacent on the right is an old chapel that became J. H. Sharp's studio, which he referred to as "the copper bell." Kibbey Couse earned respect and recognition for his design of a line of mobile equipment repair shops light and compact enough to be airlifted during World War II. (Virginia Couse Leavitt gifted this photograph to the Taos Historic Museums.)

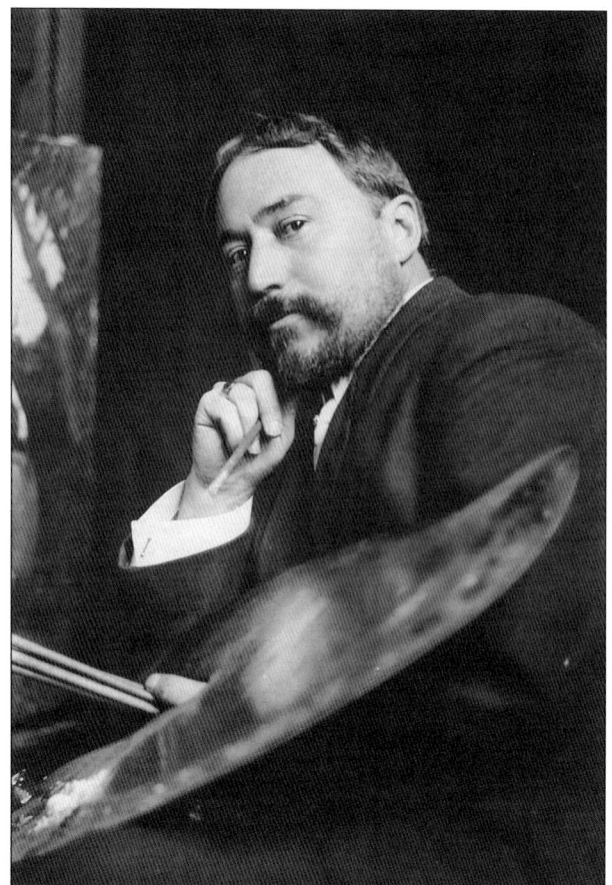

Eanger Irving Couse was born in Saginaw, Michigan, in 1866—one of three children born to Moses Snover Couse and Mary Jane (Price) Couse. Like Joseph Sharp, Couse was born with a natural artistic talent, and also like Sharp, he earned money to pay tuition to art school—first at the Art Institute of Chicago and later at the National Academy of Design in New York City. Like many of his contemporaries, Couse eventually made his way to Paris and studied at the Académie Julian, where his work won numerous prestigious awards. While in Paris he met fellow art student Virginia Walker, and the two married in 1889. They spent a number of years traveling between Oregon and France. In 1902, Couse saw Taos for the first time, and by the summer of 1905 he brought his family to live there, but it was not until 1928 that he was able to settle in Taos for good. Couse enjoyed a long and very successful painting career. (Courtesy of The Couse Family Archive.)

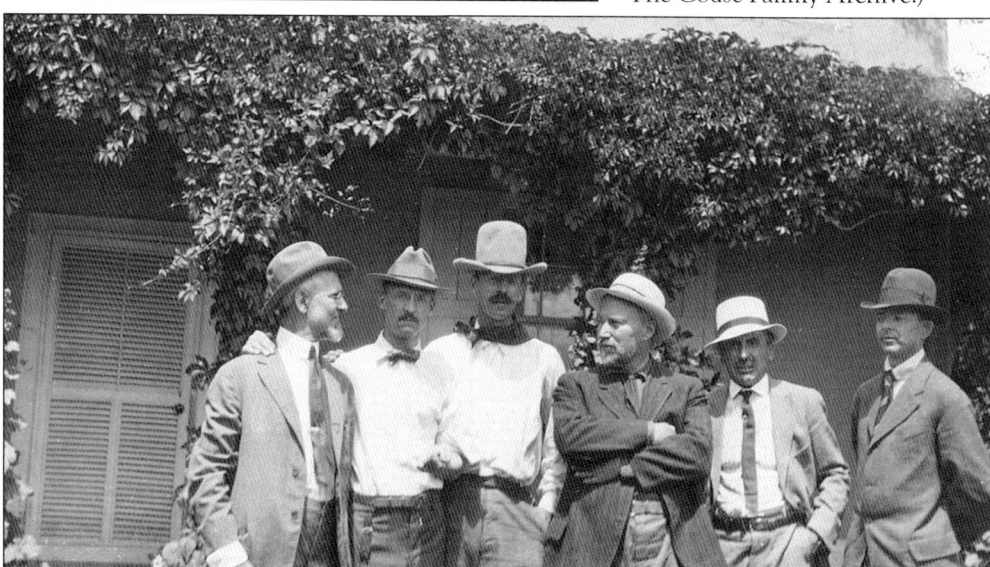

Standing in front the Couse residence portal are, from left to right, Taos Society of Artists members Joseph H. Sharp, Ernest L. Blumenschein, W. Herbert Dunton, E. Irving Couse, Bert G. Phillips, and Oscar E. Berninghaus. (Courtesy of The Couse Family Archive.)

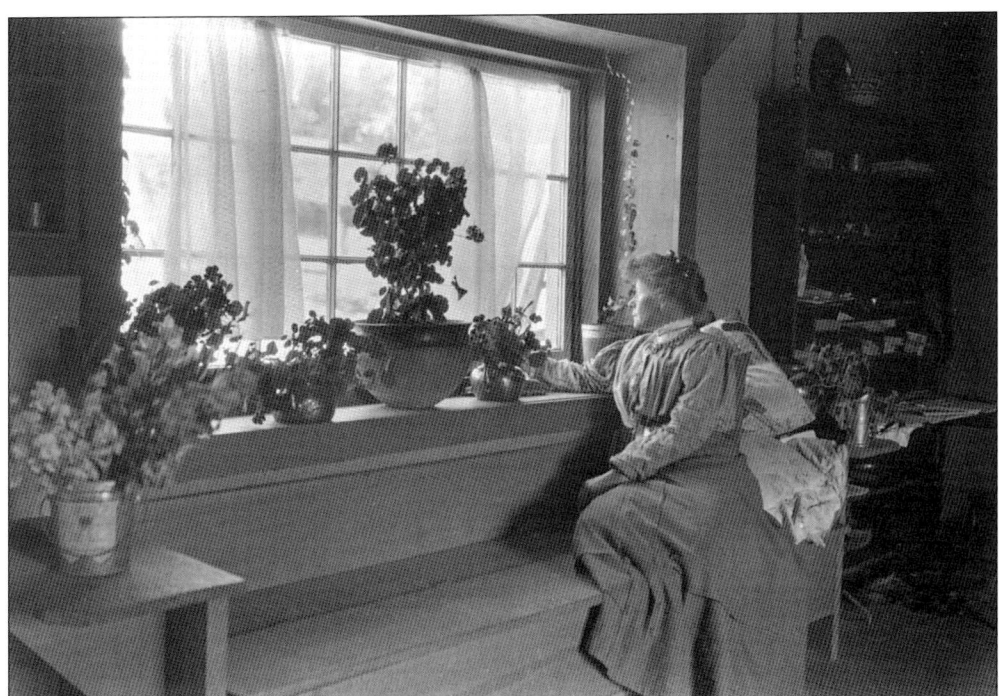

Virginia Walker was an accomplished American artist studying in Paris when she met fellow artist E. Irving Couse in 1887. The couple married in France two years later. Diminished vision forced Virginia to abandon her dream of a career in illustration, but as her granddaughter Virginia Couse Leavitt so beautifully explains, "She turned her passion to gardening; she relinquished her pen and brushes for shovel and hoe; the soil became her canvas and the flowers her colorful palette." Above Virginia Walker Couse is seated on one of the benches built for their Taos home. The plants on the windowsill reflect her passion for gardening. Taken in 1912, the photograph below shows Virginia seated on the portal of her home in Taos, overlooking the garden she began creating in 1909 when the Couses bought their house on Kit Carson Road. (Courtesy of The Couse Family Archive.)

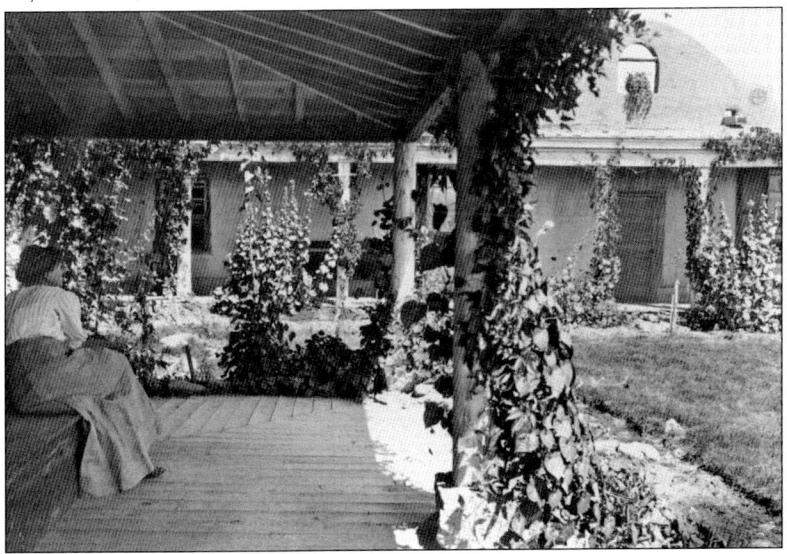

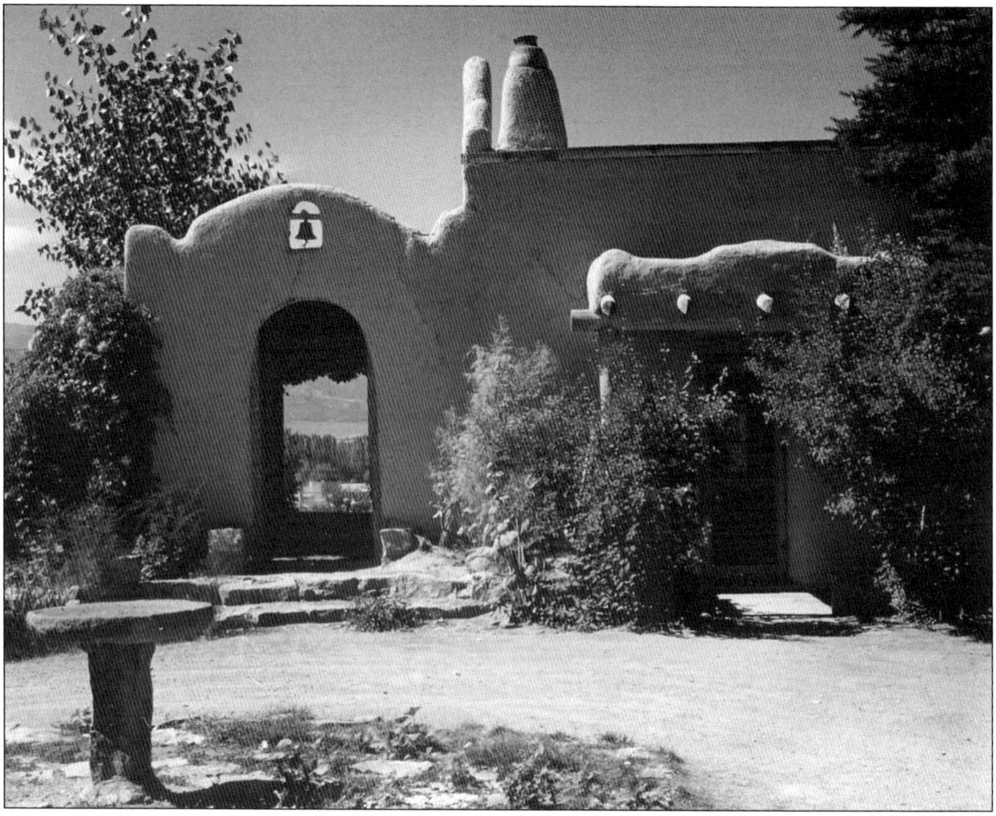

The view above is of E. Irving Couse's studio, adjacent to the Couse residence on Kit Carson Road and next to Sharp's studio. The photograph below shows the Couses' dining room, which still looks much as it did when Virginia and Irving lived there. (Courtesy of The Couse Family Archive.)

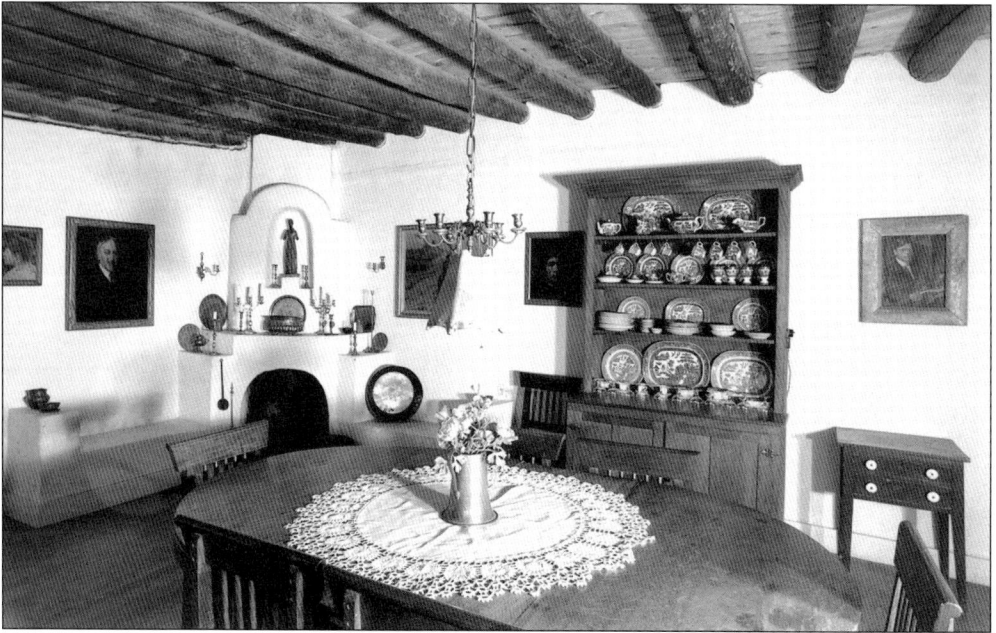

The oldest of five children, Oscar E. Berninghaus was born in St. Louis in 1874 to first-generation German immigrants Edmund O. and Augusta P. (Helgenberg). Berninghaus was a self-taught artist who received little if any formal training. On his first visit to Taos in 1899 he met Bert Phillips, who had arrived the year before and decided to stay. Berninghaus would return to Taos many times over the next few years, and around 1908 rented a house for his wife, Emilia Miller, and their two children, Charles and Dorothy. For several years the family traveled between Taos and St. Louis as Berninghaus' national reputation grew. After a long illness, Mrs. Berninghaus died in 1913. In the 1920's Berninghaus participated in a number of successful shows and his work continued to increase in popularity. In 1932, Oscar married a woman from Raton, New Mexico, and lived in Taos full-time until his death in 1952 at age 78. (Courtesy of Southwest Research Center.)

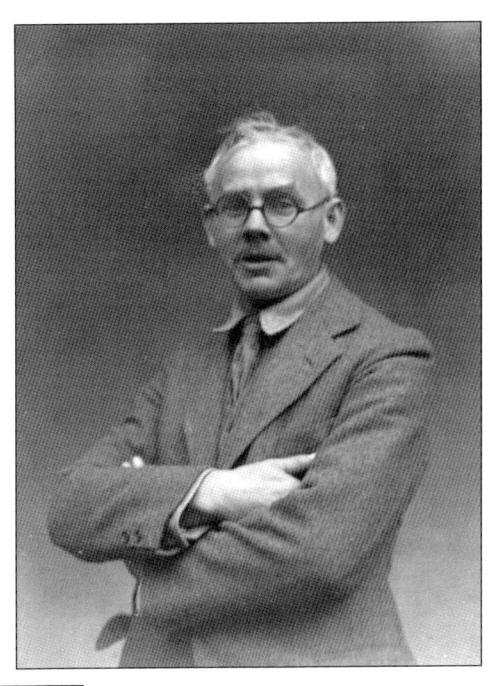

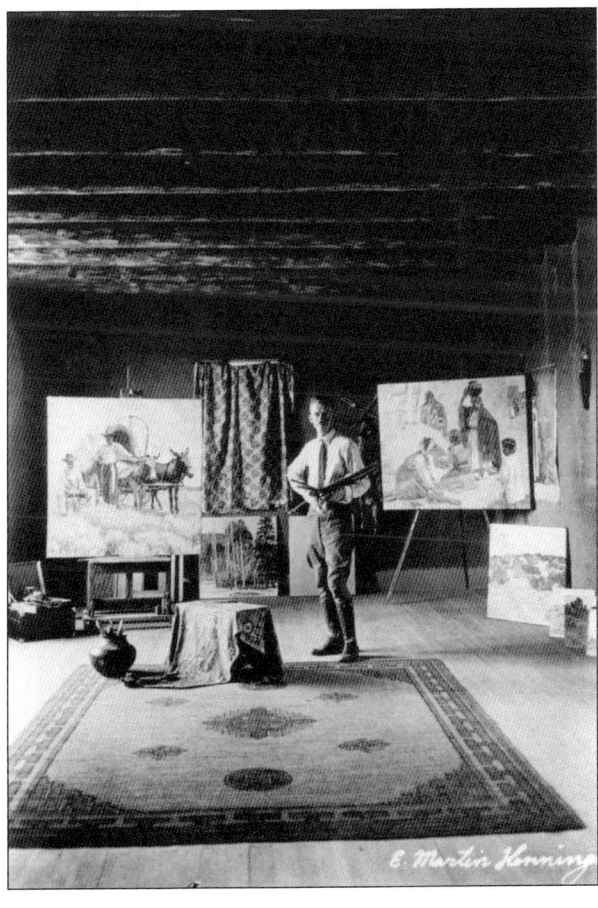

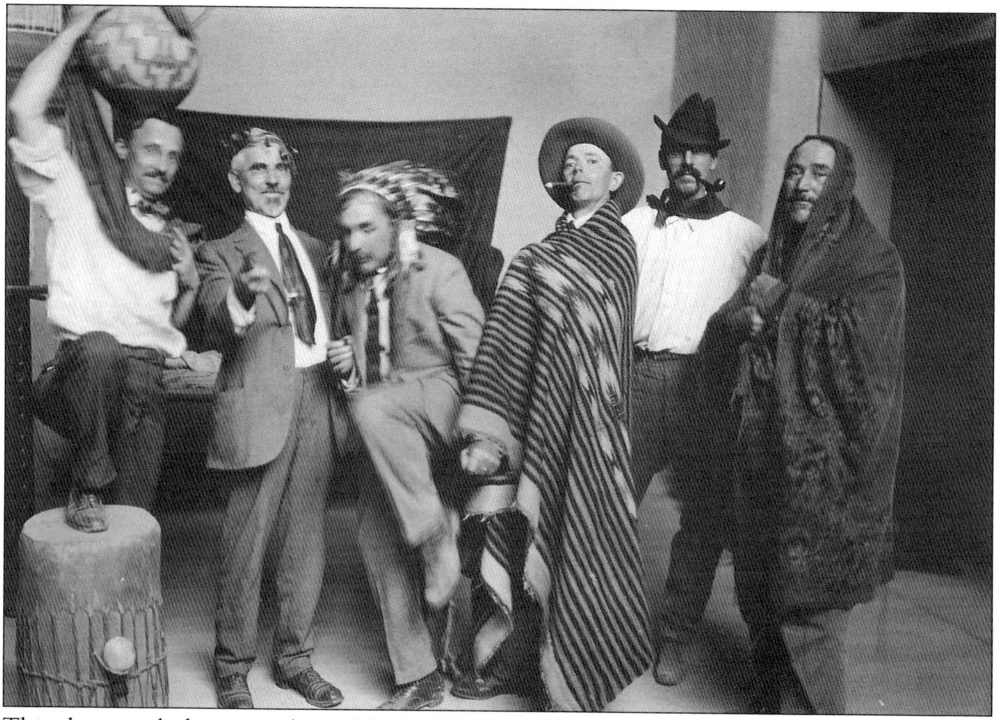

This photograph shows members of the Taos Society of Artists in a playful mood wearing costumes that were most likely studio props. Pictured here, from left to right, are Ernest Blumenschein, Joseph Sharp, Bert Phillips, Oscar Berninghaus, Herbert Dunton, and E. Irving Couse. (Courtesy of The Couse Family Archive.)

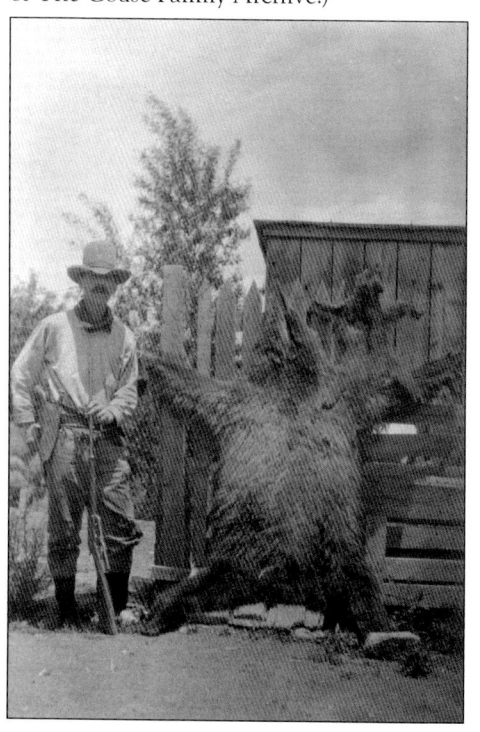

W. Herbert Dunton, known as "Buck," was the sixth charter member of the Taos Society of Artists. He was born in Augusta, Maine, in 1878 to Anna Katherine Pillsbury (whose mother was of Wedgewood lineage) and William Henry Dunton. Buck found school to be too confining so he quit at age 16 and was able to earn money selling his sketches to newspapers and magazines. He traveled extensively and spent a fair amount of time in Mexico. While Dunton enjoyed the free-range life of a cowboy, he returned to New York each winter. He managed to attend several art schools in Boston and New York while earning a living as an illustrator. Early in his career (in 1900), he married Nellie G. Hartley of Massachusetts. (Courtesy of Taos Historic Museums.)

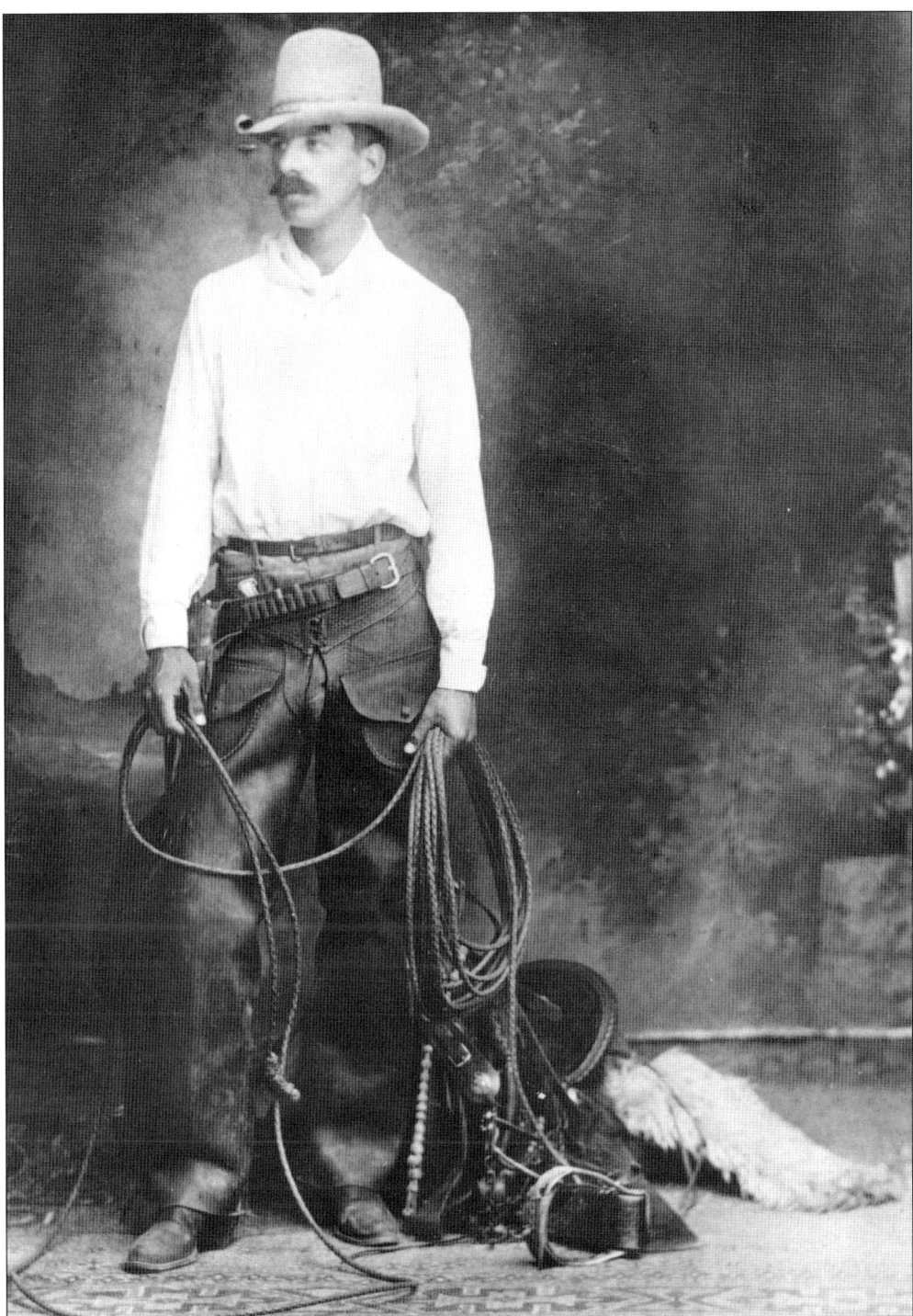

Herbert Dunton studied briefly under Ernest Blumenschein at the Art Students' League in New York City. It is believed that it was Blumenschein who urged him to visit New Mexico, and in 1912, Dunton moved to Taos. He enjoyed hunting and camping and was known for his signature 10-gallon hats and cowboy gear as shown in this photograph. (Courtesy of Taos Historic Museums.)

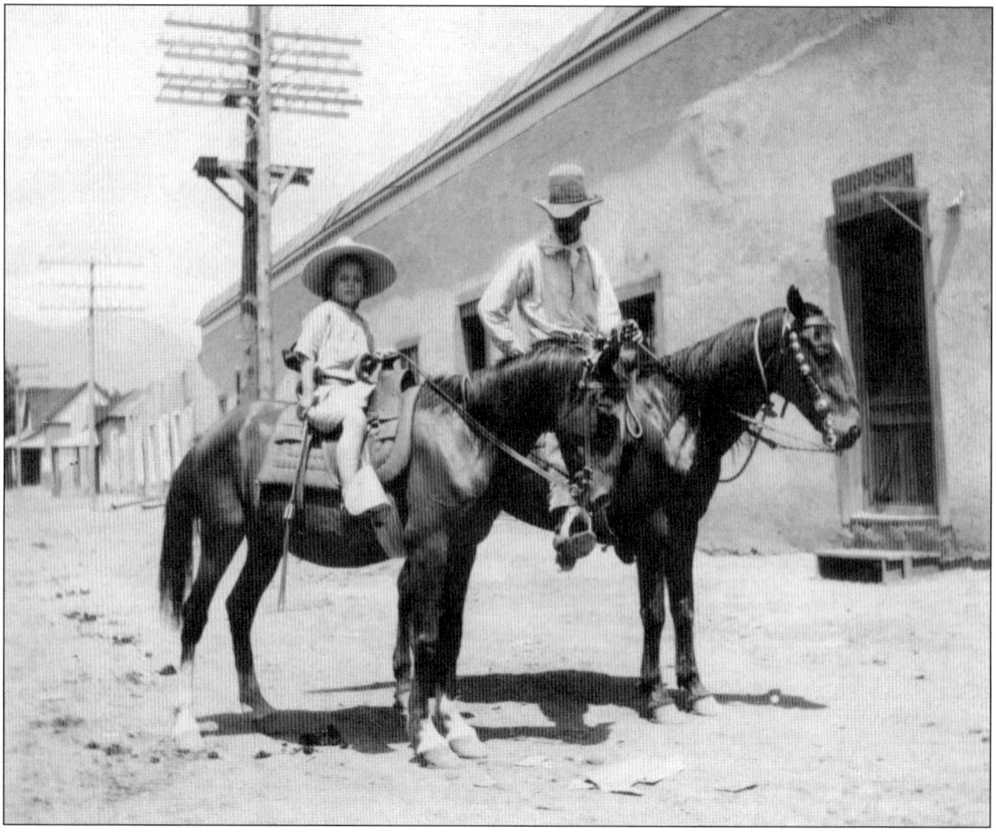

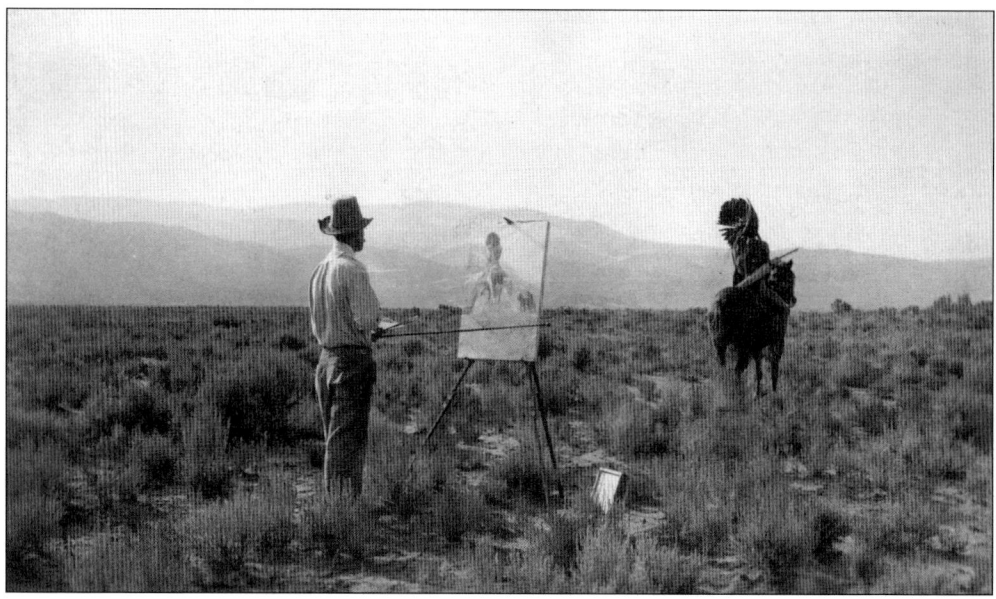

This photograph shows Dunton—a cowboy at heart—with a little girl (possibly Helen Blumenschein) on horseback. (Courtesy of Taos Historic Museums.)

With his easel and paints set up in the landscape, Dunton paints a Taos Pueblo man wearing a Plains Indian headdress. (Courtesy of Taos Historic Museums.)

Dunton enjoyed the Wild West and great outdoors. In the photographs above and below, he is using paints, easel, and canvas to capture views of the New Mexico landscape. Written across the front of one of the images is "A Taos Industry" (presumably referring to painting). (Courtesy of Taos Historic Museums.)

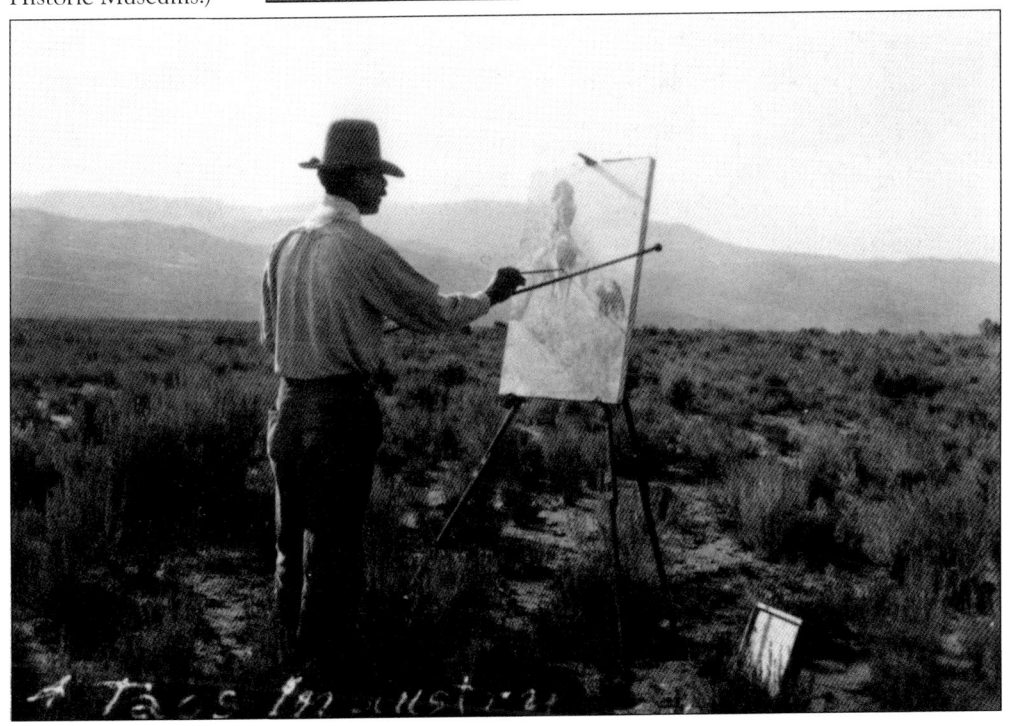

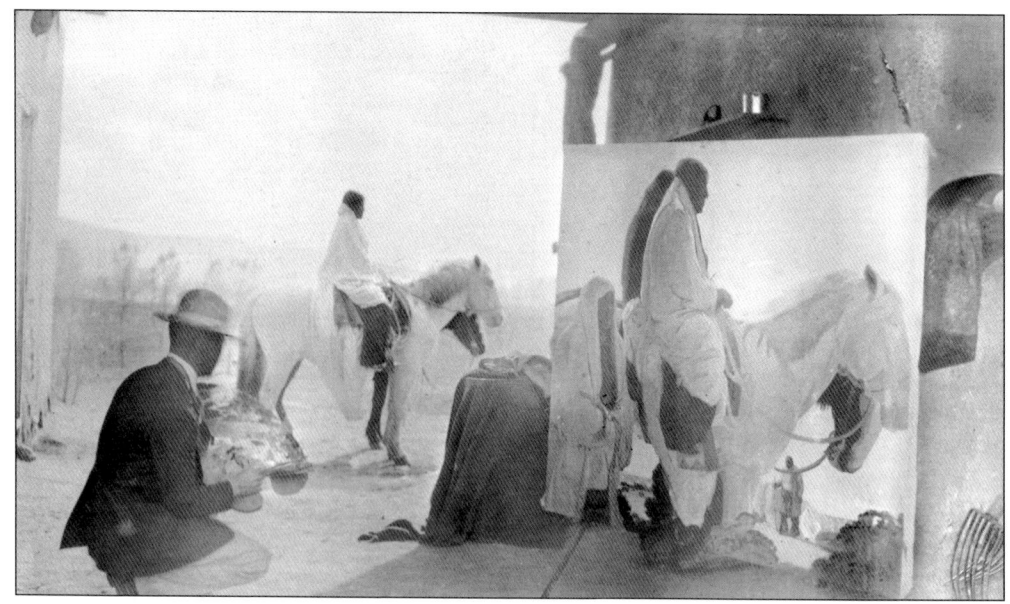

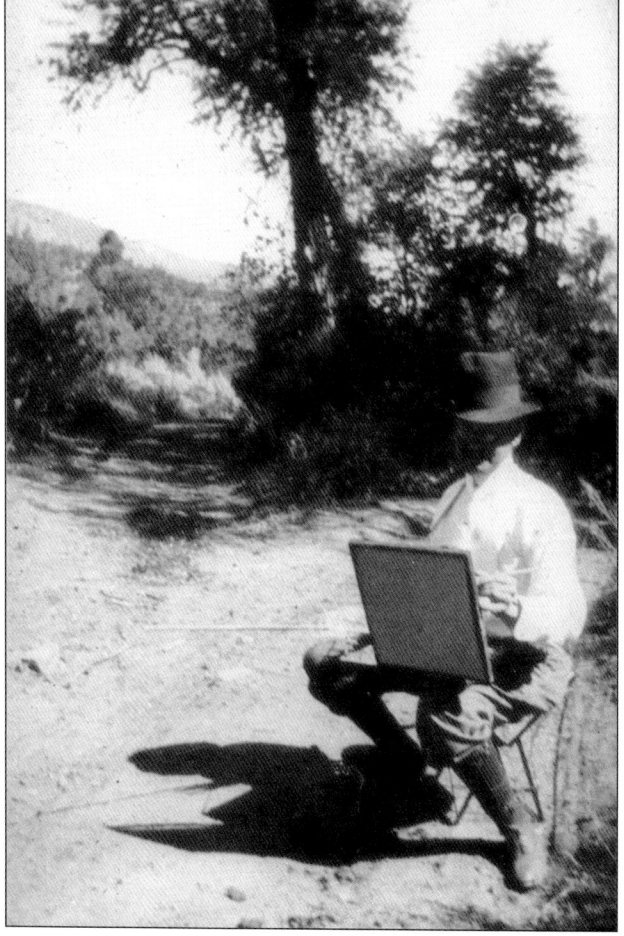

Walter Ufer was born in Kentucky in 1876 to German immigrant parents. He had already lived a good bit of life by the time he first visited Taos, having studied in Germany, lived in Chicago, and painted in France, Italy, and North Africa. Like Blumenschein and Couse, Ufer married an art student, Mary Frederiksen, who reluctantly returned to her native Denmark to live with her mother at various times during the marriage so that Walter could hopefully find a foothold in America. Through the connections he made in Taos, Ufer became a charter member of the Taos Society of Artists. (Courtesy of Taos Historic Museums.)

William Victor Higgins was born in Indiana in 1884 to Irish Catholic parents John Tilson and Rose Ellen (Dolan). Like Couse and Sharp, Higgins' talent was apparent at an early age so much so that at 15, his parents allowed him to attend the Art Institute of Chicago. After staying in the city for more than a decade, Higgins set sail for Europe to further his art training in Munich and Paris. When he returned to the states Higgins began dividing his time between Chicago and Taos. From 1937 to 1939, he was married to Marion Koogler McNay of San Antonio. Otherwise, from 1920 until his death in 1949, his primary residence was in Taos. (Courtesy of Taos Historic Museums.)

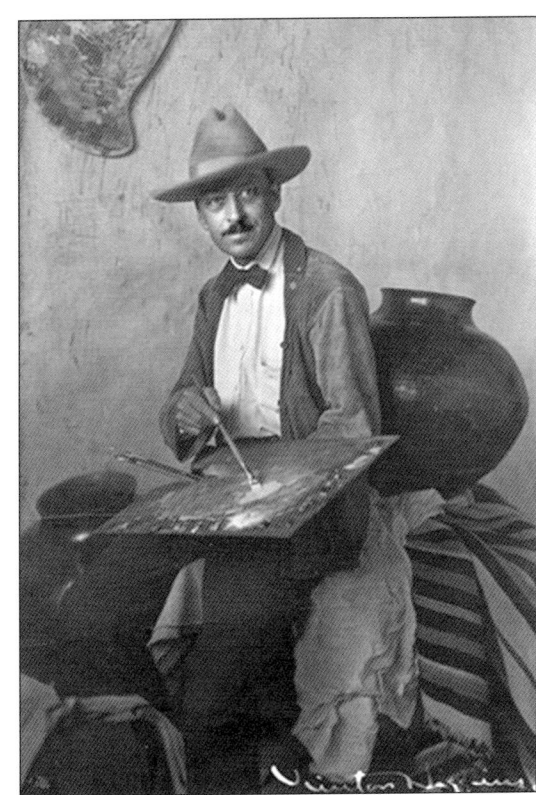

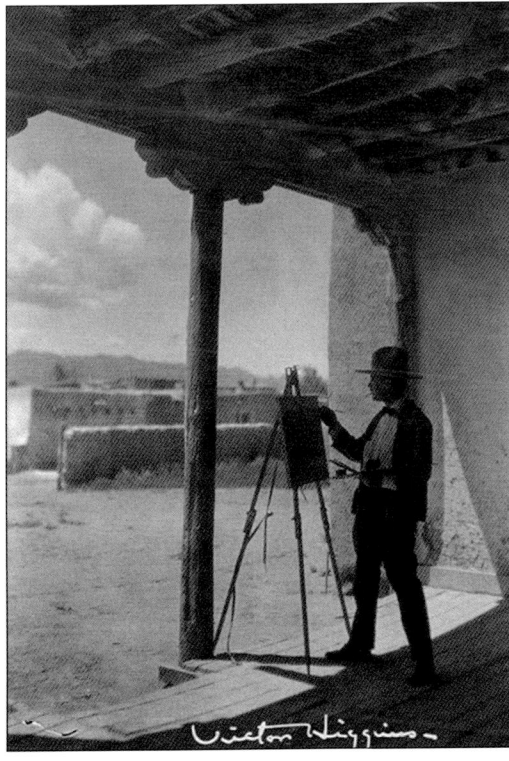

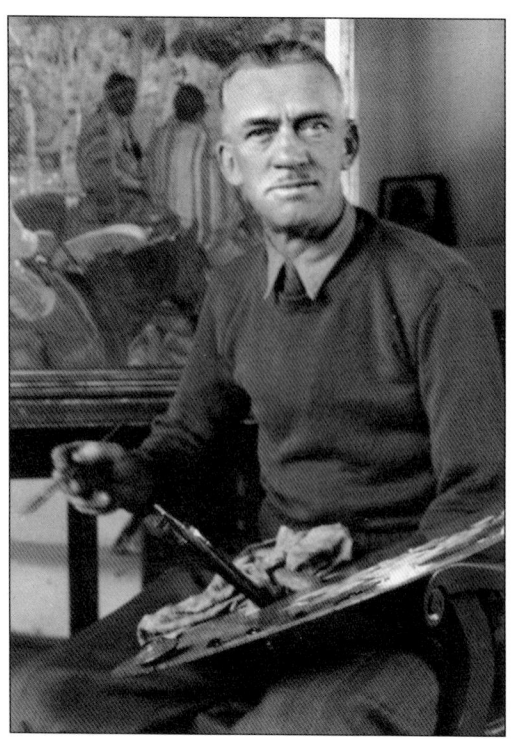

Taos Society of Artists member E. Martin Hennings was born in New Jersey in 1886 to parents who were German immigrants. He attended the Art Institute of Chicago, and eventually, like so many other artists of his time, made his way to Europe. At the American Artists Club in Munich, he met Victor Higgins and Walter Ufer. (Courtesy of Taos Historic Museums.)

This photograph shows several members of the Taos Society of Artists, including E. I. Couse and Bert Phillips. (Courtesy of Taos Historic Museums.)

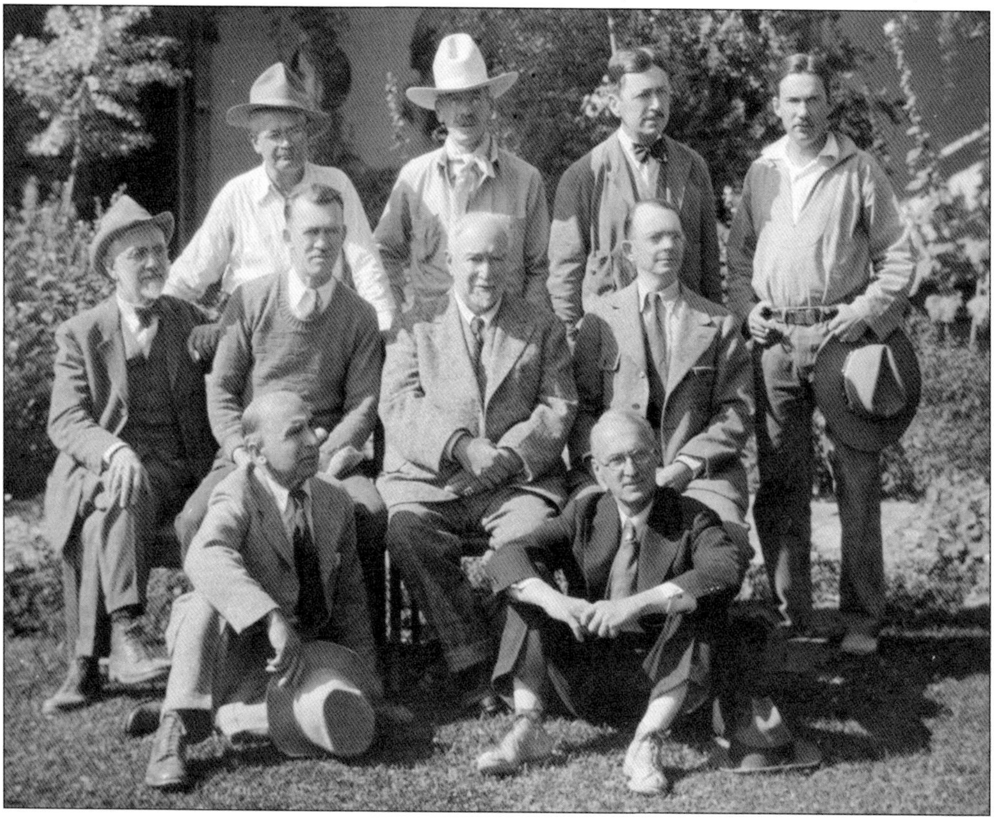

Kenneth Miller Adams was the last and youngest artist to join the Taos Society of Artists. He was born in Topeka in 1897 to Susan and Charles Adams. After graduating from high school, Adams attended the Art Institute of Chicago and later studied in Italy and France before returning to the States. He studied with Andrew Dasburg one summer in Woodstock, New York, and eventually moved to Taos to be near Dasburg and Walter Ufer. The photograph at right shows Adams with young widow Hilda Braun Bolton, with whom he was involved prior to his short marriage to Liane Hall and whom he married after divorcing Hall. Below, Adams sits with a Taos Pueblo man. (Courtesy of Taos Historic Museums.)

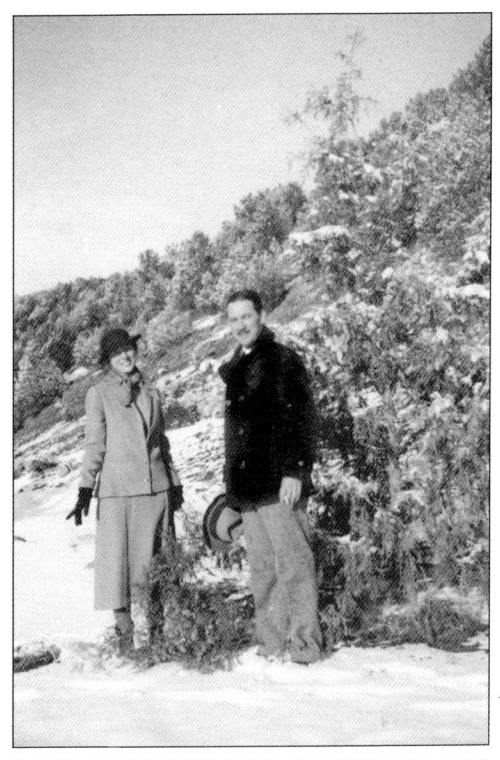

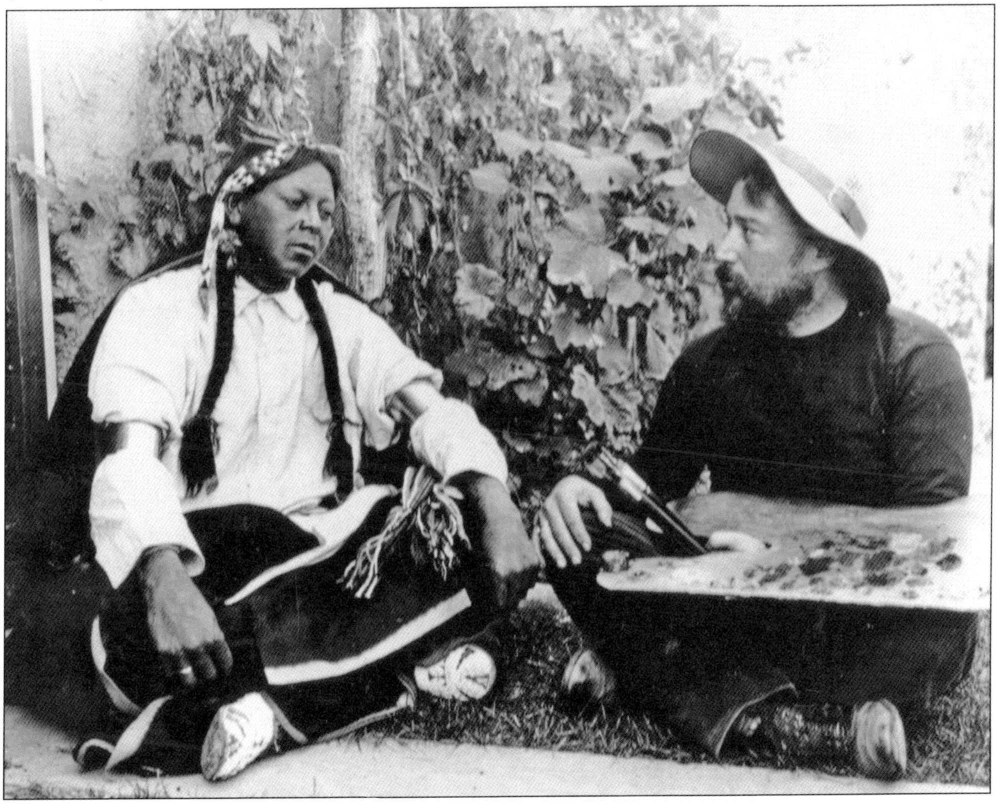

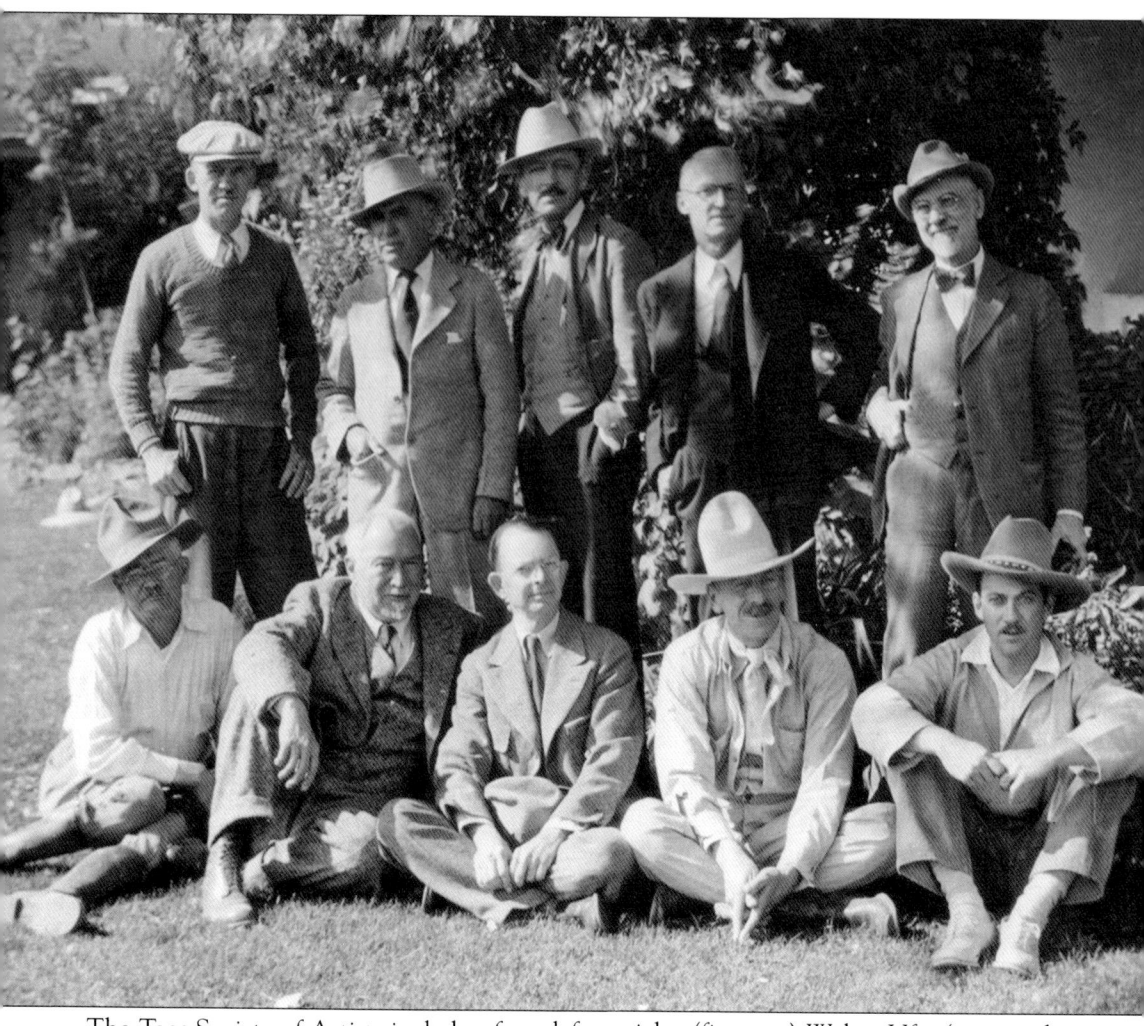

The Taos Society of Artists includes, from left to right, (first row) Walter Ufer (wearing his trademark jodhpurs), E. I. Couse, Oscar Berninghaus, W. Herbert "Buck" Dunton (wearing his signature ten-gallon hat), and Kenneth Adams; (second row) E. Martin Hennings, Bert Phillips, Victor Higgins, Ernest Blumenschein, and Joseph Sharp. (Courtesy of Taos Historic Museums.)

Five

Mabel Dodge Luhan and Friends

Mabel Ganson was born in 1879 to a wealthy family in Buffalo, New York. At 21, she married Karl Evans, and by 23 she was a widow. She then married wealthy architect Edwin Dodge, and the two lived in Florence, Italy, from 1905 to 1912. During that time, Mabel's social circle included artists and writers like Gertrude Stein, Gertrude's brother Leo, and Alice B. Toklas, many of whom were expatriates as well. Her marriage failing, Mabel returned to the United States in 1912 and set up housekeeping on Fifth Avenue in Greenwich Village, where she began holding now-legendary weekly salons that included the luminaries of the day. In 1916, she married artist Maurice Sterne, and together they moved to Taos in 1919, where Mabel promptly fell in love with Taos Pueblo Indian Tony Lujan (the spelling of which was later changed by Mabel to Luhan) whom she married in 1923. Sterne left, but Taos became Mabel's home for the rest of her life. She and Tony built an adobe home on a twelve-acre parcel adjoining Pueblo land, and Mabel established an outpost for disillusioned artists and writers of her day. Among the many notables who visited Mabel in Taos were choreographer Martha Graham, painter and poet Marsden Hartley, artist Arnold Ronnebeck, writer Willa Cather, photographer and environmentalist Ansel Adams, artist Georgia O'Keeffe, and psychiatrist Carl Jung. Thanks to Mabel, Taos still enjoys a reputation as a gathering place for intellectuals. Her home, Los Gallos, is now an active retreat center.

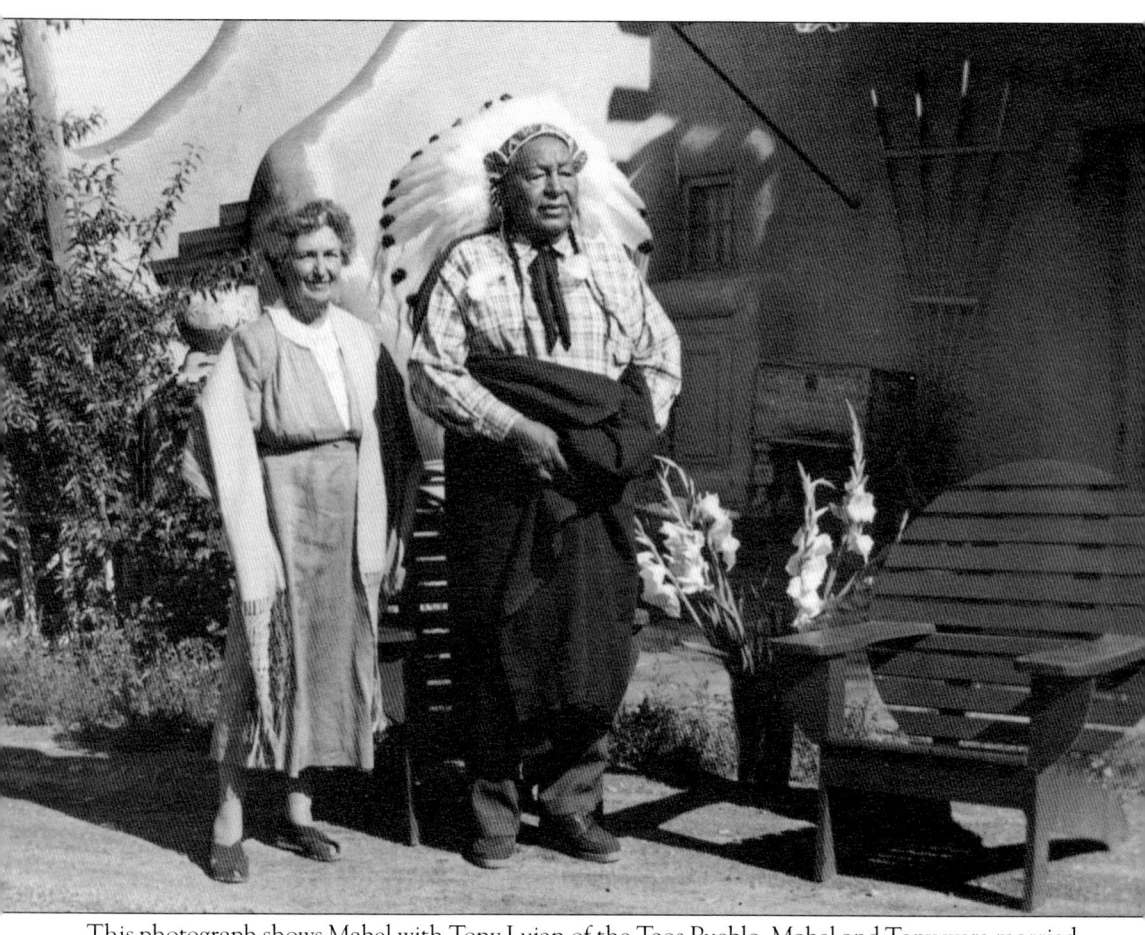
This photograph shows Mabel with Tony Lujan of the Taos Pueblo. Mabel and Tony were married in 1923. (Courtesy of the Taos Historic Museums.)

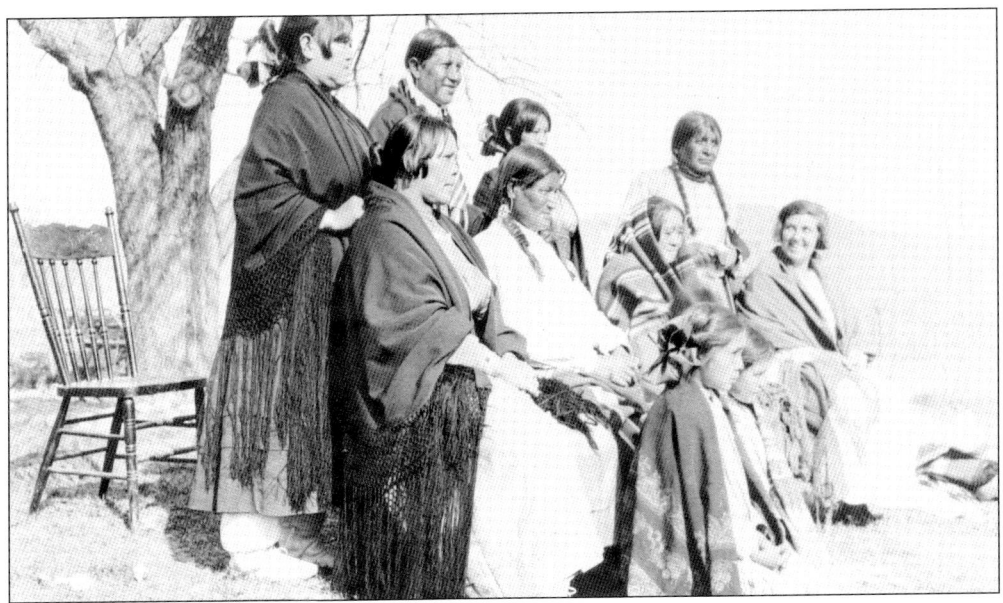

Mabel Dodge Luhan (seated on right) poses with unidentified Native American neighbors from the Taos Pueblo. Bordered by Pueblo land, Mabel and Tony Luhan's home was called Los Gallos (the roosters). Mabel occupied Los Gallos from 1918 until her death in 1962. (Courtesy of Yale Collection of American Literature, Beinecke Rare Book and Manuscript Library.)

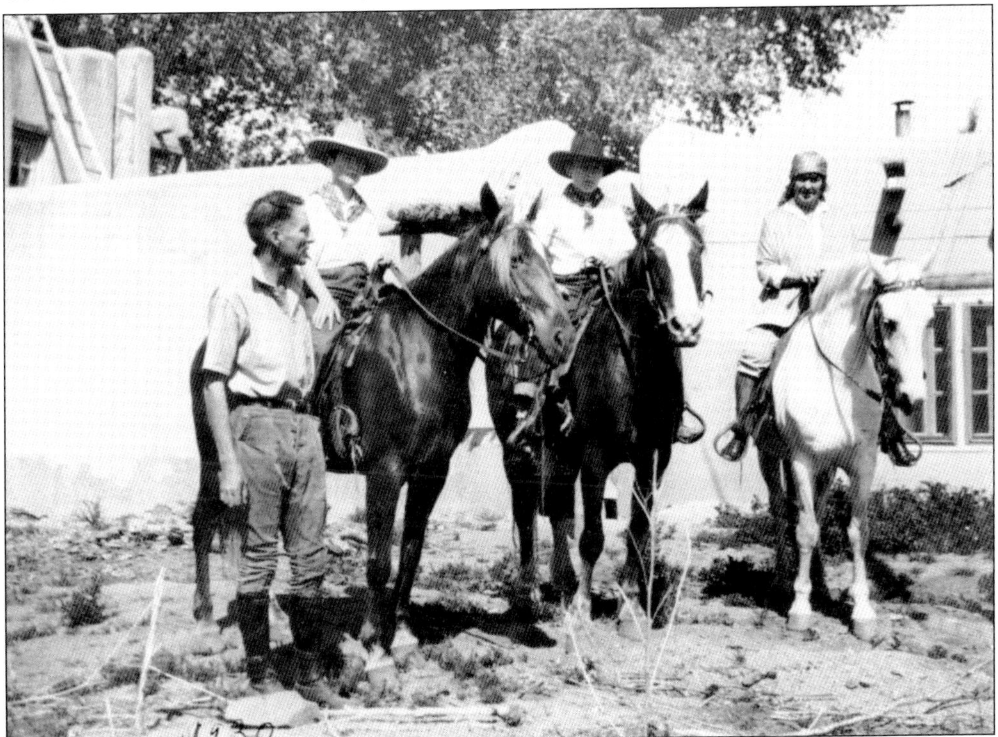

Taken in 1930, this photograph is of poet Robinson Jeffers (standing) with Mabel and his sons on horseback. Jeffers was visiting Taos from his home in Carmel, California. (Courtesy of Yale Collection of American Literature, Beinecke Rare Book and Manuscript Library.)

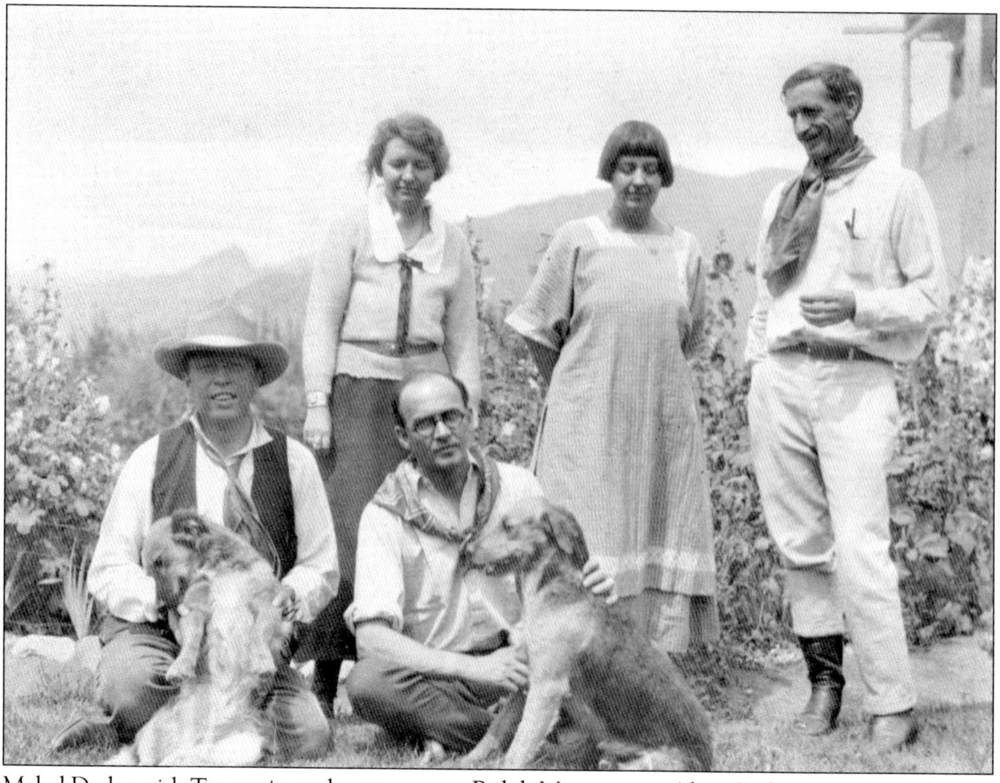

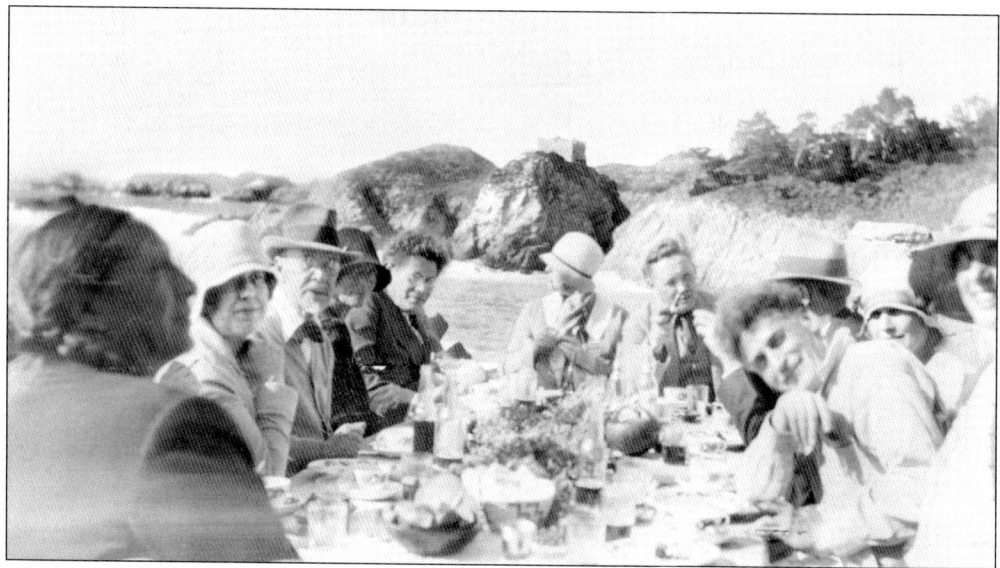

Mabel Dodge with Taos artist and entrepreneur Ralph Meyers, poet Alice Corbin, Millie Henderson, and poet Witter Bynner. (Courtesy of Yale Collection of American Literature, Beinecke Rare Book and Manuscript Library.)

This faded yet captivating photograph shows Mabel Dodge Luhan at an outdoor gathering with notables of her day poet and satirist Dorothy Parker, novelist and playwright Sinclair Lewis, journalist Lincoln Steffens, and others. Tony Luhan is shown in profile at the far left. (Courtesy of Yale Collection of American Literature, Beinecke Rare Book and Manuscript Library.)

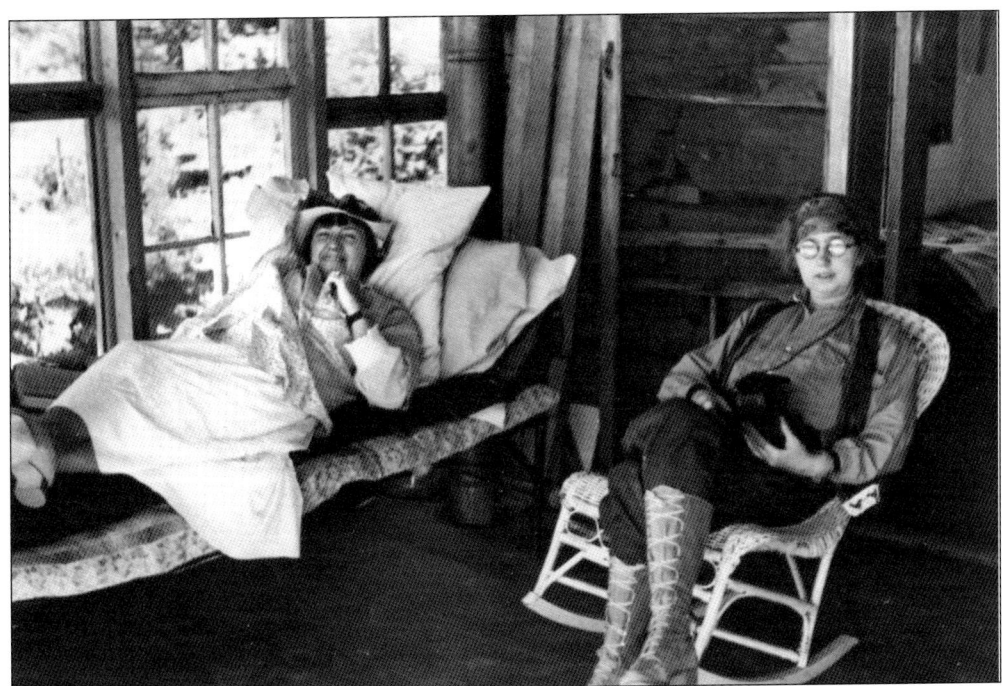

Taken by artist Cady Wells (highly respected in both Santa Fe and Taos art colonies from 1932 to 1954), the above photograph shows Mabel and Lady Dorothy Brett relaxing in Brett's northern New Mexico home. The unlikely daughter of Viscount Esher, an advisor to Queen Victoria, Dorothy Brett chose a bohemian life over that of an aristocrat and became friends with Virginia Woolf, George Bernard Shaw, Aldous Huxley, and other members of the Bloomsbury Group. Brett came to Taos in 1924 with D. H. Lawrence, became known as a local eccentric, and remained in Taos until her death in 1977. Shown at right with an unidentified friend, Brett is holding her trademark ear trumpet, which she referred to as "Toby." (Above, courtesy of Yale Collection of American Literature, Beinecke Rare Book and Manuscript Library; right, courtesy of the Taos Historic Museums.)

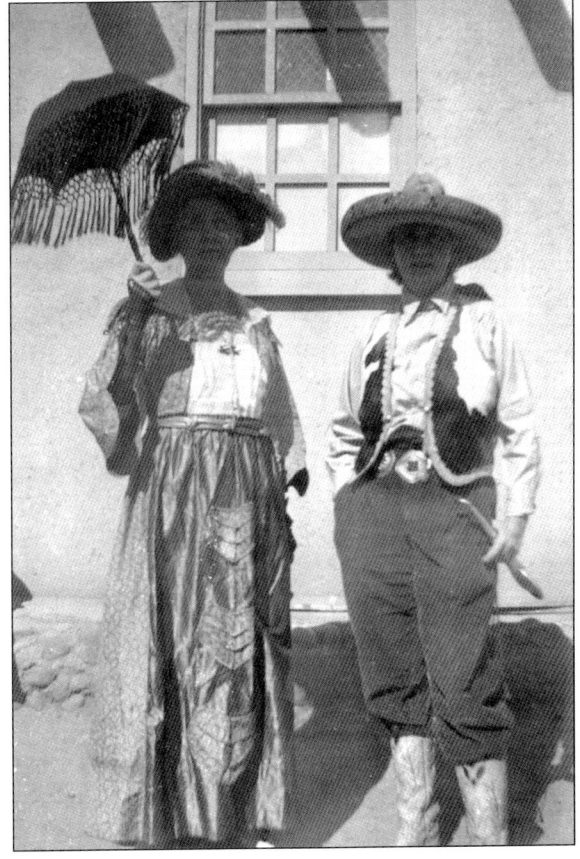

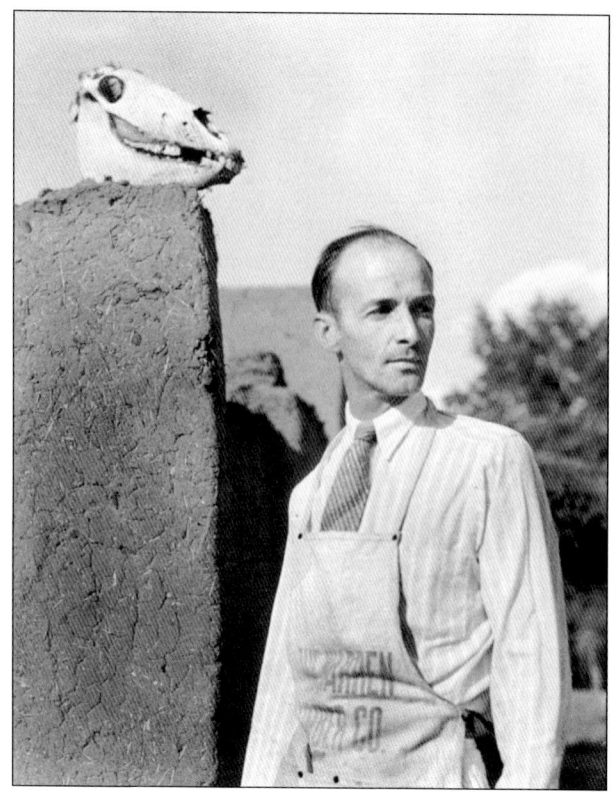

Shown here is William Willard "Spud" Johnson, posed next to an animal skull. Spud arrived in Taos in 1924, where he and his partner Witter Bynner established a magazine called *The Laughing Horse* produced in Taos using a hand letterpress. (Courtesy of Yale Collection of American Literature, Beinecke Rare Book and Manuscript Library.)

Shown here on horseback, Myron Brinig rented from Mabel and eventually based a character on her in his 1941 book *All of Their Lives*. Like Witter Bynner's, Brinig's relationship with Mabel deteriorated quickly as she had a habit of trying to control creative men. (Courtesy of Yale Collection of American Literature, Beinecke Rare Book and Manuscript Library.)

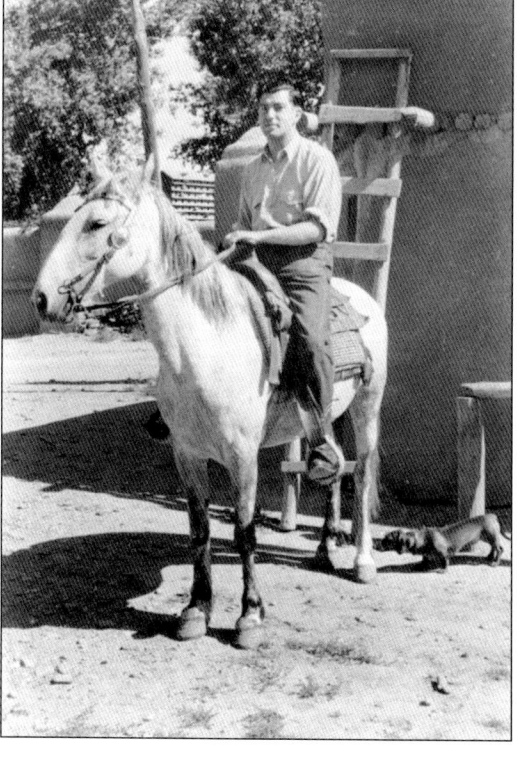

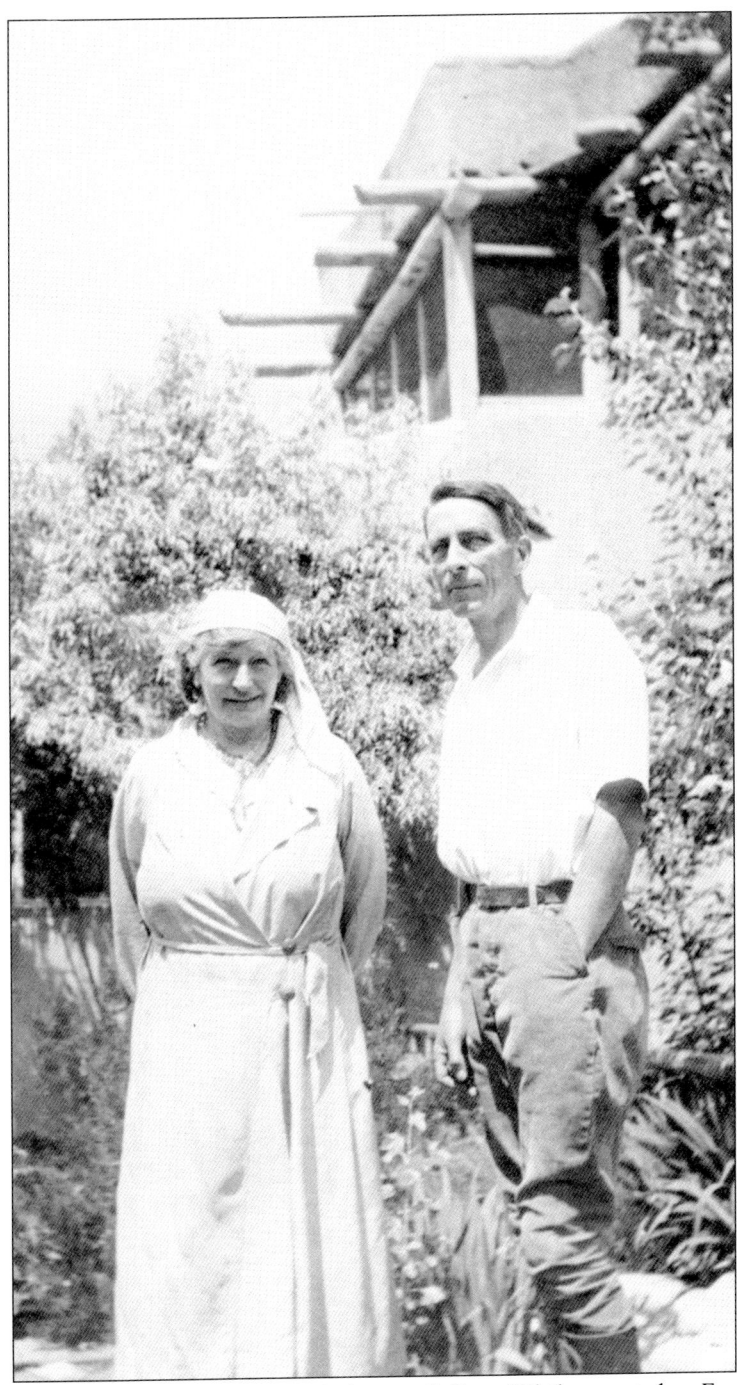

Seen here are Frieda Lawrence and poet Robinson Jeffers. While married to Ernest Weekley, Frieda fell in love with writer D. H. Lawrence. She left Weekley and their three children to be with Lawrence, whom she married in 1914. They were guests of Mabel's in Taos, and she traded a ranch in nearby San Cristobal for the manuscript to Lawrence's *Sons and Lovers*. After Lawrence's death, Frieda would spend the rest of her life on the ranch with third husband Angelo Ravagli. (Courtesy of Yale Collection of American Literature, Beinecke Rare Book and Manuscript Library.)

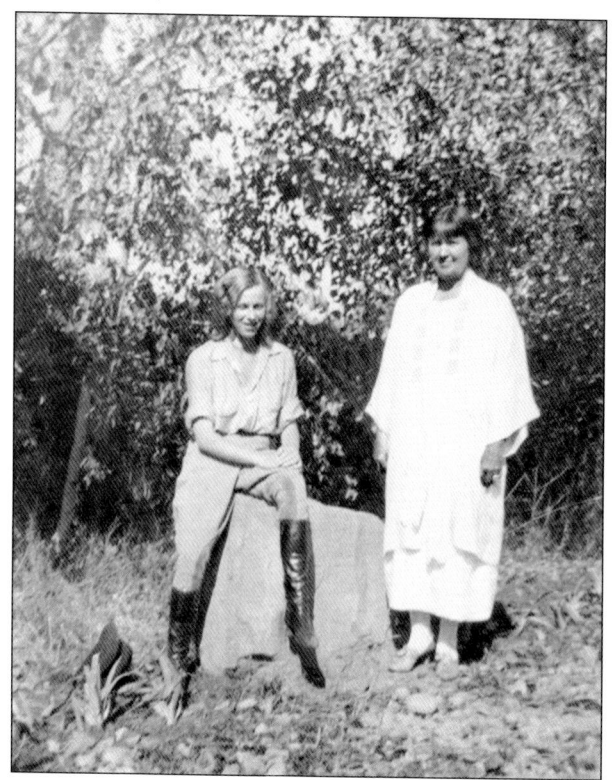

Mabel poses with Miriam Hapgood, whose parents Neith and Hutchins Hapgood were friends of Mabel's from her years in Greenwich Village. Mabel invited Miriam to visit to ease a several-year depression. It worked, and Miriam stayed in Taos for 13 years. A 1929 painting by Rebecca (Strand) Salsbury is named for her. (Courtesy of Yale Collection of American Literature, Beinecke Rare Book and Manuscript Library.)

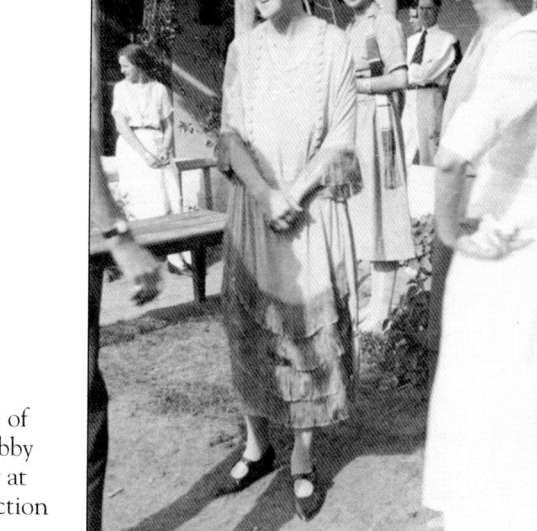

This group includes Sara Higgins (wife of artist Victor Higgins), Alice Evans, Bobby Heusk, and others at a social gathering at Mabel's home. (Courtesy of Yale Collection of American Literature, Beinecke Rare Book and Manuscript Library.)

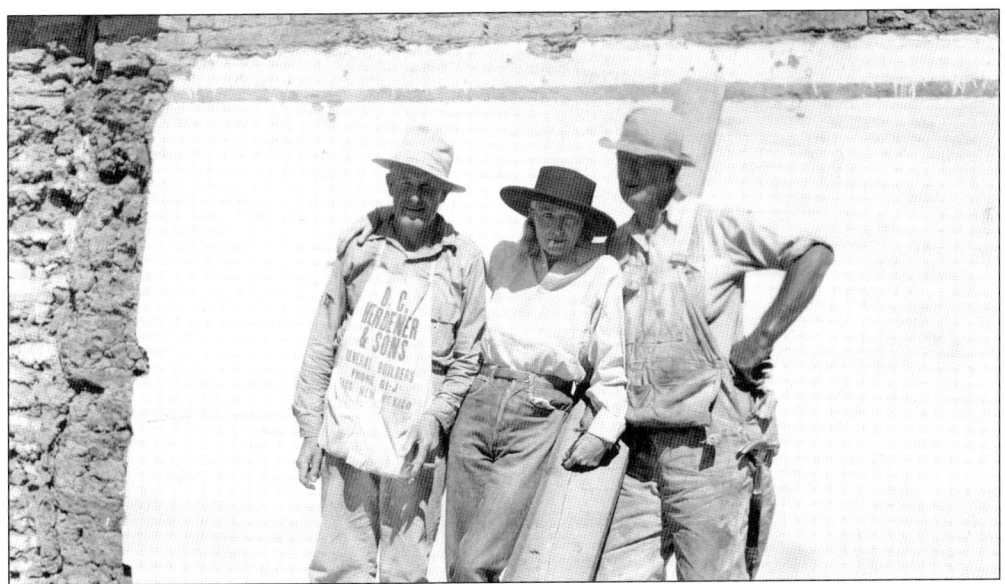

Rebecca "Becky" Salsbury James was born in London in 1891 to American parents. Her father created the wildly popular Buffalo Bill Wild West Show that was performing in London when was born. Rebecca married photographer Paul Strand in 1922, and while living with Strand in New York socialized with the New York City avant-garde that included Alfred Stieglitz and Georgia O'Keeffe. Becky visited Taos between 1926 and 1932 and moved there permanently with second husband Bill James when her marriage to Strand dissolved. She became a well-respected artist, using a reverse glass technique, as well as an accomplished colcha embroiderer and remained in Taos until her death in 1968. In the photograph above, Becky stands with two workmen, one wearing a carpenter's apron that reads "Herdener and Sons General Builders, Taos, New Mexico." Below, James stands with a group of unidentified men in front her Taos home, which she named Casa Feliz (Happy Home). (Courtesy of Taos Historic Museums.)

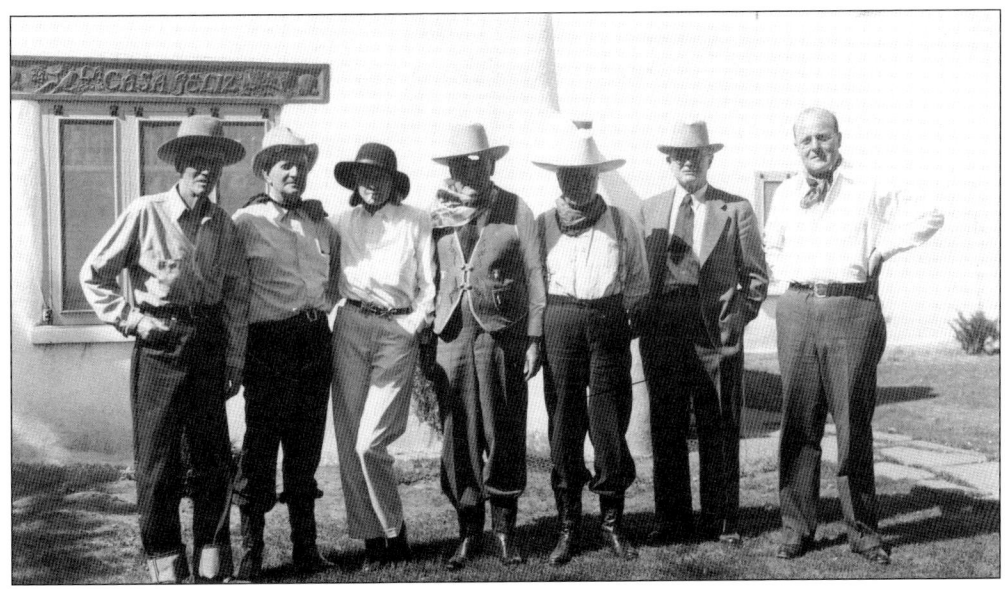

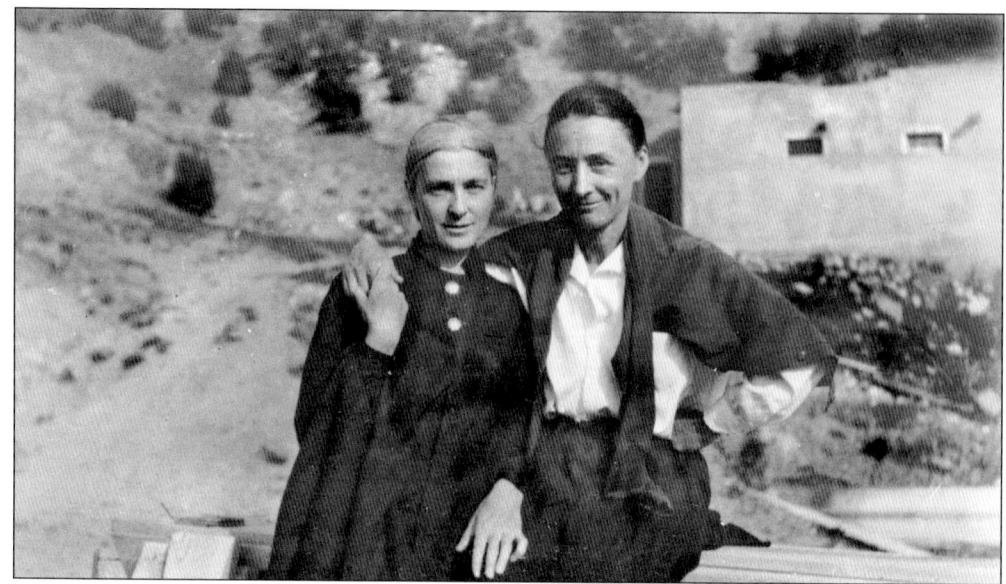

This photograph shows longtime friends Becky James (left) and artist Georgia O'Keeffe. O'Keeffe fell in love with the Southwest while visiting Mabel and ultimately moved to Abiquiu, New Mexico, where she lived for the rest of her days. (Courtesy of Yale Collection of American Literature, Beinecke Rare Book and Manuscript Library.)

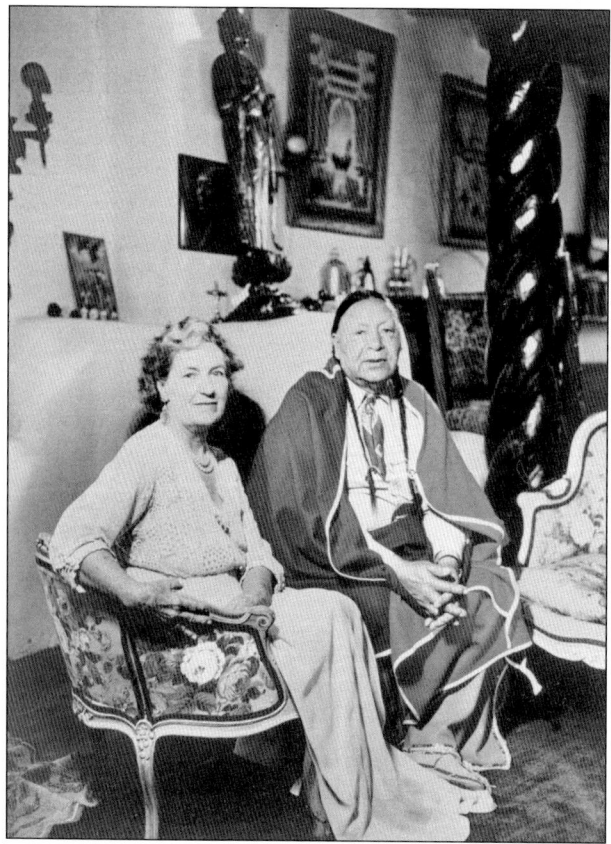

This photograph shows Mabel Dodge Luhan and Tony Luhan in their later years seated in the home they built together in Taos. Their unlikely marriage was long lasting. Tony Luhan was Mabel's fourth and final husband. (Courtesy of Yale Collection of American Literature, Beinecke Rare Book and Manuscript Library.)

Six

Taoseños y Taoseñas

The history of Taos includes the mixing of several cultures from the original residents, Taos Pueblo Indians, to descendents of Spanish explorers, to the many "foreigners" who migrated to Taos and have contributed greatly to the landscape. This chapter includes photographs of old Taos families, such as the Martinez', Salazars, Gusdorfs, Trujillos, Randalls, as well as a few colorful local characters, of which Taos has had many.

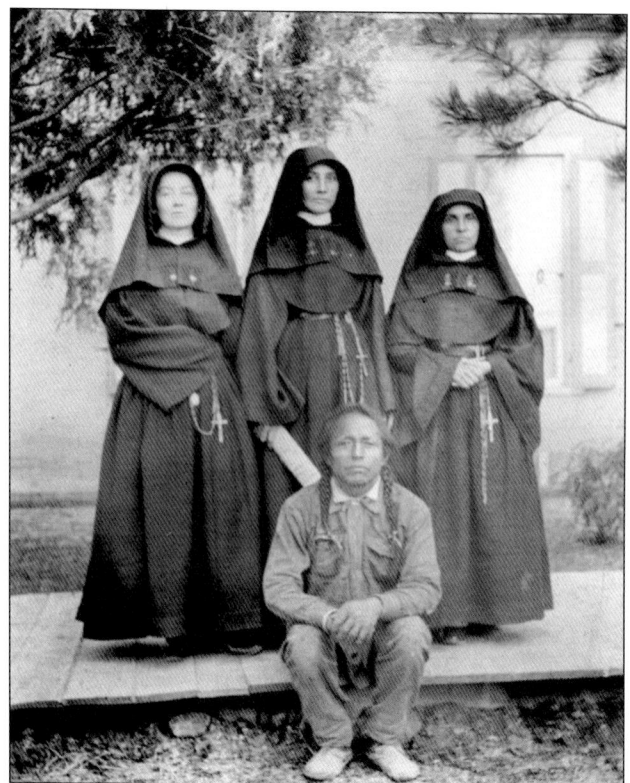

The Sisters of Loretto came from Kentucky to serve the Taos community. They taught many residents from 1863 to 1976. Many locals still recall the sisters' stern teaching methods. This photograph shows three of the nuns with a Taos Pueblo man. (Courtesy of Taos Historic Museums.)

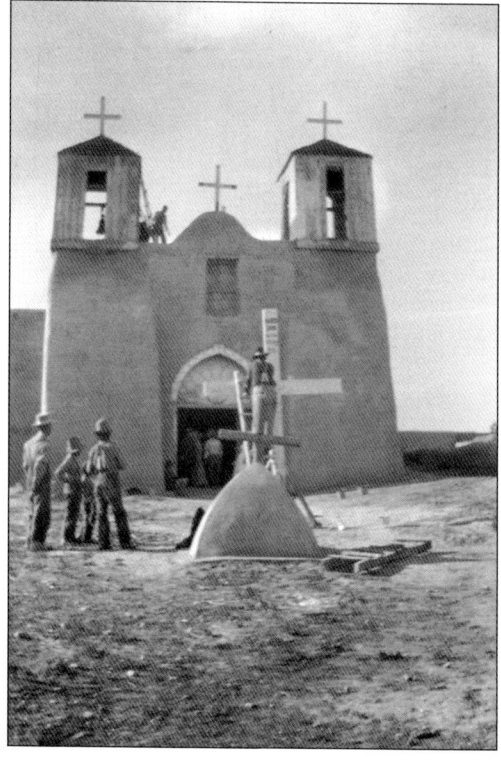

The Saint Francis of Assisi Church, located in Ranchos de Taos, has been painted and photographed by such notables as Georgia O'Keeffe and Ansel Adams. Parishioners participate in an annual mudding of the exterior to preserve the adobe building. (Courtesy of Taos Historic Museums.)

Taken in May 1918, this photograph shows Taoseños J. M. Bernal and J. A. Pachecho in track team suits. The Taos Tigers won their first New Mexico State Track and Field Championship in 1932. (Courtesy of Taos Historic Museums.)

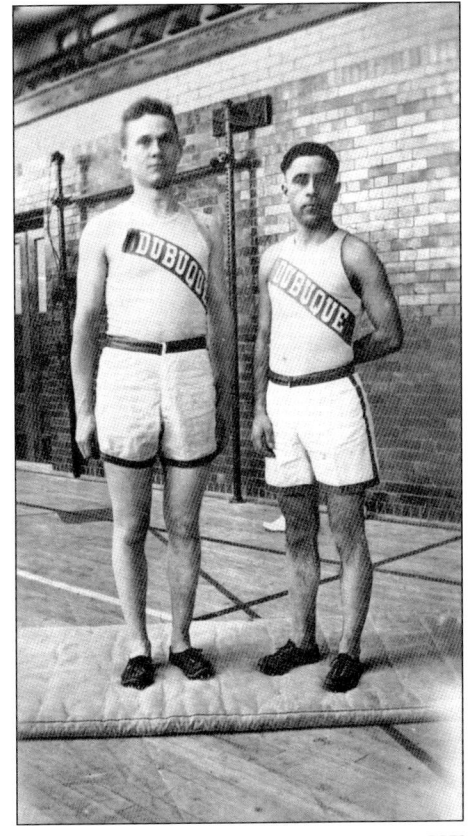

This championship St. Francis boys basketball team is photographed outside the St. Francis School in Ranchos de Taos. (Courtesy of Martinez y Montaner/Martinez y Salazar.)

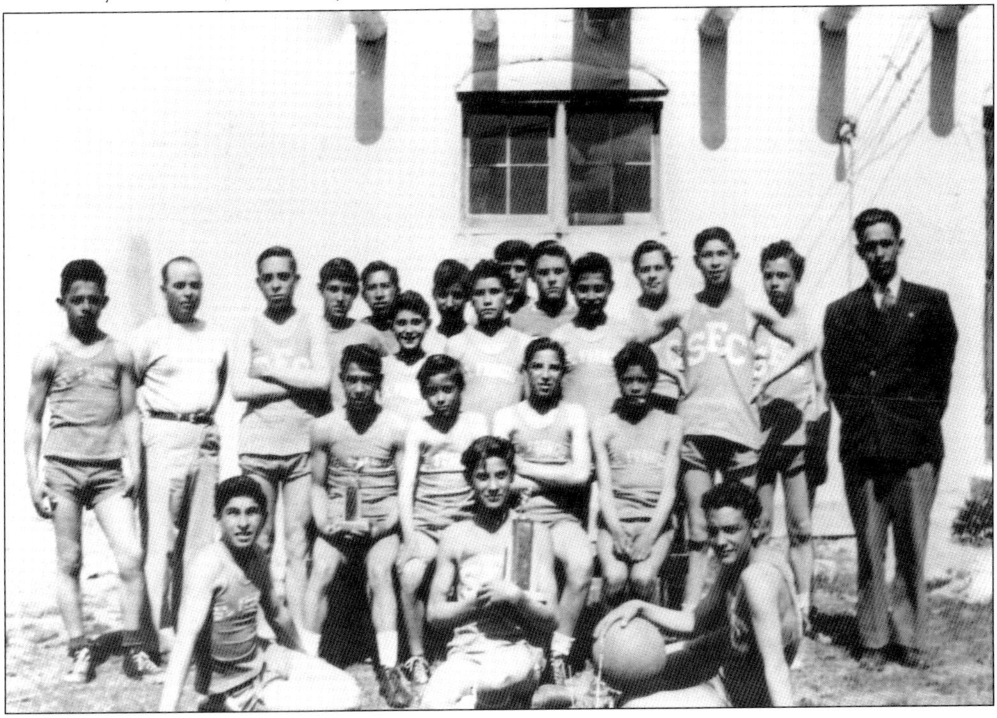

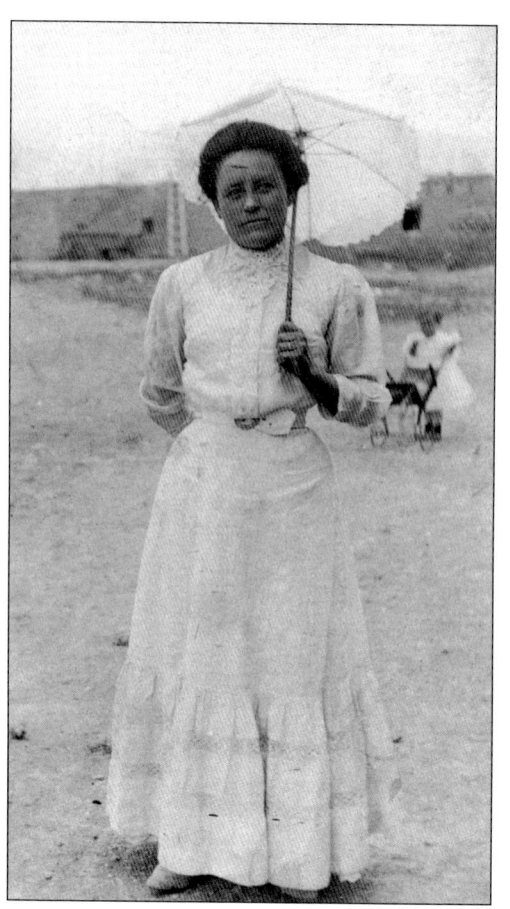

Holding a parasol, Emilia Santistevan poses while an unidentified little girl with a stroller plays behind her. Members of the Santistevan family have been Taos residents for several generations. (Courtesy of Taos Historic Museums.)

In this 1908 image, Bill T. Hinde and friend Ansel Hart are riding in Bill's first Ford past the *La Revista* newspaper office and Novelty Studio. Bill T. Hinde owned a blacksmith shop in Taos. This photograph is from Becky Salsbury James' scrapbook. (Courtesy of Taos Historic Museums.)

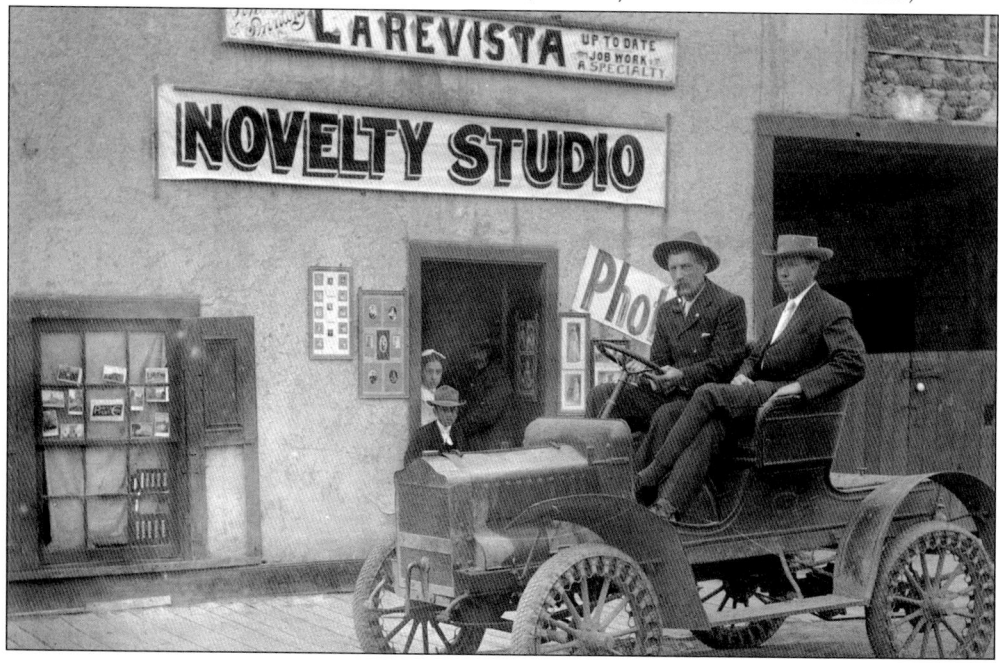

Millicent Rogers was an heiress to her grandfather's Standard Oil fortune and was a noted fashion icon and jewelry designer. Rogers, along with writers Frank Waters, Lucius Beebe, and Oliver LaFarge, traveled to Washington, D.C., in 1947 to lobby for more humane rights for New Mexico's Pueblo Indians. Her vast collection of Indian art and jewelry is housed in the Millicent Rogers Museum in Taos. In the photograph at right, Rogers wears her trademark fashionable clothing and jewelry. Below she is standing on a kitchen chair dying wool. (Courtesy of the Millicent Rogers Museum.)

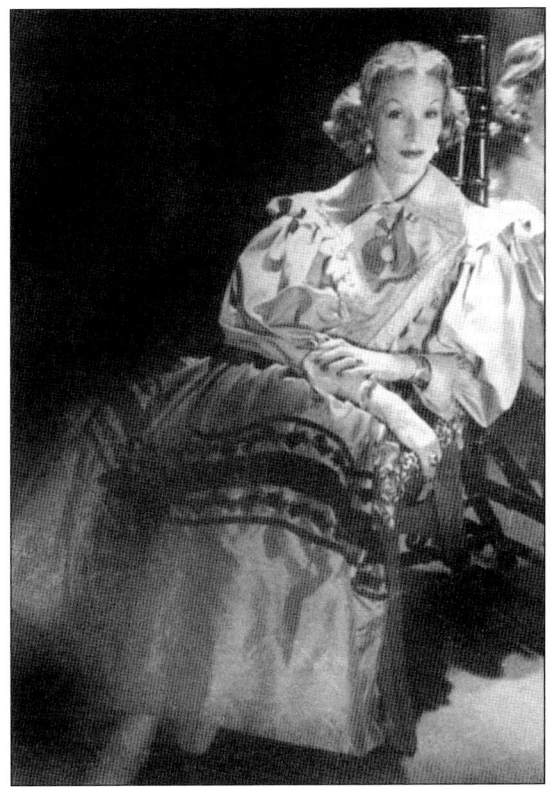

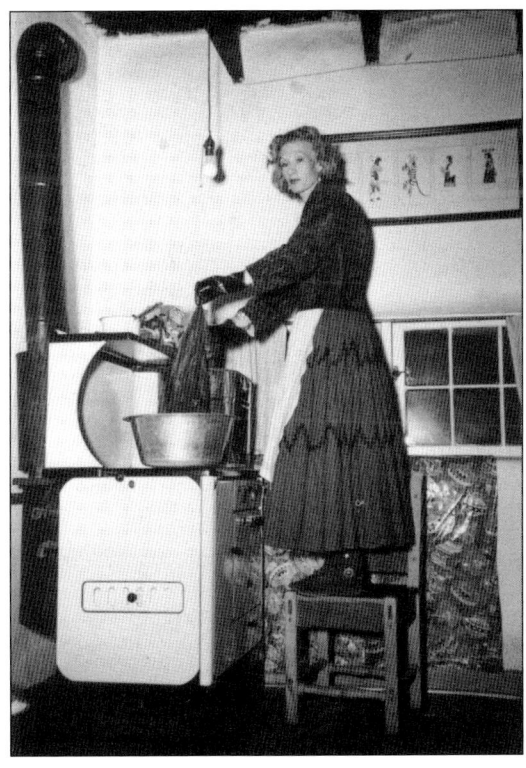

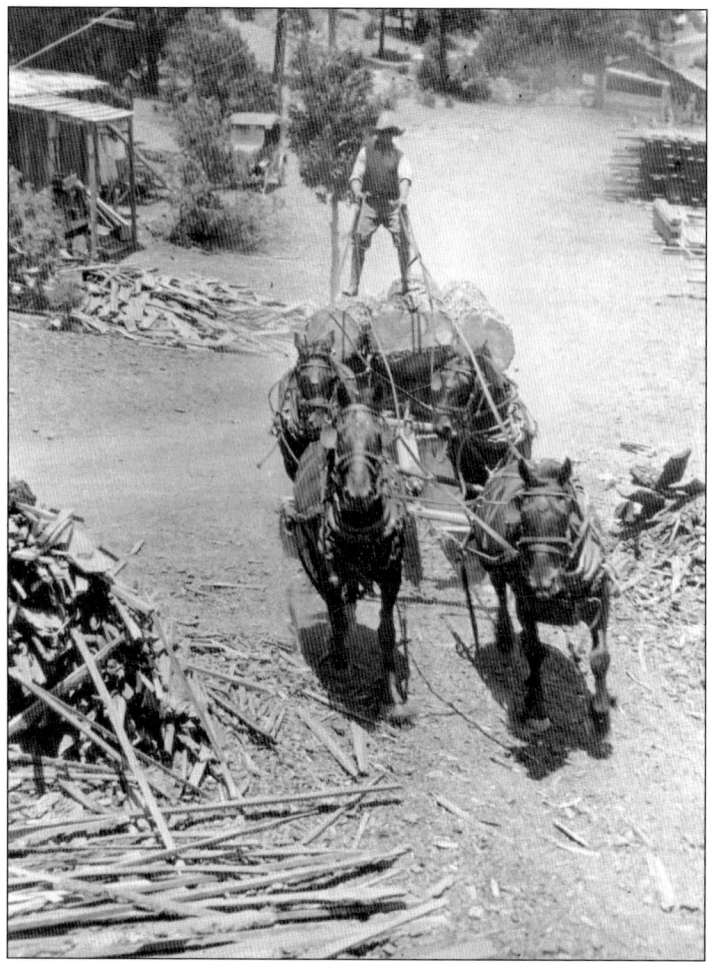

The Randall family has been part of the Taos community since New Mexico was still a territory. The Randalls left their family roots in Maine and headed west in search of fortune and adventure. When gold mining failed to pan out, Elisha P. Randall established Randall Lumber Company, now the oldest family-run business in town. He processed wood at his steam sawmill that relied on horsepower. Elisha and his wife, Erna (lovingly known by residents as "Grandma Randall"), raised three sons—John, Merlin, and Charles—and a daughter, Minnie Lou. At left, Elisha drives a horse team at the sawmill. Below is a photograph of the original sawmill office. (Courtesy of the Randall family.)

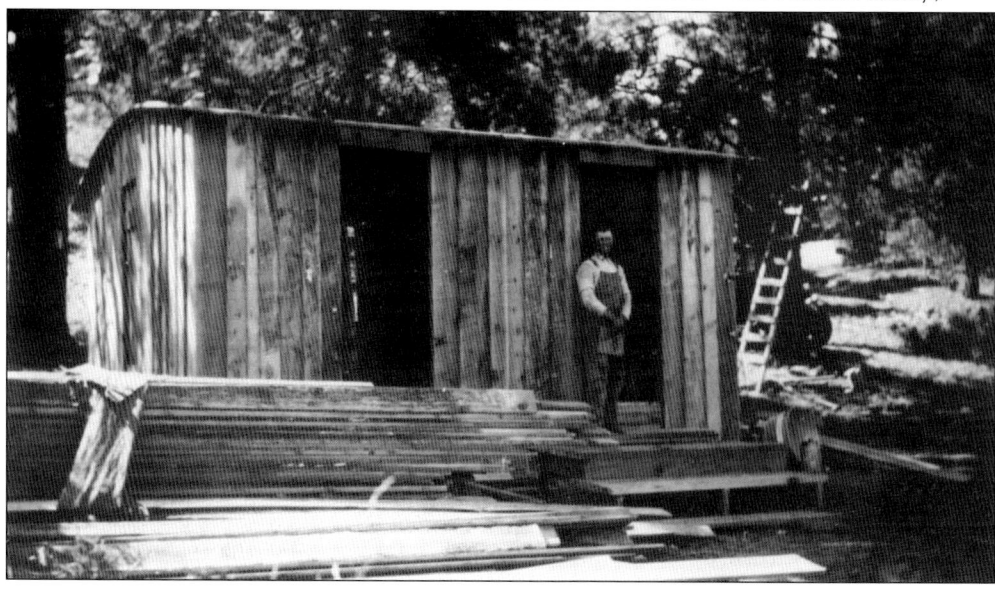

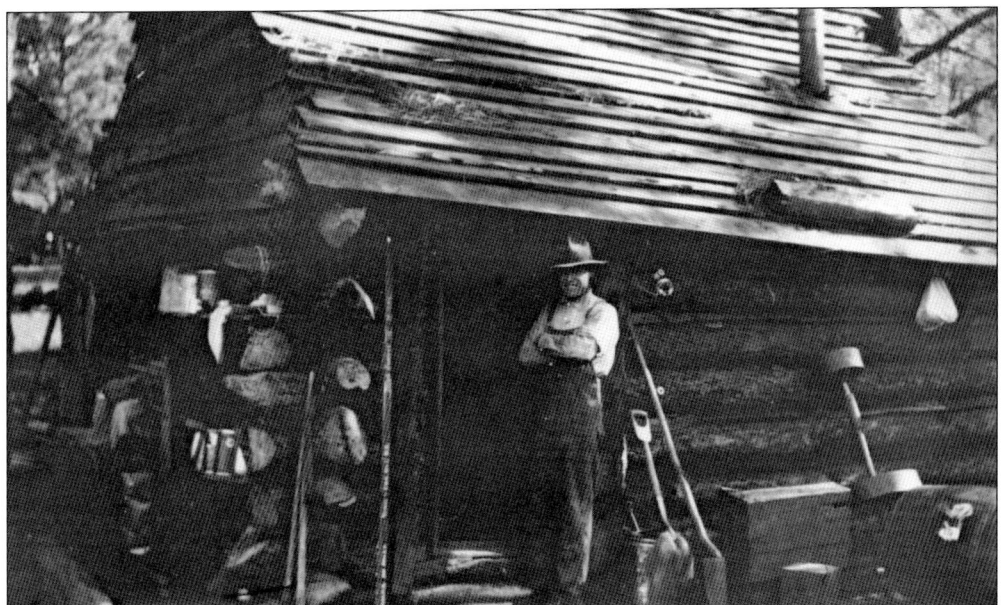

In the early days of the business, Elisha Randall lived in a log cabin on the sawmill property, as seen here. (Courtesy of the Randall family.)

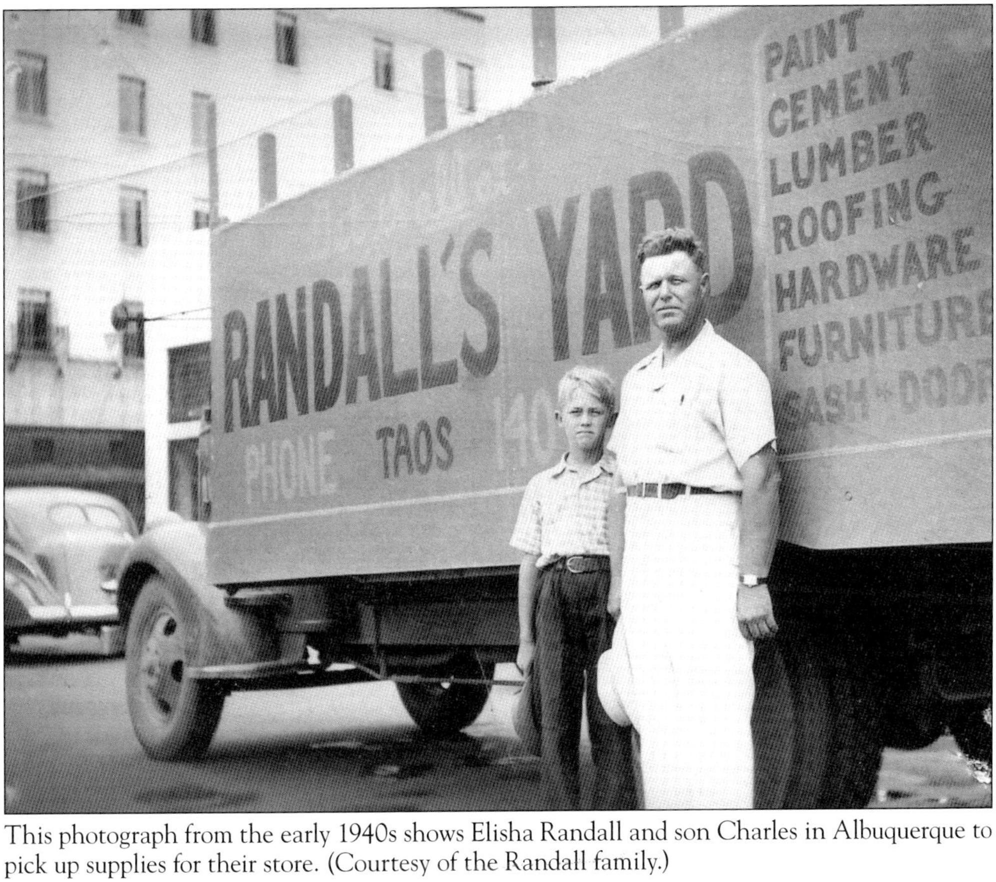

This photograph from the early 1940s shows Elisha Randall and son Charles in Albuquerque to pick up supplies for their store. (Courtesy of the Randall family.)

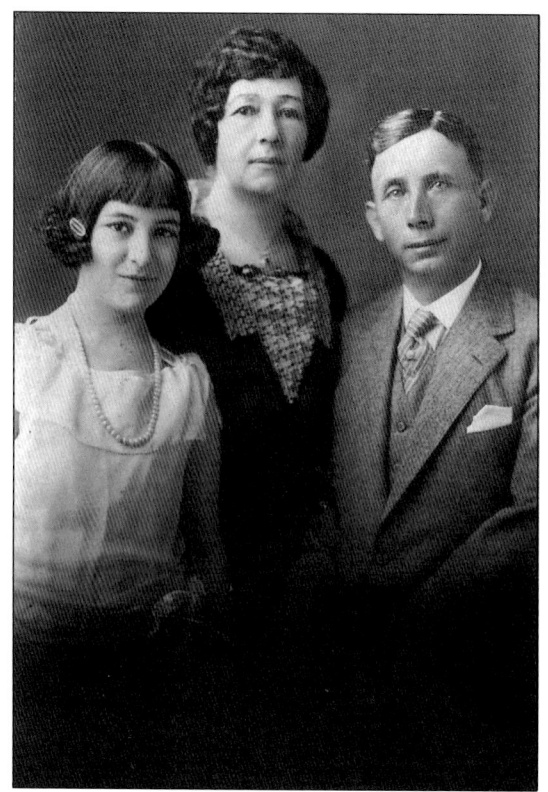

Tenth-generation Taoseña Mariquita Martinez is photographed here with daughter Teodora and husband Jose Montaner (a.k.a. Jase Montaner), whom Mariquita married in 1906. Mariquita's father, Santiago Martinez, was a soldier in the Civil War and the first legislator from Taos County under the territorial government. His son, Marquita's brother Malaquias, served in the U.S. Senate for 20 years. (Courtesy of Martinez y Montaner/Martinez y Salazar.)

Jose Montaner, shown here with his wife, Mariquita, was born in Barcelona, Spain, in 1877, the youngest of seven children. He came to the United States in 1898 with $7 in his pocket. By 1901, he had moved to Taos where, with the help of local support, he established the first newspaper in Taos County, *La Revista*, printed in Spanish. In 1933, he began publishing *The Taos Valley News*, an English-language paper. Montaner spoke fluent Spanish, English, and French. He was chosen as Taos County Schools' first superintendent, a position he held from 1912 to 1921. In the fall of 1924, he ran for a seat in the U.S. Senate and won by a landslide 1,300 votes. (Courtesy of Martinez y Montaner/Martinez y Salazar.)

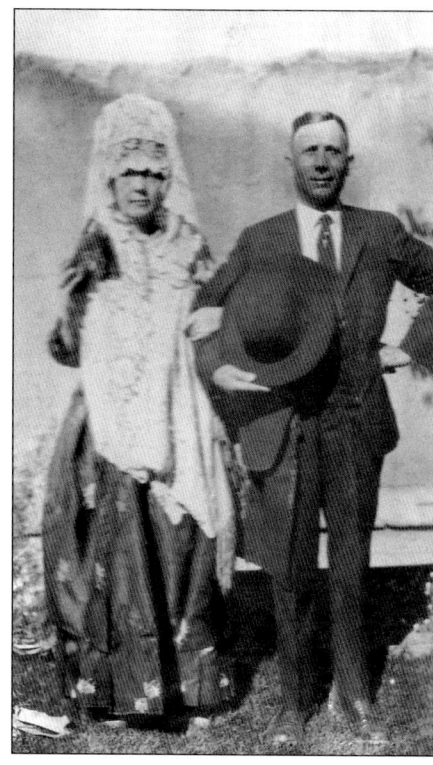

This image shows 12th-generation Taoseña Cecelia Martinez Torres as a young girl holding her grandmother Marquita's hand on the Taos Plaza. Cecelia appears in chapter three as fiesta queen. (Courtesy of Martinez y Montaner/Martinez y Salazar.)

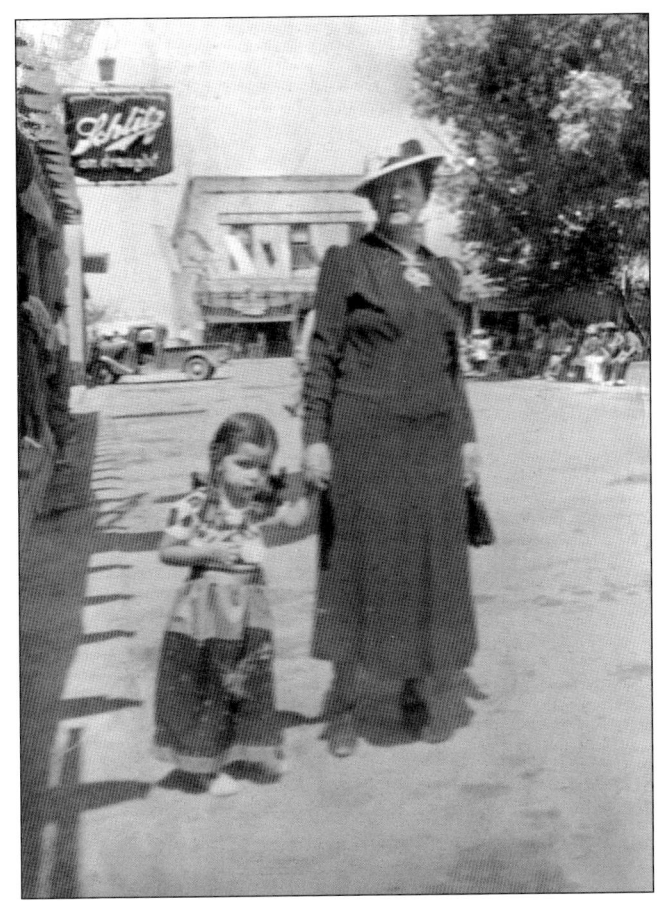

Sitting on the porch of their family home are Teodora and Arturo Martinez y Salazar with son, Vicente, daughter, Cecelia, and beloved dog, Bones. Teodora is holding a friend's infant in her arms. Set back to the right is the former home of priest and legislator Padre Jose Antonio Martinez, whom author Willa Cather fictionalized in *Death Comes for the Archbishop*. (Courtesy of Martinez y Montaner/Martinez y Salazar.)

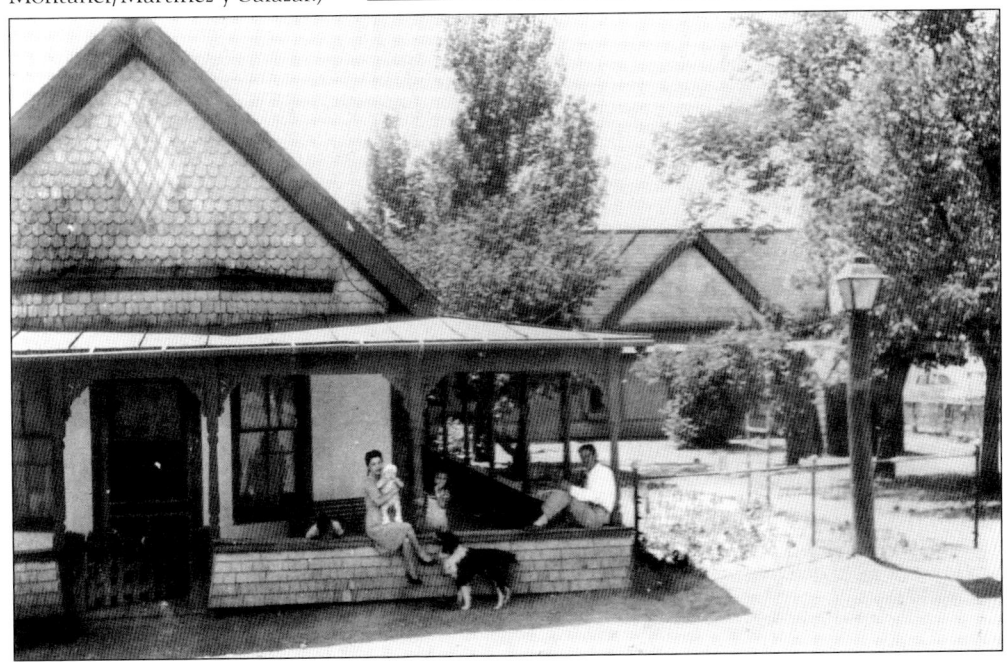

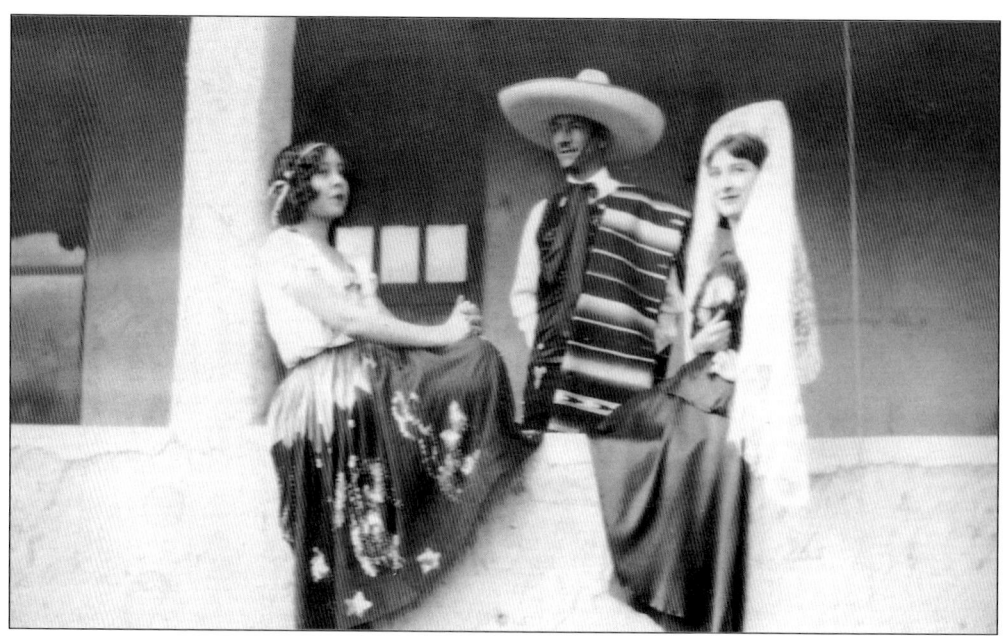

Mabel Dodge Luhan's famous Taos home, Los Gallos, is the backdrop for these festive photographs from 1935 of Escolastica Trujillo, Rudolph Liebert, and Teodora Montener. Teodora, who played piano for the silent films in the Monener Theatre on the plaza, is wearing a traditional lace mantilla and holding a fan. (Courtesy of Martinez y Montaner/Martinez y Salazar.)

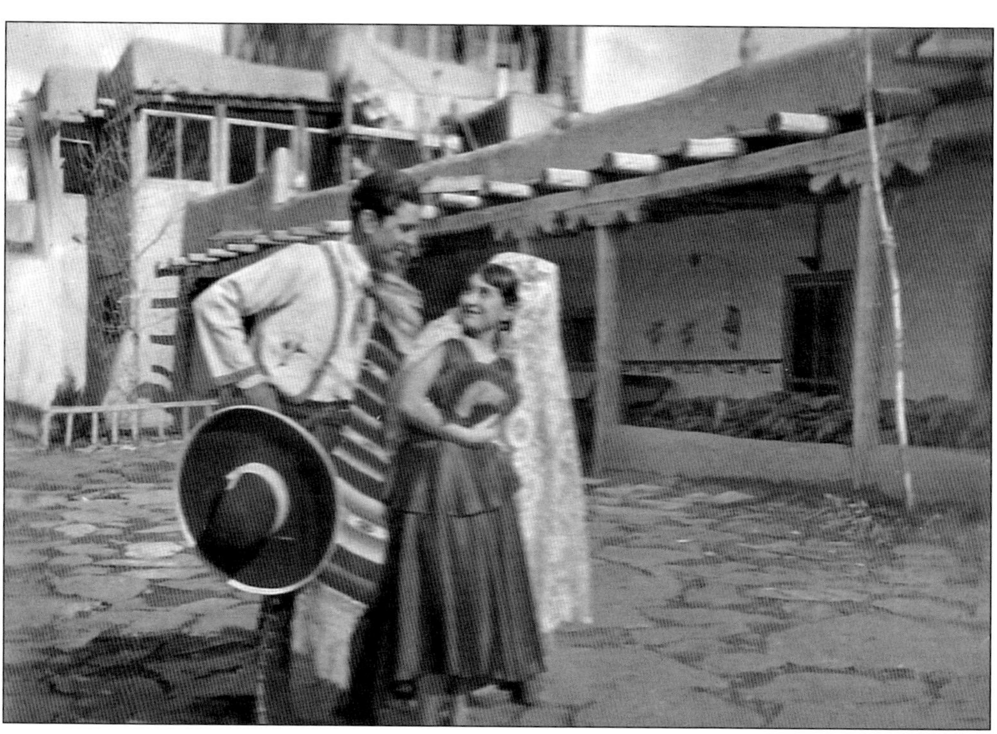

The Gusdorf family opened the first general merchandise store in Taos, and Alex Gusdorf served as president of the First State Bank of Taos. The portrait at right shows Maggie Gusdorf and daughter Margaret. Below, a rather eccentric Maggie Gusdorf poses in front her garden gate wearing a lace mantilla and holding an ostrich feather fan. (Courtesy of Taos Historic Museums.)

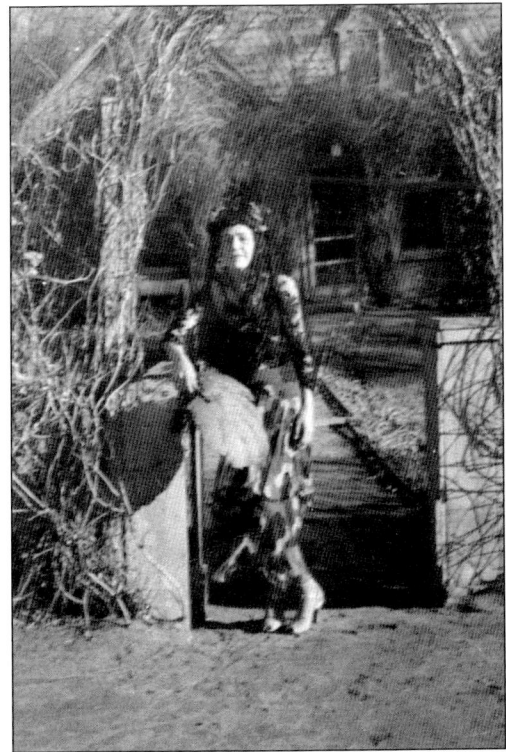

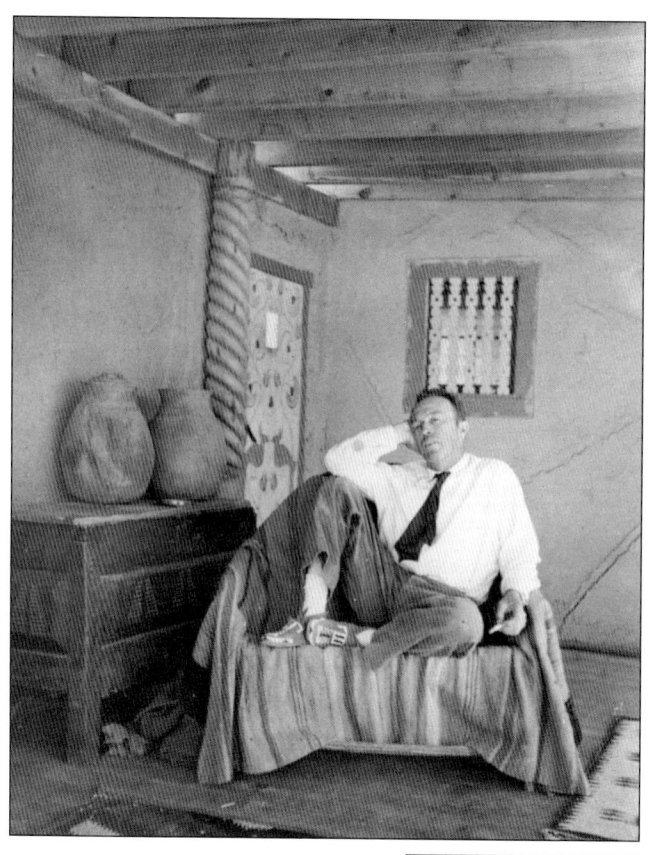

Taoseño Ralph Meyers was a well-known artist and entrepreneur who was depicted as Good White Trader in author Frank Waters classic *The Man Who Killed the Deer*, published in 1942. Meyers opened the first trading post, El Rincón (the corner), across from Kit Carson's former residence, and hired Diné and Pueblo Indians to make jewelry and crafts to sell to the growing tourist trade. In 1933, Meyers married Rowena Matteson, 25 years his junior. The couple had two children, Nina Cristina and Ouray Emerson. (Courtesy Taos Historic Museums.)

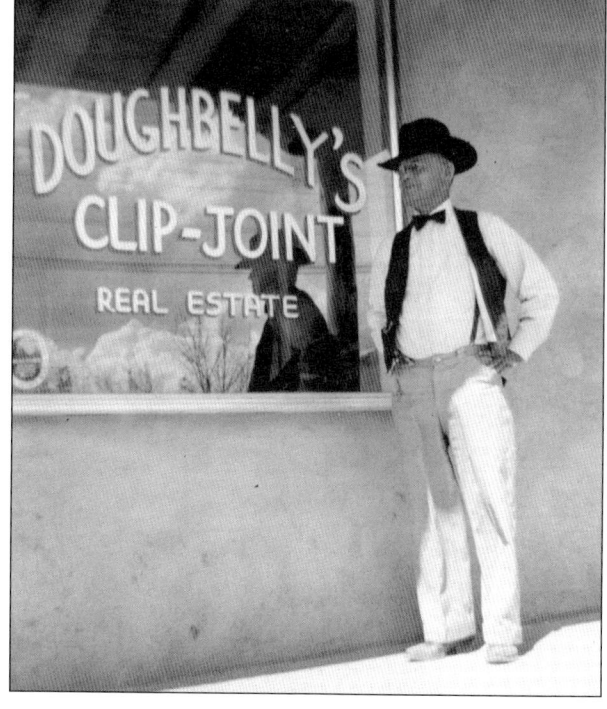

A true Taos character, Doughbelly Price was a self-professed con man, short-change artist, cowpuncher, champion bronco rider, carnival drifter, gambler, and petty thief. He earned the name Doughbelly while working as a camp cook when, according to Price, his "round little belly" was often covered with flour and dough from rubbing against surfaces he used for biscuit making. He ran a real estate company in Taos, as seen in this photograph, and wrote a popular weekly column in *El Crepusculo* and *The Taos News* in which he took creative liberty with the use of the English language. Doughbelly's book titled *Short Stirrups* was published in 1960. (Courtesy of Taos Historic Museums.)

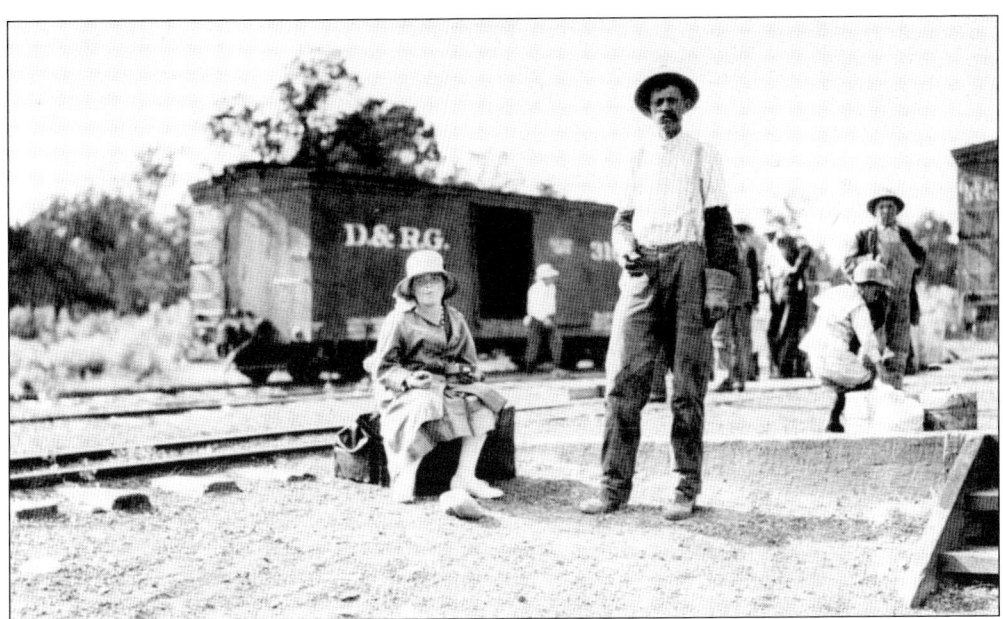

In a town of eccentrics, 6-foot-4-inch "Long" John Dunn managed to stand out. He opened two gambling houses in Taos and one in nearby Red River to cater to the gold rush crowd. Later he held a monopoly on local transportation by owning the only bridge crossing the Rio Grande (for which he charged tolls for people and cattle) and the only stagecoach/turned taxi business serving Taos for more than 30 years. When he died on May 21, 1953, his good friend Doughbelly Price wrote the following in an obituary that appeared on the front page of *El Crepusculo*: " The early part of his life was rocky and uphill. . . . He was caught in the web of law and Texas gave him 40 years in the State Pen. He had no education, but what he 'knowed' was learned from cattle, horses, natural observation and mother nature. . . . John Dunn was at his best behind a roulette wheel or a monte table, where you never got more than was coming to you and if you didn't watch, it was less." The photograph above shows John Dunn meeting Dorothy Berninghaus at the Denver and Rio Grande (D&RG) train in 1917, and below is a much later image of John at a roulette wheel. (Both courtesy of Taos Historic Museums.)

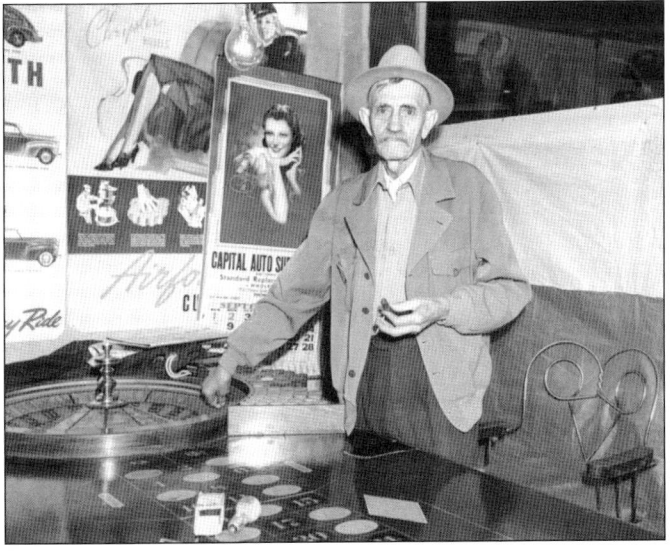

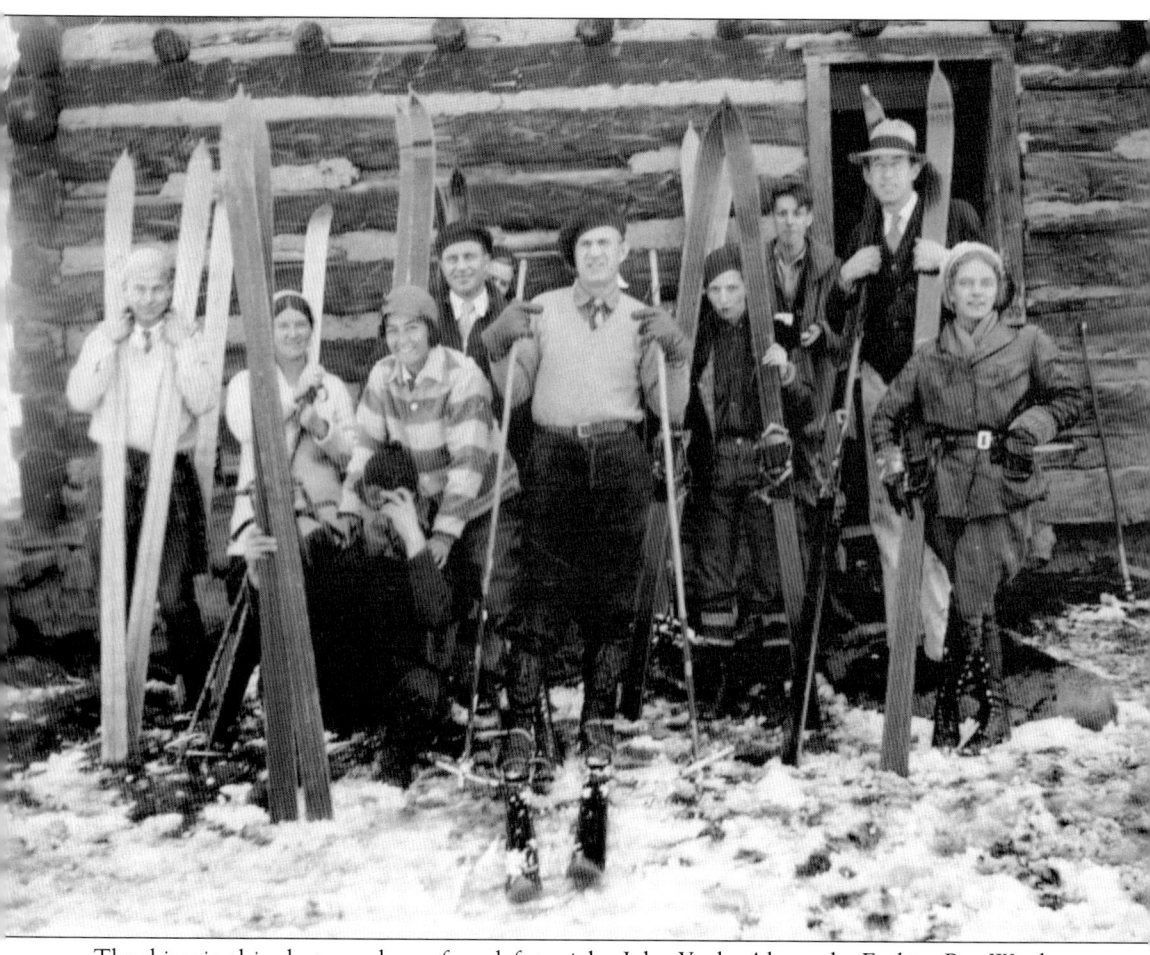

The skiers in this photograph are, from left to right, John Yaple, Alexandra Fechin, Ray Woolsey, Helen Blumenschein, George Boyd, Imil Bistrim, Avery Jean Woolsey, Edward Bright, and Eya Fechin. Nicolai Fechin (husband of Alexandra and father of Eya) was an accomplished artist who was born in 1881 in Kazan, Russia. He moved his family out of Russia shortly after the Bolshevik Revolution, arriving in New York in 1923. The Fechins moved to Taos in 1927 and built an extraordinary house and studio that Nicolai had designed. The Fechin house is now home to the Taos Art Museum. (Courtesy of Taos Historic Museums.)

Dr. Paul Thomas Martin was affectionately known to locals as "Doc" Martin. When he arrived in Taos in the 1890s (about the same time as his future friend Long John Dunn), Doc was the county's first and only physician. He made house calls by horse and wagon, and later in his tin lizzie, covering hundreds of miles to treat his patients. He was said to have healed more bullet holes than diseases. Doc's wife, Helen, was a talented batik artist who established the Hotel Martin the year Doc passed away. Now called the Taos Inn, the hotel houses a restaurant named Doc Martin's. The photograph at right shows Dr. Martin reading a newspaper in front of his office. Below Doc Martin makes a house call at the Pueblo in his tin lizzie. (Right, courtesy of Taos Historic Museums; below, courtesy of Taos Historic Museums.)

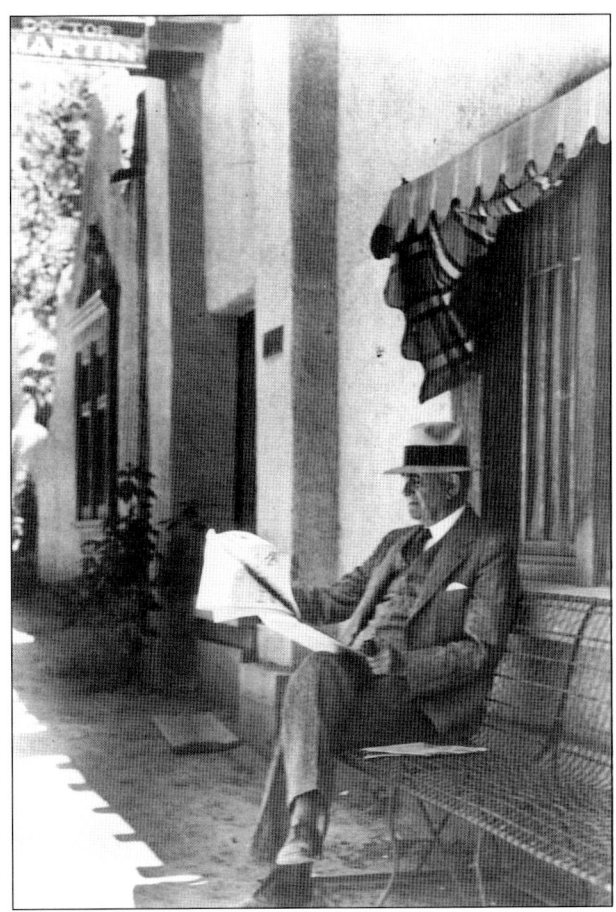

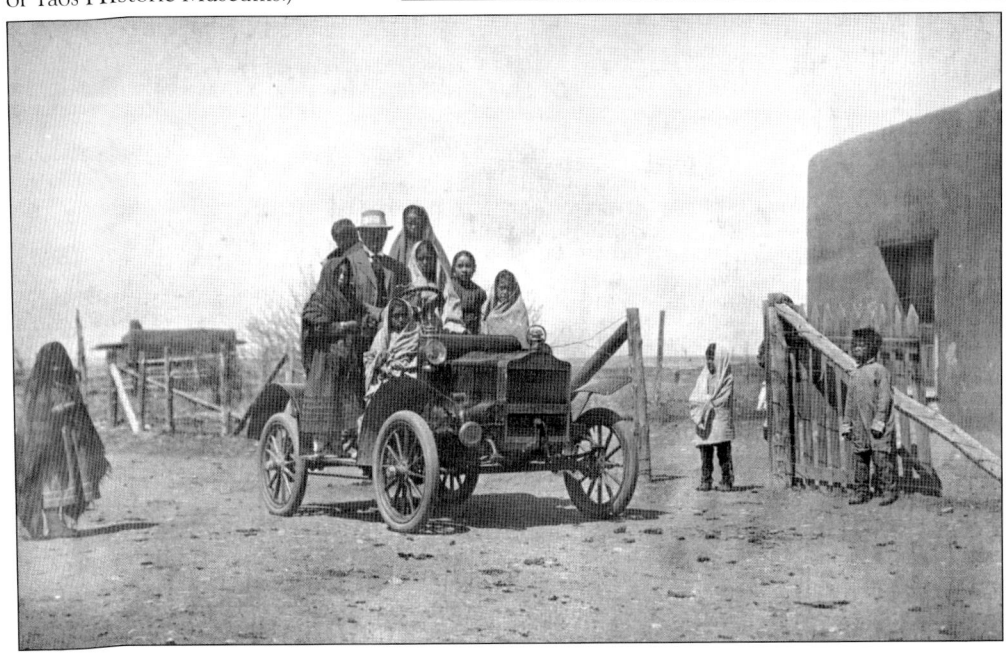

Discover Thousands of Local History Books
Featuring Millions of Vintage Images

Arcadia Publishing, the leading local history publisher in the United States, is committed to making history accessible and meaningful through publishing books that celebrate and preserve the heritage of America's people and places.

Find more books like this at
www.arcadiapublishing.com

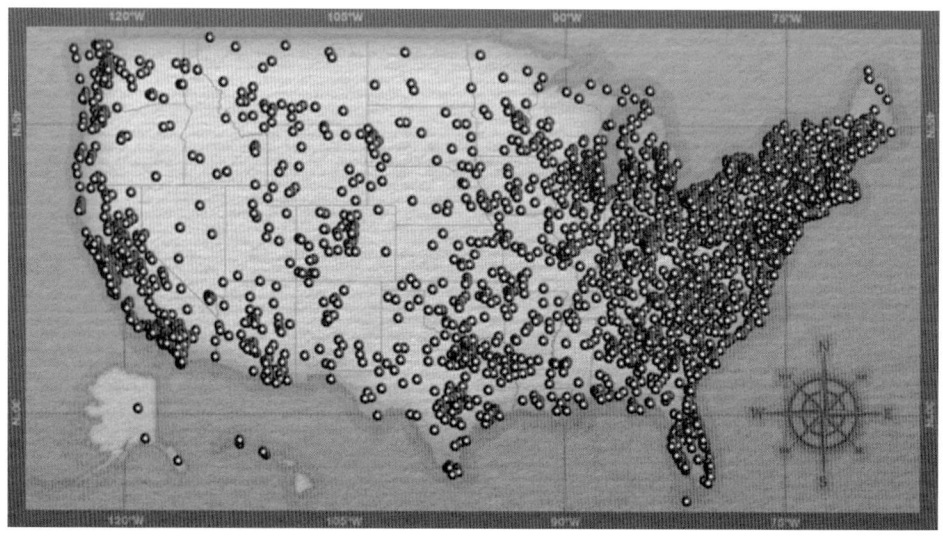

Search for your hometown history, your old stomping grounds, and even your favorite sports team.

Consistent with our mission to preserve history on a local level, this book was printed in South Carolina on American-made paper and manufactured entirely in the United States. Products carrying the accredited Forest Stewardship Council (FSC) label are printed on 100 percent FSC-certified paper.

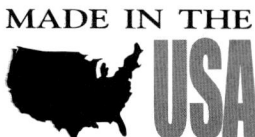